ROCKHOUNDING
New England

A Guide to 100 of the Region's
Best Rockhounding Sites

PETER CRISTOFONO

FALCONGUIDES

GUILFORD, CONNECTICUT
HELENA, MONTANA

AN IMPRINT OF ROWMAN & LITTLEFIELD

To my mother, Anita, who gave me my first book about
rocks and minerals when I was eight years old

FALCONGUIDES®

Copyright © 2014 Rowman & Littlefield

Photographs © 2014 by Peter Cristofono unless otherwise noted

ALL RIGHTS RESERVED. No part of this book may be reproduced or transmitted in any
form by any means, electronic or mechanical, including photocopying and recording,
or by any information storage and retrieval system, except as may be expressly permitted in writing from the publisher.

FalconGuides is an imprint of Rowman & Littlefield.
Falcon, FalconGuides, and Outfit Your Mind are registered trademarks of Rowman &
Littlefield.

Distributed by NATIONAL BOOK NETWORK

Maps by Alena Joy Pearce © Rowman & Littlefield

Library of Congress Cataloging-in-Publication data is available on file.

ISBN: 978-0-7627-8365-6

Printed in the United States of America

CONTENTS

Overview

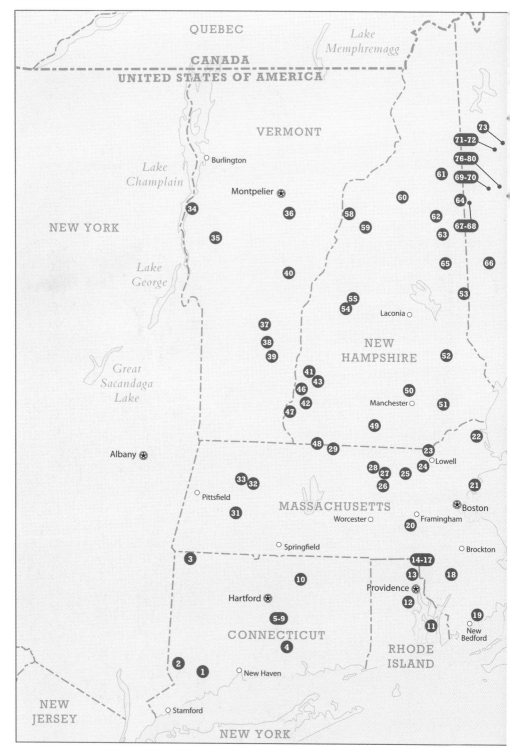

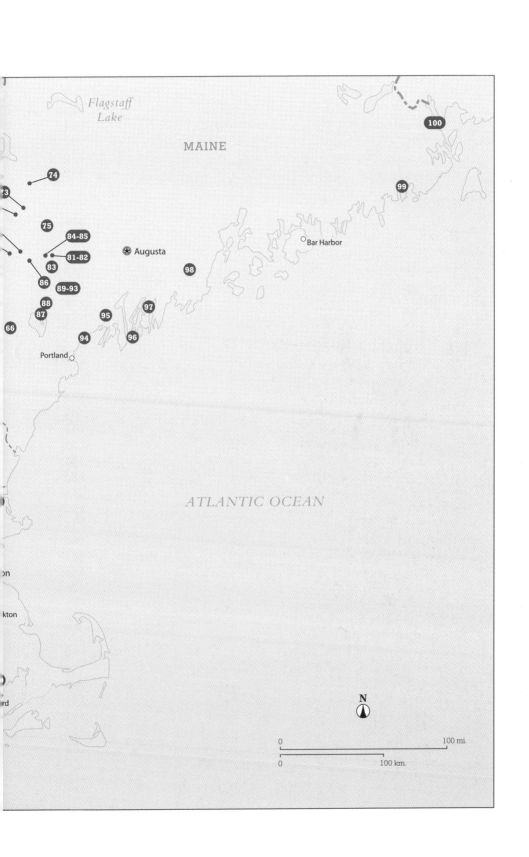

Maine Sites

ACKNOWLEDGMENTS

I gratefully acknowledge and thank the following individuals for permitting me to photograph specimens from their private collections and/or who generously donated specimens that were used in the preparation of this book: Kendrick Allen, Lynn Bannon, Patricia Barker, Gene Bearss, Ingeborg Burggraf, Jim Cahoon, John Campbell, John Chipman, Wayne Corwin, Kevin Czaja, David DeCourcey, Gabriel Dinh, Linda Frahm, Bob Janules, Melissa Jeswald, Dana M. Jewell, Dana Krueger, Barbara Liebman, Bryan Manke, Nathan C. Martin, Etienne Médard, Paul Monti, Tom Mortimer, Joe Mulvey, Jim Nizamoff, Ed Norton, Sam Pavadore, Michael Ruprecht, Stephan Segedy, Michael Shih, Don Swenson, Woodrow Thompson, Clifford Trebilcock, Linda Trebilcock, Barbara Wagner, Suzanne Wall, John P. Walsh, Anna Wilken, Robert Wilken, Ellen Young, and Paul Young.

In addition to those mentioned above, the following individuals shared their valuable time, knowledge, expertise, support, and/or assistance. I am most grateful to Patrick Bigos, Andrew Brodeur, Larry Bull, Jim Catterton, Chad Cramer, Bob Fendrich, Carl Francis, Gary Freeman, James Gage, Jim Gaudette, Michael Haritos, Hal Herard, Gordon Jackson, Van King, Anthony Mariano, Harold Moritz, Dana Morong, Jeff Morrison, James Parella, Frank Perham, Scott Reilly, Andy Simmons, Bob Sproule, Curtis Stevens, Art Wagner, Robert Whitmore, and Ted Zagwyn.

The mineralogy website Mindat.org was an invaluable resource in the preparation of this book. I would like to acknowledge and thank the following contributors for their submissions of New England mineral photos and locality data to Mindat.org, which were of great assistance to me: Anthony Albini, Adam Berluti, John Betts, Steve Bonney, Bill Bunn, Chad Cramer, Charles Creekmur, Kevin Czaja, Fred Davis, Dick Dionne, Jeffrey Fast, Paul Gilmore, Ken Gliesman, Michael Kieron, Van King, Matthew Lambert, Rob Lavinsky, Dan Levesque, Jasun McAvoy, Henry Minot, Harold Moritz, Joe Mulvey, Michael Otto, Joseph Polityka, Mike Polletta, Michael Shaw, Chris Stefano, James Tovey, Clifford Trebilcock, Doug Watts, Lawrence White, Scott Whittemore, and Jeremy Zolan.

Thanks also to my editor, Imee Curiel, for her patience and wisdom and to Jerry Butler for his expert advice and assistance, and a big thanks to Linda Frahm for her steadfast support and encouragement.

INTRODUCTION

A hot summer morning in the woods of western Maine. The air smells like pine trees and rock dust. Down in the quarry the sound of steel hitting steel rings in my ears as I carefully chisel into a crack in the ledge. Suddenly a chunk of smoky quartz starts to separate; I pull at it gently until it drops into my hands. Turning it over, I find a 3-inch-long gemmy crystal of green-and-pink watermelon tourmaline—perfectly formed and smooth to the touch, hidden for millions of years until this moment. Takes my breath away. This is rockhounding in New England. This is cool.

Despite what's depicted on television "reality" shows, cash and treasure is not what it's about. There's treasure seeking, sure, but the real reward is in acquiring a deeper connection with and appreciation for nature. When rockhounds "rescue" crystals that would have ended up in a quarry crusher or salvage rare minerals from old mine dumps, we are preserving a beautiful part of nature that would have otherwise been lost.

There is so much to explore—digging for topaz crystals in a remote New Hampshire forest; panning for gold in an icy Vermont stream; hammering out fossil ferns from the wave-battered cliffs of Rhode Island; searching tiny rock cavities in Connecticut for some of the world's rarest minerals; discovering a piece of aquamarine in an old Massachusetts quarry and having it locally crafted into an exquisite gemstone. By responsibly collecting and studying the region's minerals and fossils and by cooperating with and assisting professional earth scientists, we can be important participants in the ongoing discovery of our natural world. There is still much to be learned about the geology, mineralogy, and paleontology of New England, and as rockhounds, we are at our best when we are also "citizen scientists."

The one hundred sites profiled here represent the best of what New England has to offer and cover a range of geological environments. Each of the sites can be accessed either on your own or through participation on an authorized field trip. At all but two, you are allowed to collect rocks, minerals, or fossils; and where you can't collect, you can still bring home a souvenir. Some well-known mineral localities were excluded because the sites were closed, the status could not be determined, or in the case of operating quarries, field trips had not been held for more than a decade.

Rockhounding New England is a guidebook meant for everyone from young "pebble pups" to seniors embarking on a new adventure, from the greenest novices to the most knowledgeable earth science professionals, and my hope is that it will inspire you to go forth to seek, find, and experience for yourself New England's rich variety of minerals and fossils.

Top, left to right: Garnet (almandine), the official state mineral of Connecticut, from Roxbury; and cumberlandite, the official state rock of Rhode Island, from Cumberland. *Middle, left to right:* Babingtonite, the official state mineral of Massachusetts, from West Springfield; and tourmaline (elbaite), the official state gemstone of Maine, from Newry. *Bottom, left to right:* Beryl, the official state mineral of New Hampshire, from North Groton; and talc, the official state mineral of Vermont, from Ludlow.

NEW ENGLAND GEOLOGY

A full discussion of the geology of the New England region, with all its complexities, is well beyond the scope of this book. Suffice to say that the oldest rocks in New England are more than a billion years old, and the geological history of the region since that time is revealed in rocks that originated on several continents, micro-continents, volcanic islands, and ocean basins. The story is one of repeated tectonic plate collisions, the formation of a rift valley, and periodic mountain-building events, including some with peaks rising to Himalayan heights, then slowly eroding away, and a Greenland-like ice sheet blanketing every mountain and valley—and that's only a few of the highlights. To help make sense of it all, I recommend the four *Roadside Geology* books that cover the New England states, all written in an easy-to-read style (see bibliography).

The majority of sites described in this book are found in one of five geological environments (a few fit into more than one) that host mineral or fossil deposits. Four of these are bedrock environments. Bedrock is the solid rock that lies beneath soil, loose stones, and boulders, and sometimes is exposed at the surface as an outcrop. At rock quarries and mines, bedrock is excavated to obtain rocks and minerals. The bedrock at a particular site can consist of one or more types of rock. A rock is a solid aggregate of one or more minerals. Rocks can be classified by their geological environment as sedimentary, igneous, or metamorphic (defined below). The fifth type of geological environment consists of unconsolidated deposits. In contrast to bedrock, an unconsolidated deposit is one consisting of loose stone, gravel, sand, etc. These include stream, beach, lake, and glacial deposits.

Below are the five geological environments applicable to the sites in this book:

1. Sedimentary environment: Sedimentary rocks are formed through the deposition of sediments within bodies of water or on the earth's surface. Examples include limestone, sandstone, and shale. In many cases, rocks that are classified as sedimentary for the purposes of this book have actually been slightly metamorphosed. In New England, the vast majority of fossils and a handful of mineral species are found in sedimentary rocks.

2. Igneous environment: Igneous rocks are formed by the crystallization of magma deep within the earth (intrusive rocks) or by the crystallization of magma at or near the surface (extrusive rocks). Examples of intrusive rocks are granite, granitic pegmatite, and syenite. In New England, granitic pegmatites are the most important source of gem minerals. Seams and cavities in other types of intrusive rock can also contain interesting minerals. Extrusive rocks include andesite, basalt, and rhyolite. Cavities in basalt sometimes contain prehnite or zeolite minerals.

3. Metamorphic environment: Metamorphic rocks are those that have formed from other types of rock through the influence of heat, pressure, fluids, and/or strain. Regionally metamorphosed rocks such as schist and gneiss can contain a variety of minerals including almandine, pyrite, and kyanite. Some minerals that are hydrothermal in origin occur in veins or seams in these rocks. Metamorphosed ultramafic rocks (serpentinite, talc-carbonate rock) contain minerals such as talc and magnesite. Contact-metamorphosed rocks may contain fine crystals of vesuvianite and grossular.

4. Hydrothermal vein deposits: Water, especially hot water, can deposit minerals in fractures in rock, forming deposits of metallic ore minerals along with quartz, barite, fluorite, and carbonate minerals. Ore deposits formed through ascending water are called *hypogene*. Secondary mineral deposits formed by descending (meteoric) water are called *supergene*. Mineralized veins often occur in zones along faults.

5. Unconsolidated deposits: Silt, sand, and stone may congregate due to the action of water or ice. Unconsolidated sediments are by definition loosely bound; i.e., not consolidated into rock. These include alluvial (stream) deposits containing gold and other minerals (placer deposits), beach deposits containing heavy sands, and deposits derived from glacial-lake sediments.

Mineral (and fossil) occurrences or deposits are characterized by their geological environment and by the types of rocks in which they're found. Each site in this book has this information in the "Type of deposit" section. Knowing the geological environment and rocks at a site can be useful in understanding what minerals might be found. For example, a blue mineral in schist (a metamorphic rock) might be kyanite or cordierite. But a blue mineral in pegmatite (an igneous rock) would more likely be beryl or tourmaline, because kyanite and cordierite do not occur in an igneous environment. This is where a good mineral field guide will come in handy for learning about minerals and their environments.

MINING INDUSTRY

Most rockhounding occurs in active or abandoned mines and quarries, so knowing the area's mining industry is an important part of understanding where to look and what you might find. From an economic standpoint, the mining industry in New England is relatively insignificant compared to other areas of the United States. That said, active quarries and mines are found throughout the region.

By far, the most important products are crushed stone, sand, and gravel for construction purposes. Dimension stone—primarily granite, marble, and slate—is quarried in northern New England and Massachusetts. Marble is mined for calcium carbonate in Vermont and Massachusetts, and ground dolomitic marble is produced in Connecticut. Limestone is quarried in Maine for the production of cement. Talc is an important mining product in Vermont. Small gemstone mines operate in Maine (tourmaline) and New Hampshire (beryl).

Currently there are no active metal mines in New England. The last one, a copper and zinc mine in Maine, closed in 1977. However, there are significant untapped ore deposits in Maine that may be developed in the future. Abandoned mines exist throughout New England, some dating back to the 1600s. Iron and copper were produced in all of the New England states, and lead and silver were mined in all but Rhode Island. Gold was produced in all states except Connecticut, but never in significant amounts. Ores of arsenic, bismuth, cobalt, manganese, molybdenum, nickel, tin, tungsten, and zinc were also mined, mostly to a minor extent. A pyrite mine operated near the now-abandoned village of Davis, Massachusetts.

New England pegmatite deposits were once important sources of mica and feldspar; some mines also produced minor amounts of beryllium, cesium, lithium, niobium, tantalum, or tin ore. Nonmetallic minerals formerly mined in New England include anthracite, asbestos, barite, emery, fluorite, garnet, graphite, quartz, and serpentine. Today old mine and quarry dumps are favorite hunting grounds for rockhounds, particularly those in pegmatites.

CONNECTICUT

State mineral: Garnet. State fossil: Dinosaur footprints *(Eubrontes)*.

Mineralogy: Connecticut has a prominent place in the history of American mineralogy. In particular, Yale University was instrumental in the rise of mineralogy as a science in America. Today collectors and scientists, both amateur and professional, continue to add to the knowledge of the mineralogy of the state.

The first major mineralogical discovery in Connecticut began when a crystal of a heavy black mineral (probably from the Middletown area) was acquired by the British Museum in 1753. Charles Hatchett, a chemist, analyzed the specimen in 1801 and discovered that it contained a brand-new element, which he named columbium (later renamed niobium). The mineral itself was named columbite by the mineralogist Robert Jameson in 1805. Connecticut is also known for the first chrysoberyl locality in America (Haddam, 1810); the first topaz locality in America (Trumbull, 1826); and the discovery of the mineral danburite, found in Danbury and described in 1839.

Some of the most famous Connecticut mineral occurrences are in granitic pegmatites. One site, the long-abandoned Branchville quarry in Ridgefield, is the original, or *type*, locality for nine new mineral species, the second-highest number in New England, after the Palermo No. 1 mine in New Hampshire. All of the new minerals at Branchville were discovered between 1878 and 1890, and one wonders if a modern investigation would turn up any others. The Gillette pegmatite in Haddam is famous for fine pink beryl (morganite) and gem elbaite, and the Slocum quarry in East Hampton produced superb golden beryl crystals. The Strickland quarry in Portland was a famous pegmatite site where more than ninety minerals could be found, including fine elbaite and fluorapatite (regrettably it is now under a golf course).

Traprock (basalt) quarries, notably in Southbury, Woodbury, Wallingford, and East Granby, have produced world-class specimens of calcite, datolite, apophyllite, babingtonite, and prehnite. The Thomaston Dam railroad cut, Thomaston, produced more than sixty-five minerals in metamorphic rocks, pegmatites, and hydrothermal veins. The Bristol copper mine's chalcocite crystals are the best in the world. The Becker quarry in West Willington has produced fine Tessin-habit quartz crystals.

Many famous sites in Connecticut are now closed to the public or no longer exist. Fortunately specimens from these sites can be seen in museums and are sometimes available for purchase through mineral dealers. Collectors who investigate (with permission, of course) new construction sites often turn up interesting material; some of the state's finest specimens have been discovered at such temporary sites.

Paleontology: The Connecticut Valley in the central part of the state has long been known for Early Jurassic fossils, including dinosaur tracks, fishes, insects, and plants. Plant fossils were found in Westfield in 1816 and dinosaur fossils in East Windsor in 1818. Superb displays of Connecticut fossils can be viewed at Dinosaur State Park in Rocky Hill and at the Yale Peabody Museum of Natural History in New Haven.

RHODE ISLAND

State mineral: Bowenite. State rock: Cumberlandite.

Mineralogy: Famous mineral localities in Rhode Island include the Conklin quarry in Lincoln, where more than seventy minerals have been found, including fine specimens of bowenite; the Dexter quarry in Lincoln, the original bowenite locality; and Diamond Hill in Ashaway Village, known for exceptional specimens of amethyst on milky quartz.

Paleontology: Pennsylvanian-age plant and insect fossils can be found in the eastern part of the state; the Museum of Natural History at Roger Williams Park in Providence sponsors several fossil-collecting field trips each year. Contact the museum for details.

MASSACHUSETTS

State mineral: Babingtonite. State rock: Roxbury puddingstone. State gem: Rhodonite. State fossil: Dinosaur footprints.

Mineralogy: Massachusetts was at the forefront of the rise of mineralogy in America, and many of the state's mineral sites are steeped in history. The Tantiusques graphite mine in Sturbridge was worked by Native Americans long before colonists arrived at Plymouth in 1620. The Manhan mine in Easthampton dates to the 1670s, and the dumps still produce fine examples of wulfenite and pyromorphite. The Devil's Den quarry in Newbury was opened in 1697 and is famous for precious serpentine and wollastonite. The Clark Ledge pegmatite in Chesterfield was the original locality for both the albite variety cleavelandite (1822) and microlite (1835). The first vesuvianite locality in America was discovered in Worcester in 1822. By 1825 chiastolite was well-known from the Lancaster-Sterling area, and by the 1830s rhodonite was being collected in Plainfield and gem-quality aquamarine was found in Royalston. Museums around the world have specimens of the exceptional spodumene crystals from Walnut Hill in Huntington, found since 1850. World-class margarite occurs at the old emery mines in Chester, opened in the 1860s. The Russell garnet mine in Russell produced some of the finest almandine crystals in the United States beginning in the 1880s.

In the twentieth century, the Acushnet quarry became known for world-class fluorapatite. The traprock quarries of the Connecticut Valley, particularly the Lane quarries in Westfield, became famous for babingtonite, datolite, and prehnite. Massachusetts has some of the best babingtonite in the world; however, one of the most famous localities—Blueberry Mountain in Woburn—is now the site of an industrial park.

Paleontology: Fossils in Massachusetts include Pennsylvanian-age plant and insect fossils in the southeastern part of the state; marine fossils at scattered sites in the east and northeast; and Jurassic fossils in the Connecticut Valley, including dinosaur tracks, fishes, insects, and plants.

VERMONT

State mineral: Talc. State rocks: Granite, marble, and slate. State gemstone: Grossular garnet. State fossil: A Beluga whale skeleton.

Mineralogy: Asbestos (chrysotile) mines on Belvidere Mountain in Eden and Lowell near the village of Eden Mills operated from about 1900 to 1993. From a collector's point of view, this was the most important mineral locality in the state. Many superb specimens of grossular, diopside, vesuvianite, and other minerals were collected; more than sixty mineral species were reported from the mines. Another famous Vermont locality was the Carlton mine, Chester, the type locality for three of the four minerals discovered in Vermont. The Carlton mine was well-known for fine specimens of pyrite and magnetite, but is now inaccessible. A road cut on I-89 in Montpelier produced many large, high-quality pyrite crystals. The Vermont Verde Antique quarry in Rochester, an active site, has produced world-class specimens of talc. Recently a quarry near Enosburg Falls in northern Vermont has produced exceptional specimens of albite and hematite from an alpine-vein-type deposit.

Green Mountain National Forest covers more than 400,000 acres in Vermont. Mineral collecting and hobby gold panning are allowed in the national forest, as long as it is for personal, noncommercial use and done by hand.

Paleontology: Marine fossils are abundant in Ordovician rocks in northwestern Vermont. You can view fossils of the 480-million-year-old Chazy Reef at the Fisk Quarry and Goodsell Ridge preserves on Isle La Motte in Lake Champlain.

NEW HAMPSHIRE

State mineral: Beryl. State rock: Granite. State gem: Smoky quartz.

Mineralogy: New Hampshire has several famous pegmatite localities, which are of great interest to mineral collectors. The best known is the Palermo No. 1 mine in North Groton, which has produced more than 150 minerals, more than any other single site in New England. Palermo is the type locality for twelve minerals, and more will likely be discovered as research into the pegmatite continues. The Fletcher mine, also in North Groton, is known for world-class hydroxylherderite crystals. Ruggles mine in Grafton is a classic locality for uraninite and gummite, and a destination for thousands of tourists every year. The Chandlers Mill quarry in Newport is famous for fine specimens of hurlbutite and brazilianite. The Parker Mountain mine, Strafford, is well-known among fluorescent mineral collectors for the rare mineral eucryptite. Beryl Mountain, Acworth, has been a producer of beryl and rose quartz for collectors ever since the 1820s.

Several localities in the White Mountains are noted for outstanding mineral specimens originating in miarolitic granite, including Black Cap Mountain, Conway (smoky quartz and amazonite); Hurricane Mountain, North Conway (arfvedsonite); Moat Mountain, Hales Location (smoky quartz); South Baldface, Chatham (topaz); and South Percy Peak, Stratford (topaz).

Two metamorphic rock localities are widely known: Pond Hill (Pearl Lake/Mink Pond), Lisbon, is famous for fine staurolite specimens, while the Richmond soapstone quarry, Richmond, is a classic locality for cordierite. And lastly, the William Wise mine, Westmoreland, is known the world over for fine emerald-green fluorite.

Paleontology: Fossils are very rare in New Hampshire, but Silurian- and Devonian-age marine fossils have been found in metamorphic rocks in the western part of the state, and Devonian plant fossils occur near the border with Quebec.

MAINE

State gemstone: Tourmaline. State fossil: A Devonian fernlike plant, *Pertica quadrifaria.*

Mineralogy: If New England is a rockhound's paradise, then surely Maine is a paradise within a paradise. Collectors come from far and wide to experience firsthand the thrill of rockhounding in the gem-bearing hills of the state, particularly in Oxford County. Businesses have sprung up to cater to these eager collectors, such as Poland Mining Camps, Maine Mineral Adventures, and Maine Mineralogy Expeditions (see Appendix D). Professional and amateur mineralogists converge on the state for annual events like the Maine Pegmatite Workshop and the New England Mineral Conference. The new Maine Mineral and Gem Museum in Bethel is the most significant mineralogical institution to be established in New England in a very long time; it's a "must" for anyone visiting mineral-rich Oxford County.

The largest gem pocket discovered in North America was found in 1972 at the Dunton mine in Newry. The tourmaline pocket was so rich that at times the miners were removing tourmaline crystals by the shovelful. While the Dunton mine is no longer active, several other Oxford County pegmatite properties are currently being worked for gem tourmaline, including Mount Mica and Mount Marie in Paris and the Havey mine in Poland. Other famous pegmatite localities in Oxford County include the Bennett quarry (morganite); Black Mountain (rubellite); Bumpus mine (beryl and rose quartz); Emmons quarry (fluorapatite and perhamite); Songo Pond mine (aquamarine); Plumbago Mountain (world-class rose quartz crystals); Pulsifer quarry (royal purple fluorapatite); Lord Hill (smoky quartz, topaz, and phenakite); and Deer Hill, site of a major amethyst discovery in 1993. Well-known pegmatite localities outside of Oxford County include the Fisher quarry, Topsham (beryl, elbaite, microlite, and topaz); Swamp No. 1 quarry, Topsham (world-class uraninite crystals); and the Estes quarry, West Baldwin (world-class fairfieldite).

Maine also has some notable non-pegmatite mineral localities, including a famous sodalite locality in Litchfield; the Pitts-Tenney prospects, Minot (grossular); and the Webster prospects, Sanford (vesuvianite). Many other mineral sites could be mentioned; see the bibliography for more resources on Maine mineralogy.

Paleontology: Marine fossils are fairly common in some areas of Maine. Local clubs sometimes conduct field trips to Devonian and Silurian fossil-collecting sites in Somerset and Piscataquis Counties. For those interested in learning more, I recommend *Maine's Fossil Record: The Paleozoic* by Lisa Churchill-Dickson.

ROCKHOUNDING BASICS

Before you head out, it's important to make sure that you are fully pre-pared. Here are a few basic tips that all rockhounds—beginner and veteran alike—should always keep in mind.

Educate yourself. A rock and mineral (or fossil) field guide or two (yes, in addition to this one) is a must. Websites are useful, but not as comprehen-sive as the best books. If I had to recommend one book for rock and mineral identification, it would be *A Field Guide to Rocks and Minerals* by Frederick Pough. (Appendix E lists additional state-specific recommendations.) Mindat .org is the single best online resource for the mineral collector. Though interna-tional in scope, the website has more than 10,000 photos of minerals from the New England region alone. More than just a database, Mindat.org is a friendly online community of like-minded rockhounds and professional mineralogists from around the world. For a list of additional useful websites, see Appendix D.

Every rockhound should have an inexpensive reference collection. While this book is geared toward those who want to find their own specimens in the field, even the most die-hard field collector does a little "silver-picking" now and then. Purchasing representative specimens of what you hope to find is a great idea. There are many opportunities to buy minerals and fossils online, of course, but I recommend seeing some in person. Appendix C has a list of shops that sell rocks, minerals, and fossils. Mineral club shows are another excellent source of specimens, and many museums throughout New England have displays of rocks, minerals, and fossils (see Appendix B).

Join a club. The best advice I can give a new collector (or even a veteran one) is to join a club. Whether you live in New England or anywhere outside of it, belonging to a club is the single best way to learn about rockhounding. In addition, being a member of a club in New England can help you gain access to some of the very best sites in the region, many of which would not be possible to visit otherwise. Dues range from $10 to $25 per year for an individual, and most clubs have substantial family discounts. Some collectors join more than one club in order to be able to participate in field trips and programs in different areas.

Clubs tend to be very welcoming organizations, open to anyone with an interest in the earth and its treasures. Members are typically mineral and fossil collectors, gem cutters, jewelry makers, and science and nature enthusiasts. Club members range in age from toddlers to seniors, and in experience level from novice to PhD mineralogists, geologists, and paleontologists. Field collecting is a major focus of most clubs; some even own or lease mineral rights to one or more collecting sites. Monthly meetings are generally open to the public and may feature expert speakers on a variety of topics.

Many clubs have committees for educational outreach to local schools and libraries, and scholarships for students in earth science–related programs. Most have an annual gem and mineral show open to the public. A few have public auctions. Some clubs offer training in gem cutting and polishing and jewelry making. Clubs are also frequently active in programs to aid in conservation and protection of the environment.

There are also clubs that cater to collectors with specialized interests. Members of the Micromounters of New England collect micromounts—mineral specimens that are viewed with the aid of a microscope and are often quite beautiful and rare. Gold-prospecting clubs cater to those interested in seeking gold in the streams of New England. There are no fossil clubs in New England, but the New York Paleontological Society based in New York City conducts occasional field trips to western New England in addition to fossil-rich New York State. See Appendix A for a list of New England clubs. Visit club websites for information on membership, field trips, and other activities. In general, most clubs will accept you as a member no matter where you live, and you do not need to attend monthly meetings.

FIELD COLLECTING

Clothing: Proper clothing is essential for a successful collecting trip. For sites in wooded localities, dress as if you were going hiking. Wear layers, bring rain gear, and bring a change of clothes in case you get wet. In active quarries and mines, you will almost always be required to wear a hard hat, reflective safety vest, long pants, and sturdy boots. I strongly recommend wearing steel-toed boots for all rockhounding situations—you'll need rugged protection for your feet. Never wear sneakers or sandals.

Maps and GPS: Topographic maps and a compass are essential if you plan to hike for any significant distance. Topo maps can be purchased as downloads or hard copies. You should also have a handheld GPS unit, but don't rely on GPS alone. Geological maps are not essential, but are useful if your goal is to prospect in new areas.

Tools: In most rockhounding situations you'll be using a hammer. You'll need one (or more) capable of safely breaking rock, not the kind you'd use for driving nails into wood. A geologist's or prospector's pick is popular with many collectors, and is ideal in many situations, but often you'll need something that packs a little more punch. A crack hammer (also called a hand sledge) or a larger sledgehammer is often necessary. In most cases, I find that I can get by with a crack hammer and an assortment of chisels. *Always* use safety goggles when hammering. I recommend the kind that protect your eyes in all directions from flying rock fragments.

Other tools that can be useful in certain situations include steel wedges, a gad, pry bars, and a bent screwdriver (for cleaning out pockets). Digging tools are often necessary. Keep a full-size shovel with a pointed tip in your vehicle in case you need it. If a hike is required, take a small collapsible army-type shovel with you. Various gardening tools such as hoes, hand rakes, and trowels may be useful.

Wear leather gloves to protect your hands, especially where you might encounter sharp fragments of minerals such as quartz and mica. A whisk broom and an old toothbrush are handy for cleaning off rocks. Sifting screens are recommended for many sites with loose gem material. Bring a camera to document your collecting efforts—you never know when you'll make a big find!

To carry equipment and specimens, you'll need collecting bags and/or buckets. If hiking, a backpack with a small plastic wastebasket inside works well. A knapsack is okay for short hikes. A 5-gallon paint bucket is standard for carrying tools and specimens, and is fine if you are reasonably close to your vehicle. Be sure to bring wrapping material to protect the specimens you find—newspaper and paper towels are ideal. Wrap up delicate crystals and put them into ziplock bags.

One of the most important pieces of equipment for rockhounding is a magnifying lens or loupe. At some sites it is indispensible for identifying the minerals you might encounter. I specifically recommend a good-quality 10-power (10x) triplet loupe. Why 10-power? Any higher, and the decreased depth-of-field makes it difficult to use. So 10x is about the right amount of magnification to get a clear close-up view of any small crystals you might find at a mine or quarry, or any small flakes of gold that turn up in your gold pan.

Geiger counters and other radiation detectors are useful for collecting in pegmatites where you might encounter or are seeking radioactive minerals. Portable UV lights can be used to collect fluorescent minerals, and they are

Many rockhounds enjoy collecting mineral specimens that fluoresce under ultraviolet light.

also valuable tools for mineral identification. Some collectors use a blackout cloth to create a dark enclosure to enable them to test minerals for fluorescence during daylight hours.

Labeling: When you return home from a rockhounding trip, immediately put your finds in a box labeled with the site location and date. The identification of minerals can be done anytime, but locality information is all too easy to forget. Minerals and fossils without locality information have far less value than those with. Plastic bead boxes from craft stores and egg cartons work well for storing small specimens. Beer or soda flats are preferred by many collectors for larger ones. Later you can catalogue, label, and display your best specimens in a way that suits your needs and space limitations.

COLLECTING ETIQUETTE

On private property, you are a guest and need to have permission to collect. (When in doubt about land ownership, inquire at the local town or city hall.) Be sure to comply with all rules provided by the landowner. It's vitally important to abide by regulations governing mineral and fossil collecting on public lands as well. All too many sites have been closed due to the carelessness and misbehavior of a tiny percentage of collectors.

Never leave trash—this is a common landowner complaint. In fact, it's a good idea to pick up any trash you see at the site, if it's not too inconvenient to do so, in the spirit of good landowner-rockhound relations. Leave gates as you found them, closed or open. Collect only what you need for your personal use; leave something for the next collector. Do not use power equipment (rock saws, drills, etc.) without express permission. Never use blasting materials in collecting areas. Be careful with matches, cigarettes, etc., to avoid starting brush or forest fires.

SAFETY

No matter where you go, always have a first-aid kit with you. Cuts and scrapes will happen. Use sunscreen and insect repellent when appropriate. Bring plenty of water.

Mines and quarries: Quarries and mines are inherently dangerous places. At most active quarries, you will be required to sign a liability waiver in order to collect. Quarry walls may be unstable; do not climb walls or collect beneath them—a hard hat will not protect you from heavy rock crashing down on you. At abandoned mines and quarries, be aware of the possibility of encountering old blasting caps, dynamite, and unstable rock. Do not enter old mine tunnels or shafts. When hammering, always wear safety goggles. Warn others around you before you start to hammer to alert them of potential flying fragments. Do not collect above or below other collectors, to avoid having rock fall on them or you.

Remote areas: It's really not a good idea to go rockhounding alone, especially to remote sites. You never know when an accident or medical emergency might occur. All of the same safety measures that apply to hikers and campers apply to rockhounds as well. Let someone know where you are going and when you expect to return. Always bring a cell phone, but keep in mind that service can be spotty, especially in northern New England.

Hunting season: Dress in bright orange when collecting in forests during hunting season, in areas and on days where hunting is allowed. Hunting is not allowed on Sunday in Massachusetts and Maine; Connecticut prohibits hunting on Sunday on all public land.

Poison ivy: Sometimes it seems as if the best specimens are underneath poison ivy! Unfortunately this nasty weed is ubiquitous on the dumps of old mines and quarries in New England. Keep an eye out for it, and wear gloves and appropriate clothing if you are susceptible.

Weather Hazards

Summer heat: It's all too easy to get sunburned while collecting in the summer. For protection, wear sunscreen with a sun protection factor (SPF) of at least 30, and wear a hat, long-sleeved shirt, and long pants. Drink sufficient water to avoid dehydration. On hot days, collect as early in the morning as you can, or else late in the day.

Cold weather: Hypothermia is a risk even at cool temperatures if you become chilled from rain or sweat. Bring rain gear when collecting in damp weather or heading out on a long hike; change out of wet clothing as soon as you can.

Lightning: In case of a thunderstorm, find shelter in a safe place—inside your vehicle with windows closed is a good option. Do not remain in open areas, under trees, or near water or metal objects. As a last resort, crouch down low to the ground, at least 15 feet from anyone else.

Insects, Spiders, and Ticks

Flies and mosquitoes: In many areas, particularly in northern New England in late spring and early summer, blackflies can be a major annoyance. Mosquitoes, too, commonly pester rockhounds, especially in shady locations and near water. There are at least two serious diseases that mosquitoes in New England can transmit. Eastern equine encephalitis (EEE), a rare and often fatal disease transmitted by the bite of an infected mosquito, occurs primarily in southern New England. The risk of contracting EEE is highest from late July through September. West Nile virus (WNV) is another disease transmitted by mosquitoes in New England, but only a tiny percentage of people become seriously ill. The risk for WNV is highest from July through early October. Use sufficient insect repellent and wear long-sleeved shirts and long pants to help reduce your risk.

Bees and wasps: Bees and wasps will usually leave you alone if you leave them alone, but when digging in old dumps, you should be aware of the possibility of encountering a nest of ground hornets or yellow jackets. They do not take kindly to being disturbed!

Spiders: Spiders and rockhounds like to hang around in the same places. Fortunately most spiders in New England are pretty harmless. One exception is the female northern black widow, which could be encountered under stones or in embankments in southern New England. If disturbed, black widows would usually rather escape than attack, but it's a good idea to wear gloves when collecting in their range, just to be safe.

Ticks: Ticks are all too common in New England, particularly in areas with high deer populations. Lyme disease, a tick-transmitted disease first recognized in Lyme, Connecticut, in 1975, is now widespread in the region. The deer ticks that transmit this disease are most active in May, June, and July, but can be encountered throughout the year. For protection, use an insect repellant containing DEET on your skin and clothing (shirts, pants, socks, shoes). Try to avoid sitting in, or walking through, brushy and grassy places. After collecting, wash your clothes in hot water, and dry them in high heat. Check your body for ticks, and remove any that you find immediately with fine-tipped tweezers. Lyme disease is generally curable with antibiotics, but can have serious health consequences if left untreated.

Wildlife Dangers

Snakes: Though venomous snakes are rare in New England, the timber rattlesnake occurs in all states except Maine, and the northern copperhead is native to southern New England. Human encounters with these species are infrequent. Use common sense—don't reach into holes.

American black bear: Black bears rarely exhibit aggressive behavior; they would much rather flee from humans than attack. Just the same, keep your distance if you see one. Make your presence known by talking or making other noise. When in bear country, always keep food where bears won't see or smell it.

Moose and deer: Hitting a moose with your vehicle can be deadly for both you and the moose. Use abundant caution while driving at night

A harmless maritime garter snake slithers over rocks at the Tamminen quarry (Site 78) in Greenwood, Maine.

or at dusk in moose country. If you see one in the forest, appreciate it from a distance. Never approach a moose—they are unpredictable, and if they feel threatened can attack with little or no warning. Deer-car collisions are a significant hazard throughout New England. Drive slowly in high-risk areas and remain alert for deer, particularly at dawn and dusk.

Eastern coyote: Coyote attacks on humans are extremely rare. One incident occurred in New Hampshire in 2012, possibly involving a rabid animal. But coyotes are definitely a threat to your pet, so don't leave dogs unattended.

HOW TO USE THIS BOOK

Each site in this book has the following:

Status: The inclusion of a site in *Rockhounding New England* does not guarantee that the site is available for collecting, or that if it is open, it will remain accessible in the future. Inclusion of a site in this book is only an indication that past collecting has taken place, and does not constitute permission to access any site without the permission of the owner. Please be aware that the status of a site can change at any time.

"Open" means the site is *believed* (though not guaranteed) to be open for collecting, usually subject to certain restrictions. If a fee, permit, and/or schedule apply, this information will be indicated here.

"Restricted" means that the site is *closed* to collectors, with the exception of those participating on an authorized field trip conducted by an organization such as a mineral club, school, museum, or commercial guide service. These organizations generally carry the necessary liability insurance often required by owners. Managers of some sites might allow several field trips per year, while others only rarely authorize them. See Appendix A (clubs) and Appendix D (commercial guides) for organizations that conduct field trips. If you are interested in visiting a particular "restricted" site, contact one of these organizations for more information.

Land manager: Most sites are on private property; the remainder are on federal, state, or city/town land. The land manager indicated is the owner, leaseholder, property manager, or other responsible party.

Land type: This is a general description of the landscape and topography.

Type of deposit: The geological environment or rock types in which minerals or fossils at the site are found.

Location: City/town and county. If a site is in a national, state, or town forest or park, or on conservation land or in a wildlife management area, that information is indicated here as well.

GPS: GPS coordinates are provided in decimal degrees format. Before heading out into the field, I recommend plugging these coordinates into Google Earth to view the satellite imagery of the site. If you're heading to an area obscured by trees, try using Google Earth's "historical imagery" feature to find a satellite image taken in the winter or early spring, when there was no foliage on the trees, in order to get a better view of the site.

Elevation: Given in feet, as one number or as a range where appropriate.

Vehicle: The majority of sites in New England are accessible to any type of vehicle, but in many cases a 4WD or high-clearance 4WD vehicle is recommended.

Best season: The range of months listed here is the recommended "best season" for planning purposes. The collecting season is a bit longer in southern New England than in mountainous northern regions, where snow may linger well into spring and unpaved roads can be muddy, washed out, or otherwise impassable. Throughout the region, flooded quarries may need to be pumped out in the spring before operations can resume. Keep in mind that weather in New England is notoriously unpredictable, and a hot, humid day in May or a cool, damp one in July is not unusual.

Tools: Recommended tools and collecting gear. The tools listed here are only the essential ones needed for a particular site. It's a good idea to carry an assortment of tools in your vehicle to use as the need may arise. If specific safety gear is *required,* it is listed under "Rules and regulations."

Minerals (or fossils): For mineral sites, a list (as complete as possible) of reliably reported species is provided in alphabetical order. For fossil sites, some of the more commonly found fossils are mentioned. Lists were compiled using the following sources: books and articles listed in the bibliography, mineral- and fossil-related websites, museum and private collection resources, personal communications from knowledgeable collectors, and my own personal collecting efforts. As much as I would like to reference each and every entry, that is not practical in a book of this size. For further information about the mineralogy of a particular site, I recommend consulting the sources listed in the bibliography and the online resources listed in Appendix D.

When seeking to identify a mineral you've found, use this list to help narrow down the possibilities. Keep in mind that a mineral list may well be incomplete, especially for little-explored sites, and you may have discovered something new for the locality. In some cases (hopefully not many), the inclusion of a mineral or fossil on a list may be an error.

Special attractions: Local attractions that would appeal to those interested in the earth sciences, nature, history, and archaeology are listed here.

Accommodations: Nearby locations for camping and lodging.

Finding the site: Directions are provided beginning at a nearby highway junction, with distances to the nearest 0.1 mile. Hiking distances and times are approximate.

Rules and regulations: All sites have rules and regulations; those listed here do not necessarily constitute a complete list. "Restricted" sites, in particular, often have additional rules that will be provided to you when you register for a field trip. Rules and regulations are subject to change at any time. It is the responsibility of each collector to learn and abide by all applicable rules and regulations for each site to be visited.

Rockhounding: Details about the history and geology of each site and the notable gems, minerals, and/or fossils that can be found are provided in this section, along with tips to help you make the most of your visit.

ABOUT THE PHOTOGRAPHS

All of the specimens shown in *Rockhounding New England* are from personal collections. I decided to exclude specimens obtained by professional miners or displayed in museums. I wasn't looking to feature glamorous specimens that would be virtually unobtainable by the average rockhound. The quality of the specimens in this book ranges from average to superb, but all of them are typical of what can be found by a well-prepared and industrious rockhound collecting at the sites in this book.

ABOUT THE AUTHOR

Peter Cristofono has been a field collector of minerals, gems, and fossils for more than thirty-five years. A native New Englander, he began assembling a large collection of self-collected specimens from the region during his high school years in New Hampshire and later while majoring in geology at Boston College. Peter has served as president of the Boston Mineral Club and is currently a director of the Micromounters of New England. He has authored mineralogical articles for various publications and websites. He is well-known for his macro photos of minerals and insects, which have appeared in major newspapers, magazines, books, scholarly journals, museum exhibits, and various websites, including over 3,700 mineral photos on Mindat.org. Peter spends as much time as he can in the field. His home base is Salem, Massachusetts.

Map Legend

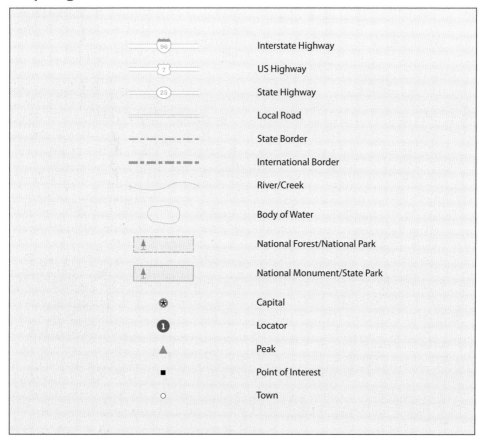

	Interstate Highway
	US Highway
	State Highway
	Local Road
	State Border
	International Border
	River/Creek
	Body of Water
	National Forest/National Park
	National Monument/State Park
	Capital
	Locator
	Peak
	Point of Interest
	Town

CONNECTICUT

Elbaite from the Strickland quarry, Portland, Connecticut

1. Old Mine Park

This specimen of non-gem white topaz is from the topaz pit area. (Paul Young collection)

Status: Open with town permit; available at police station—158 Edison Rd., Trumbull
Land manager: Town of Trumbull
Land type: Dumps of abandoned mines on a wooded hillside
Type of deposit: Hydrothermal ore veins, metamorphic (amphibolite, marble), igneous (granitic pegmatite)
Location: Long Hill, Trumbull, Fairfield County
GPS: Parking, N41.2871 / W73.2289
Elevation: Parking, 288 feet; collecting areas, 350 to 470 feet
Vehicle: Any
Best season: Apr through Oct
Tools: Crack hammer, chisels, safety goggles; UV light and blackout cloth (optional)
Minerals: Actinolite, albite, arsenopyrite, barite, beryl, biotite, bismuth, bornite, brookite, calcite, chalcopyrite, clinochlore, clinozoisite, copper, diaspore, diopside,

epidote, ferberite (wolframite), fluorapatite, fluorite, galena, graphite, grossular, gypsum, hematite, hornblende, malachite, marcasite, margarite, melanterite, microcline, muscovite, opal (hyalite), phlogopite, pickeringite, pyrite, pyrrhotite, quartz, rutile, scapolite, scheelite, siderite, sphalerite, titanite, topaz, tourmaline, tungstite, uraninite

Special attraction: Yale Peabody Museum of Natural History, New Haven

Accommodations: Camping at Kettletown State Park, Southbury. Lodging available along I-95, Fairfield to West Haven.

Finding the site: From the junction of CT 25 and CT 111 in Trumbull, follow CT 111 north for 1 mile. Turn right onto Old Mine Road; proceed 0.3 mile. Follow trail signs.

Rules and regulations: Rules provided with permit. Some mine areas are fenced off and closed to entry.

Rockhounding

The first topaz deposit in the United States was discovered at this site and publicized in the *American Journal of Science* in 1826. But it was tungsten ore that led to the first serious mining attempt, when the American Tungsten Mining and Milling Company opened a mine in 1899. The tungsten mine operated for several years, was sold, and in 1916 was destroyed by a suspicious fire. The town of Trumbull acquired the property in 1937 and later named it Old Mine Park. Today visitors enjoy an 11-mile loop trail for mountain biking and hiking, two pavilions, and a picnic area with grills. Rockhounds come to explore four main mineral areas in the 72-acre park: the topaz pit, tungsten mine (upper pit), lower dump, and an old lime quarry.

Topaz in the topaz pit area occurs as gray, white, or pale yellow masses and only rarely as crystals. It can be distinguished

Top: Scheelite and quartz are almost indistinguishable in ordinary light. Bottom: Under shortwave UV light, scheelite glows bright bluish white.

Sites 1–2

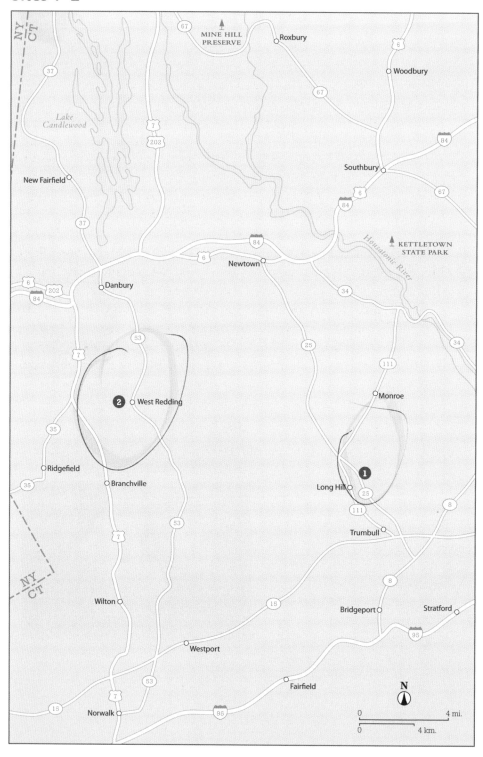

from quartz by its higher specific gravity, greater hardness, and perfect basal cleavage. The dumps also contain fluorite, sphalerite, and scapolite. Fluorite occurs as pink to purple crystals and masses that exhibit green to blue-green fluorescence under UV light. A reddish-brown variety of fluorite known as chlorophane exhibits a property known as thermoluminescence—when heated or placed in hot water, it emits an eerie greenish glow.

The old tungsten mine dumps contain ores of tungsten—scheelite, wolframite, and tungstite. Scheelite is commonly white or tan and massive; like topaz, it is difficult to distinguish from quartz, but it glows strongly (blue-white) under shortwave ultraviolet light. Ferberite (wolframite) occurs as pseudomorphs after scheelite, and these are classics of New England mineralogy. Tungstite occurs as lemon-yellow coatings on quartz but is not common. These tungsten minerals can also be collected in the lower dump. Associated minerals include fluorite, green to black actinolite and hornblende, green epidote, pale brown clinozoisite, red-brown grossular, white scapolite, massive gray arsenopyrite, brassy pyrite, bronze-colored marcasite, and metallic-brown pyrrhotite.

An old "lime" quarry in marble was first worked prior to 1803. Ruins of an old kiln can be seen near the pit. Brown phlogopite, grass-green diopside, dark green clinochlore, and brassy pyrite occur in the marble. Calcite is massive and white, gray, or pink; it exhibits red fluorescence under shortwave ultraviolet light.

2. West Redding Grossular Locality

Cavities in the bedrock contain lustrous crystals of grossular.

See map page 26.
Status: Restricted; no access, unless on an authorized field trip
Land manager: Connecticut Yankee Council, Boy Scouts of America
Land type: Two rocky, wooded knolls
Type of deposit: Metamorphic (skarn)
Location: John Sherman Hoyt Scout Reservation, Redding, Fairfield County
GPS: N41.3226 / W73.4381
Elevation: 440 feet
Vehicle: Any
Best season: Apr through Oct
Tools: Crack hammer, sledgehammer, chisels, safety goggles, shovel, rake
Minerals: Andesine, calcite, clinozoisite, diopside, fluorapatite, graphite, grossular, quartz, scapolite, titanite, tremolite
Special attraction: Mine Hill Preserve, Roxbury

Accommodations: Camping at Kettletown State Park, Southbury. Lodging available off of I-84 in Danbury and in cabins on the Hoyt Scout Reservation.
Finding the site: From I-84, exit 3, in Danbury, follow US 7 south for 2.8 miles; turn left onto Starrs Plain Road and proceed 0.5 mile. Turn left onto West Redding Road; continue for 1.6 miles. Turn right onto Long Ridge Road; continue for 0.6 mile to the train station. Turn right onto Simpaug Turnpike; proceed about 0.3 mile to a rocky knoll on the left.
Rules and regulations: No parking allowed on Simpaug Turnpike.

Rockhounding

The unusual bedrock at this site is composed almost entirely of one mineral—grossular, a calcium-aluminum garnet. The deposit, essentially a skarn, covers about 60 acres. The grossular is mostly massive, but occasional cavities can be found lined with orange-brown or cinnamon-colored crystals. Some of the crystals have a rather gemmy luster, and have been called by the varietal names hessonite, essonite, or cinnamon stone.

This site has long been popular with individual mineral collectors and as a field trip locality for mineral clubs. As long ago as 1923, the Philadelphia Mineralogical Society visited and collected "brilliant red" garnets, which they called essonite. Mineral clubs still conduct field trips to the locality, sometimes including an overnight stay at the campground. Despite having been visited for generations, there is plenty of garnet left. First, survey the area for interesting rock fragments. Dig into the tailings below where others have prospected. If you decide to work the exposed bedrock, use a good hand sledge and chisel, but be forewarned that this is *very* hard rock and won't break easily. Safety goggles and gloves are a must to avoid injury from sharp rock fragments.

Minerals other than grossular are difficult to find. However, radiating groups of pale green or pale brown clinozoisite crystals sometimes occur in massive grossular. Diopside can be found as small, well-formed green crystals embedded in white calcite; frequently it is associated with gemmy grossular.

Mine Hill Preserve in Roxbury, 27 miles north of West Redding, is the site of eighteenth-century lead-silver mines, nineteenth-century iron mines and an iron-making complex, and nineteenth- to twentieth-century building stone quarries. You can take a self-guided tour of the 360-acre preserve on trails marked with interpretive signs and get a close view of the old quarries as well as the remains of a blast furnace and roasting ovens.

3. Falls Village Marble Quarries

This specimen, consisting of large white tremolite crystals on marble, was collected on a mineral club field trip.

Status: Restricted; no access, unless on an authorized field trip
Land manager: Private
Land type: Two separately owned open-pit quarries
Type of deposit: Metamorphic (dolomitic marble)
Location: Town of Canaan, Litchfield County
GPS: Century Aggregates, N41.9891 / W73.3529; Conklin, N41.9838 / W73.3544
Elevation: Century Aggregates, 663 to 860 feet; Conklin, 658 to 850 feet
Vehicle: Any
Best season: May through Oct
Tools: Crack hammer, chisels, digging tools
Minerals: Aragonite, calcite, chalcopyrite, chlorite, diopside, dolomite, goethite, grossular, phlogopite, pyrite, pyrrhotite, quartz, rutile, scapolite, tremolite, wollastonite
Special attraction: Connecticut Museum of Mining & Mineral Science, Kent

Site 3

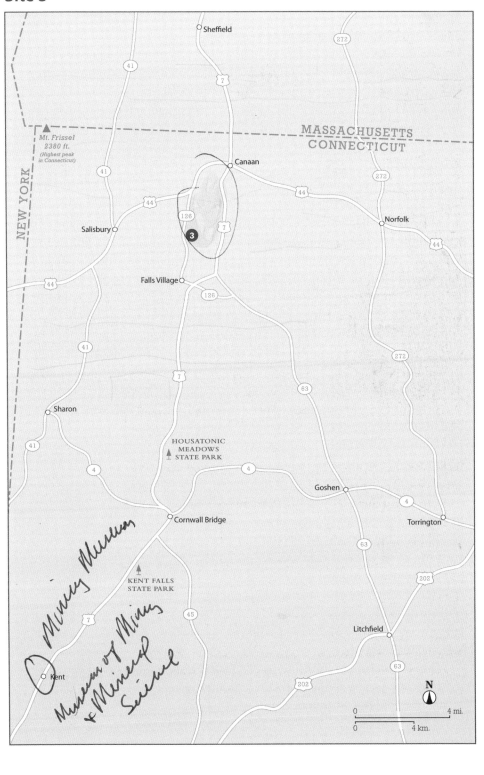

Accommodations: Camping at Housatonic Meadows State Park, Sharon. Lodging available in Falls Village and Torrington.

Finding the site: From the junction of US 7 and CT 126 in Falls Village, follow CT 126 north for 2 miles. Turn right onto Sand Road; proceed 0.6 mile to the Conklin quarry and 0.4 mile farther to the Century Aggregates quarry.

Rules and regulations: Safety gear is required: hard hat, reflective safety vest, steel-toed boots, safety goggles, and gloves.

Rockhounding

There are two marble quarries on Sand Road, a couple of miles north of the historic village of Falls Village, which is part of the town of Canaan. (Locally, the name *Falls Village* is also used to refer to the entire town.) The older of the two quarries, operated by Century Aggregates, was opened long ago, sometime before 1866. The United States Gypsum Company worked the site for a while, mining it for dolomitic marble, which was ground up and used in products like Sheetrock and plaster. Red Wing, the name of another former operator, is still frequently seen on specimen labels. The second quarry on Sand Road has been continuously operated by one company, Conklin Limestone Company, since it opened in 1938. The stone at both sites is the Cambrian- to Ordovician-age Stockbridge marble, named for Stockbridge, Massachusetts, where it was first studied.

The main attraction for collectors at these sites is tremolite, which can be found in radiating groups of white, gray, or light green crystals as long as several inches, embedded in a matrix of fine-grained marble. Canaan is a classic locality for this mineral; specimens are commonly displayed in museums and pictured in mineralogy books. Tremolite is not rare, but such large, attractive crystals (quarry workers used to call them "dog's teeth") are very uncommon. Collectors of fluorescent minerals, in particular, prize these crystals for their strong blue-white fluorescence under shortwave ultraviolet light. Careful trimming is important to produce good specimens that will show off the crystals in an aesthetic manner. As always, practice on some lesser-quality specimens first.

A brand-new mineral was thought to have been discovered in the Canaan area, way back in the early nineteenth century. The massive, white to gray mineral was named canaanite in honor of the town. Unfortunately for the local residents, canaanite was soon determined to be nothing new, just an unusual-looking diopside.

If time permits, visit the Museum of Mining & Mineral Science in Kent. The museum features an extensive collection of Connecticut minerals, one of the best in the state, as well as artifacts from the area's historical iron-mining industry.

4. CCC Quarry and Prospect

Golden beryl is relatively abundant at this site. (John Chipman collection)

Status: Open to the public, but mineral collecting is allowed only with a state permit, which may be granted to mineral clubs and other organizations.

Land manager: State of Connecticut, Department of Energy & Environmental Protection

Land type: Abandoned open-pit quarry and prospect in a forest

Type of deposit: Igneous (granitic pegmatite)

Location: Cockaponset State Forest, Haddam, Middlesex County

GPS: Parking, N41.4589 / W72.5162; quarry, N41.4587 / W72.5146; prospect, N41.4575 / W72.5147

Elevation: Parking, 155 feet; quarry, 170 to 175 feet; prospect, 190 feet

Vehicle: Any

Best season: Apr through Oct

Tools: Crack hammer, chisels, safety goggles, pry bar, screen, garden trowel

Minerals: Albite, almandine, beryl, biotite, columbite, fluorapatite, microcline, muscovite, quartz (smoky), schorl, uraninite

Special attraction: Devil's Hopyard State Park, East Haddam

Accommodations: Camping at Hammonasset Beach State Park, Madison. Lodging available in Middletown.

Finding the site: From I-91, exit 22, follow CT 9 south for 15.5 miles. Take exit 8; turn left onto Beaver Meadow Road. Continue for 1 mile; turn right onto Turkey Hill Road. Continue for 0.4 mile to Filley Road; turn right and park on the right just west of the large red barn on the left. Walk back to the east side of the barn to a gate. Take the path behind the gate 300 feet to the quarry on the left; the beryl prospect is about 250 feet farther on the right.

Rules and regulations: Small hand tools only. Minerals may not be sold or used for any commercial purpose. Complete regulations are available at www.ct.gov/dep.

Rockhounding

The Civilian Conservation Corps (CCC), the Great Depression–era economic recovery program, operated a camp near this old pegmatite quarry and prospect. However, it's likely that the outcrops were known much earlier than the 1930s, perhaps as early as the mid-nineteenth century. The site consists of a small quarry and an even smaller beryl prospect in a thickly wooded part of the state forest. The pegmatite is mineralogically simple, with relatively few species reported to date.

The CCC prospect is a well-known source of golden beryl.

Sites 4–10

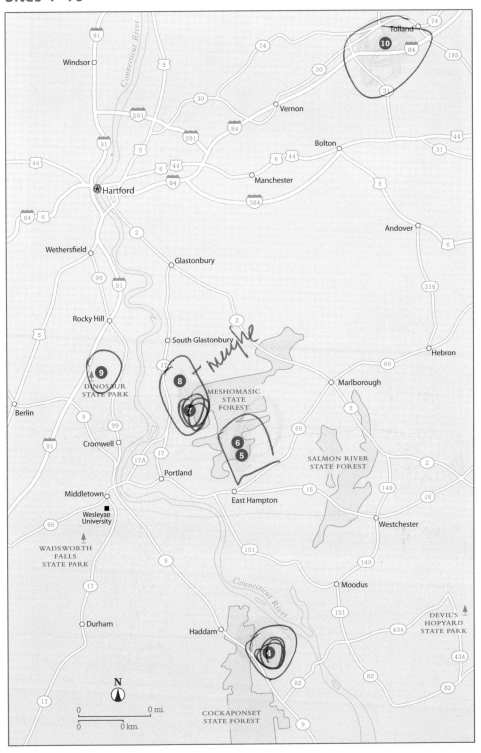

Large crystals of muscovite can be collected at this site. (John Chipman collection)

Collectors have found choice crystals of black schorl, red almandine garnet (up to an inch across), and large books of muscovite in the quarry and adjacent dumps. But most collectors skip the quarry and make a beeline to the beryl prospect, located just south of it on the slope of a rocky knoll. The prospect has been worked for many years, but first-rate mineral finds are still being made. Beryl is relatively abundant, mostly as the common opaque, non-gem variety. Crystals as long as 6 inches have been found, in pale shades of green, yellow, or blue. Gem-quality yellow beryl (golden beryl or heliodor) is the most sought-after prize; try screening the tailings to find some cuttable gem material.

Black platy crystals of columbite, often with bluish iridescence, have turned up as well. Large books of muscovite occur in sharp, pseudohexagonal crystals. Almandine crystals can be found both in the prospect area and in the surrounding schist country rock, where they are common. Collectors of radioactive species should bring a Geiger counter to scan the dumps for small crystals of uraninite.

Cockaponset State Forest is the second-largest state forest in Connecticut, encompassing 16,696 acres in eleven towns and two counties. Other recreational opportunities in the forest include swimming, fishing, canoeing, hiking, horseback riding, mountain biking, and rock climbing.

5. Nathan Hall Quarry

This crystal of almandine exhibits a stepped-growth pattern. (Linda Frahm collection)

See map page 35.

Status: Open to the public, but mineral collecting is allowed only with a state permit, which may be granted to mineral clubs and other organizations.

Land manager: State of Connecticut, Department of Energy & Environmental Protection

Land type: Dumps of an abandoned quarry in a forest

Type of deposit: Igneous (granitic pegmatite)

Location: Meshomasic State Forest, East Hampton, Middlesex County

GPS: Trailhead, N41.5913 / W72.5400; site, N41.5936 / W72.5403

Elevation: Parking, 746 feet; site, 726 to 736 feet

Vehicle: Any

Best season: Apr through Oct

Tools: Crack hammer, chisels, safety goggles, digging tools

Minerals: Albite, almandine, autunite, beryl (golden, aquamarine), biotite, columbite-(Fe), fluorapatite, microcline, monazite-(Ce), muscovite, opal (hyalite), quartz, schorl, torbernite, uraninite, uranophane, zircon

Special attraction: Brownstone Exploration & Discovery Park, Portland

Accommodations: Camping at Devil's Hopyard State Park, East Haddam. Lodging available in Cromwell, Middletown, and Hartford.

Finding the site: From the junction of CT 16 and CT 66 in East Hampton, follow CT 66 east for 0.4 mile. Turn left onto Cone Road; proceed 0.5 mile. Turn left onto Abbey Road, then immediately right onto North Cone Road and proceed 0.3 mile. Turn right onto Clark Hill Road; continue for 0.7 mile. Turn left onto Woodchopper Road; proceed about 0.3 mile to a clearing. Park and follow logging road on right 850 feet to mine dumps on left.

Rules and regulations: Small hand tools only. Minerals may not be sold or used for any commercial purpose. Complete regulations are available at www.ct.gov/dep.

Rockhounding

The long-abandoned Nathan Hall quarry was noted for an abundance of rose quartz in its dumps, according to Wilbur Foye in a 1922 *American Mineralogist* article. Maybe so, but then subsequent collectors must have scooped up every scrap of it that they could get their hands on. Fortunately there are still plenty of other minerals in the dumps for today's collectors (but keep your eyes open for rose quartz, just in case).

Beryl is the star of the Nathan Hall quarry—it can be found in the dumps as yellow, green, or blue-green crystals and crystal fragments, many transparent and gem quality. It's amazing that for such an old quarry, collectors are still finding great beryl specimens at this site every year. Almandine occurs in orange-red to red crystals that frequently exhibit complex stepped-growth patterns. Muscovite can be found in large platy crystals and as pseudomorphs after schorl. Black mica (biotite) is abundant as elongated crystals up to several inches. Quartz is rarely found in crystals, but attractive reddish-brown masses colored by iron oxide inclusions are present on the dumps. Uraninite occurs as crude black crystals, frequently surrounded by thin flakes of pale yellow–green autunite, yellow uranophane, and/or green torbernite. Massive gray to pale green manganoan fluorapatite (fluoresces bright yellow) is relatively common. Cavities in the pegmatite are almost nonexistent, but tiny vugs can be found that contain glassy, striated albite crystals and sometimes sharp micro-muscovite crystals.

A lucky young collector found this terminated crystal of beryl on his first rockhounding field trip ever.

Meshomasic State Forest is a known habitat of the endangered (and protected) timber rattlesnake, *Crotalus horridus*. The snakes hibernate through the winter in dens in rock ledges, emerge in April, and like to bask on rocks in the sun during the day. If you happen to suddenly come upon one, back away slowly—snakes are attuned to rapid movements. Use caution while rockhounding here, but consider yourself fortunate if you happen to observe this rare species in the wild.

6. State Forest No. 1 Quarry

Black biotite is common at this site, often associated with red almandine. (Paul Monti collection)

See map page 35.

Status: Open to the public, but mineral collecting is allowed only with a state permit, which may be granted to mineral clubs and other organizations.

Land manager: State of Connecticut, Department of Energy & Environmental Protection

Land type: Abandoned open-cut workings and adjacent dumps on a forested hillside

Type of deposit: Igneous (granitic pegmatite)

Location: Meshomasic State Forest, East Hampton, Middlesex County

GPS: Trailhead, N41.5913 / W72.5400; site, N41.5956 / W72.5413

Elevation: Trailhead, 747 feet; site, 690 to 724 feet

Vehicle: Any

Best season: Apr through Oct

Tools: Crack hammer, chisels, safety goggles, digging tools

Pegmatite outcrops at the State Forest No. 1 quarry contain beryl and other interesting minerals.

Minerals: Albite, almandine, beryl (aquamarine, golden), biotite, columbite-(Fe), fluorapatite, microcline, muscovite, opal (hyalite), quartz, schorl, spessartine, torbernite, uraninite

Special attraction: Wadsworth Falls State Park, Middletown

Accommodations: Camping at Devil's Hopyard State Park, East Haddam. Lodging available in Cromwell, Middletown, and Hartford.

Finding the site: From the junction of Clark Hill Road and Woodchopper Road in East Hampton, follow Woodchopper Road about 0.3 mile to a clearing. Park and follow logging road on right 0.3 mile; dumps are to the left and ledge workings are on the right.

Rules and regulations: Small hand tools only. Minerals may not be sold or used for any commercial purpose. Complete regulations are available at www.ct.gov/dep.

Rockhounding

The State Forest No. 1 quarry and the Nathan Hall quarry (Site 5) are sometimes grouped together under the name Clark Hill quarries. Clark Hill was named after Jabez Clark (1717–1765), who settled in this part of the town of East Hampton, formerly known as Chatham, back in 1742. The quarry is noted for big books of muscovite mica—as large as 15 inches across—that can be found in the dumps. In fact, for a brief period in the 1940s, the State

Forest No. 1 quarry was mined for mica. Feldspar (microcline) was also mined and can still be found in large masses.

An interesting variety of granite, known as graphic granite because of its hieroglyphic-like markings, is abundant at the State Forest No. 1 quarry and makes a nice decorative stone. Biotite mica is also very common and can be found in large black crystals. Pockets in the pegmatite outcrop on the ledge have produced albite crystals, colorless to smoky quartz, and gray-green fluorapatite. Black schorl is occasionally found in well-terminated crystals. Beryl is usually light green or yellow-green, but purer shades of yellow and rarely blue-green or blue crystals have been found as well. While gem-quality beryl is uncommon, some choice aquamarine crystals have been collected. Excellent specimens of red almandine and black columbite have also turned up, but are rare. Some of the almandine at this site has been partially altered to a tan color. You'll need to do a little digging here, as much of the easily accessible dump material has been picked over, but don't be discouraged—every year collectors find new and often high-quality specimens.

Columbite-(Fe) is a black mineral but sometimes has a multicolored tarnish. (Paul Monti collection)

This blue-green beryl crystal was found by digging into the quarry dumps. (John P. Walsh collection)

The rock ledges at this site could be a habitat for timber rattlesnakes, and ground hornets are known to inhabit the dumps. Please be careful while collecting in this area, especially if you are allergic to bees and wasps.

7. Case Quarries

Silvery muscovite pairs well with blue-green beryl .

See map page 35.

Status: Open to the public, but mineral collecting is allowed only with a state permit, which may be granted to mineral clubs and other organizations.

Land manager: State of Connecticut, Department of Energy & Environmental Protection

Land type: Small excavations on a rocky forested hill

Type of deposit: Igneous (granitic pegmatite)

Location: Meshomasic State Forest, Portland, Middlesex County

GPS: Parking, N41.6216 / W72.5819; No. 1 quarry, N41.6251 / W72.5802; No. 2 quarry, N41.6249 / W72.5798; No. 3 quarry, N41.6262 / W72.5797; No. 4 prospect, N41.6255 / W72.5797

Elevation: Parking, 253 feet; site, 358 to 400 feet

Vehicle: Any

Best season: Apr through Oct

Tools: Crack hammer, chisels, safety goggles, screen; Geiger counter (optional)

Minerals: Albite, almandine, autunite, beryl (aquamarine, golden), biotite, bismite, bismuthinite, bismutite, bismutoferrite, chalcopyrite, columbite-(Fe), cordierite, cuprobismutite, fluorapatite, goethite, gummite, liandratite, microcline, monazite-(Ce), muscovite, opal (hyalite), petscheckite, pyrite, quartz, samarskite-(Y), schorl, thorogummite, torbernite, uraninite, uranophane, uranpyrochlore, zircon (cyrtolite)

Special attraction: Wadsworth Falls State Park, Middletown

Accommodations: Camping at Devil's Hopyard State Park, East Haddam. Lodging available in Cromwell, Middletown, and Hartford.

Finding the site: From the junction of CT 2 and CT 17 in Glastonbury, follow CT 17 south for 6.3 miles. Turn left onto Isinglass Hill Road; proceed 0.7 mile. Turn right onto Thompson Hill Road; continue for 0.8 mile. Turn left onto East Cotton Hill Road; proceed 0.3 mile and park. Walk uphill along the power lines for 1,340 feet. A trail on the left leads to the site.

Rules and regulations: Small hand tools only. Minerals may not be sold or used for any commercial purpose. Complete regulations are available at www.ct.gov/dep.

Rockhounding

The Case quarries have long been a popular destination for mineral clubs, largely because of the abundance of beryl. Three small quarries on the site were worked for feldspar and mica during the 1930s and '40s and were

The trench at the No. 3 quarry is filled with leaves in late autumn.

investigated for possible beryl production during World War II, and so are often called the Case beryl prospects. In 1983 a new excavation—the No. 4 prospect—was opened by mineral collectors, who were able to extract some fine beryl crystals.

The extensive dumps at this site are in the woods and partially covered with leaves and muck, so you should be prepared to get dirty. Beryl is found as well-formed crystals up to 3 inches in diameter and in colors ranging from pale to deep blue to green, white, and yellow. Quartz is abundant, and though crystals are rare, massive milky quartz is sometimes lapidary grade. Fluorapatite is commonly white and hard to recognize in the field, but can be identified by its bright yellow fluorescence under shortwave ultraviolet light. Almandine has been found in red crystals over an inch across, but is not common. Columbite-(Fe) occurs in black prismatic crystals up to 1½ inches long, sometimes with greenish-blue iridescence on crystal faces. Several bismuth minerals are relatively common here, and the opportunity exists to add some unusual minerals to your collection: Gray metallic bismuthinite and its alteration products—green bismutite (and bismutoferrite) and earthy yellow bismite—are associated with brown goethite in massive white quartz.

The Case quarries are popular with collectors of radioactive species. A good place to search for them is in the dumps of Quarry No. 2, where uraninite crystals have been found embedded in pink microcline and dark smoky quartz. Other radioactive minerals include samarskite-(Y), a pitch-black mineral with a conchoidal fracture resembling obsidian; red-brown monazite-(Ce); and liandratite, a rare mineral that occurs as small, bright yellow grains associated with columbite-(Fe). Tiny yellow, square-shaped crystals of the uranium mineral autunite exhibit bright yellow-green fluorescence, and colorless coatings of hyalite glow yellow-green under shortwave ultraviolet light due to traces of uranium.

The trail to the site runs beneath power lines.

8. Simpson Quarry

Blue-green hyalite opal is sometimes found as coatings on feldspar.

See map page 35.

Status: Restricted; no access, unless on an authorized field trip
Land manager: Private
Land type: Dumps of abandoned open-cut mine in a wooded area
Type of deposit: Igneous (granitic pegmatite)
Location: South Glastonbury, Hartford County
GPS: Parking, N41.6363 / W72.5921; site, N41.6387 / W72.5946
Elevation: Parking, 258 feet; site, 304 to 328 feet
Vehicle: Any
Best season: Apr through Oct
Tools: Crack hammer, chisels, safety goggles, digging tools, 10-power loupe
Minerals: Albite, almandine, autunite, beryl (aquamarine, golden), chalcopyrite, columbite, elbaite, fluorapatite, gahnite, grayite, lepidolite, microcline, microlite, muscovite, opal (hyalite), pyrite, quartz, samarskite-(Y), schorl, spessartine, thorite, torbernite, uraninite, zircon
Special attraction: Connecticut State Museum of Natural History, Storrs
Accommodations: Camping at Devil's Hopyard State Park, East Haddam. Lodging available in Rocky Hill and Hartford.

Finding the site: From the junction of CT 2 and CT 17 in Glastonbury, follow CT 17 south for 6.1 miles. Turn left onto Michelle Drive and proceed 0.7 mile to sharp curve; park beyond curve on the left-hand side of the street. Walk back to curve, but continue straight ahead (NNW) on old woods road for about 500 feet. Follow faint trail on left another 500 feet (NW) to the site.

Rules and regulations: Hand tools only. Do not leave any trash.

Rockhounding

Sky-blue, transparent aquamarine is the stuff of rockhound dreams, and you *might* actually find some here. But alas, most of the beryl at the Simpson quarry is a more down-to-earth, pale green color and rather opaque. Just the same, the dream of finding aquamarine keeps collectors coming back again and again. Digging into the dumps is the best way to find beryl, and crystals have been unearthed up to several inches long. However, most crystals are broken, or if not, they'll break when you try to trim the matrix around them. Once in a while, though, you'll find an intact crystal that you'll be proud to display.

Most other collectible minerals at the Simpson quarry occur in small sizes suitable as thumbnail or micromount specimens. Black, rectangular columbite crystals, often with a bluish iridescence, are not uncommon. Microlite occurs as yellow-brown to dark brown isometric crystals somewhat resembling garnet; it can be distinguished by its color and often by its radioactivity. Hyalite opal is found as highly fluorescent, transparent coatings on feldspar and beryl, and also as non-fluorescent, blue-green, copper-bearing coatings. Crystal pockets are almost never found in this pegmatite, but very small cavities occur that contain white or pale blue albite. Lithium minerals like elbaite and lepidolite have been found, but they're pretty much just curiosities. Garnet, ranging from bright orange spessartine to deep red almandine, is abundant as small, lustrous crystals. Gray fluorapatite is very hard to spot in the field, but will glow bright yellow under shortwave ultraviolet light.

If you are interested in rare microminerals, you're in luck. Most collectors come here to search for large, showy crystals of beryl, and it's not uncommon for them to discard anything not showing blue or green color. In the rubble they leave behind, it's possible to find excellent small crystals of microlite, columbite, and spessartine, among other species. You might say one rockhound's trash is another's treasure!

A word of caution: Snakes have been encountered by collectors on the rock dumps, and the surrounding area is a known habitat for the endangered timber rattlesnake. Bug spray is recommended as protection against ticks, mosquitoes, and other insects, which are common pests at this wooded locality.

9. Dinosaur State Park

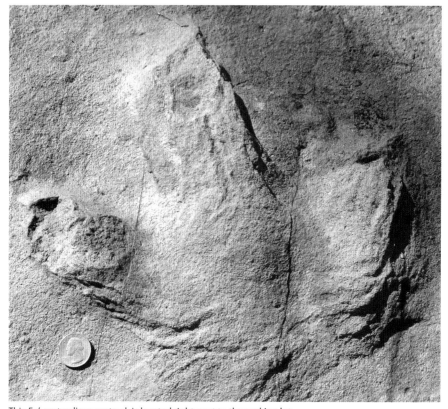

This *Eubrontes* dinosaur track is located right next to the parking lot.

See map page 35.

Status: Open to the public. No collecting is allowed, but plaster casts of dinosaur footprints can be made for free, May through Oct, 9 a.m. to 3:30 p.m. Exhibit center is open year-round (except Mon and major holidays) for a small fee.

Land manager: State of Connecticut, Department of Energy & Environmental Protection

Land type: 63-acre park with nature trails and a large exhibit center

Type of deposit: Sedimentary (sandstone, siltstone, mudstone)

Location: Rocky Hill, Hartford County

GPS: N41.6526 / W72.6562

Elevation: Exhibit center, 213 feet

Vehicle: Any

Best season: May through Oct

Tools: To make casts, bring 10 pounds plaster of Paris, ¼ cup cooking oil, a 5-gallon bucket, and paper towels or cloth rags.

Fossils: Dinosaur footprints: *Eubrontes* (plaster casts can be made of these), *Anchisauripus, Batrachopus,* and *Grallator*

Special attraction: Yale Peabody Museum of Natural History, New Haven

Accommodations: Camping at Devil's Hopyard State Park, East Haddam. Lodging available near I-91, exit 24, Rocky Hill.

Finding the site: Take I-91, exit 23, to West Street; turn right and proceed 0.7 mile.

Rules and regulations: Limit of 1 cast per family or group.

Rockhounding

In 1966 one of the largest dinosaur track sites in North America was discovered by a bulldozer operator preparing the ground for a new state building. Construction was immediately halted so that scientists could study the tracks, and eventually a state park was created to preserve them. An exhibit center, built under a geodesic dome, opened in 1978; it contains roughly 600 dinosaur tracks as well as fossils, interactive exhibits, and dioramas of the natural world that existed during the Triassic and Jurassic periods.

The dinosaurs that created the trackways lived nearly 200 million years ago during the Early Jurassic period. As they crossed what was once a mudflat, they left tracks that hardened, were buried, and survived for all this time. Based on the appearance of the trackways, the dinosaurs were probably large and quick on their feet, able to run at speeds of up to 10 miles per hour. And because their footprints have no toe impressions, some researchers believe that they were swimmers as well. The trackways also suggest that the dinosaurs traveled in herds. No fossil bones have been found to positively identify the species that left the tracks, but the genus name *Eubrontes* has been assigned to the track makers. A good candidate for their identity is *Dilophosaurus,* a medium-size carnivorous bipedal dinosaur famously depicted in the 1993 movie *Jurassic Park.*

To make your own plaster cast of a dinosaur track, bring the items listed in the "Tools" section. It's best to make your cast in dry weather because it will harden faster. Kids love this activity, but bring a change of clothes for them because the process can get very messy. To make a cast: Clear off the track and

Jurassic-age dinosaur tracks are exhibited beneath the exhibit center's geodesic dome.

metal ring in the outdoor casting area using a broom and/or rags. (Do not use water.) Use your hands to spread cooking oil on the dinosaur track and metal ring. Place the ring on the center of the track, and put rags or paper towels all around it. Pour 3 quarts of water into your 5-gallon bucket, and then add the 10 pounds of plaster of Paris. Use your hands to mix it to a smooth consistency. Pour the plaster of Paris mixture into the metal ring, and wait until it dries. Remove the ring and rags and—voila! You have your very own cast of a *Eubrontes* track.

Dinosaur State Park also has nature trails and an arboretum containing hundreds of plant species, including katsuras, ginkgoes, and magnolias, whose ancestors first appeared during the age of the dinosaurs.

10. Burgundy Hill Quarry

Large garnets from Burgundy Hill are often partially coated with green chlorite. This crystal is 1½ inches across.

See map page 35.

Status: Restricted; no access, unless on an authorized field trip

Land manager: Private

Land type: Active stone quarry and a former garnet mine

Type of deposit: Metamorphic (schist, quartzite, gneiss, granofels, amphibolite)

Location: Tolland, Tolland County

GPS: Entrance, N41.8638 / W72.4009

Elevation: Entrance, 899 feet; quarry, 880 to 942 feet

Vehicle: Any

Best season: May through Oct

Tools: Crack hammer, chisels

Minerals: Actinolite, almandine, biotite, calcite, chlorite, epidote, graphite, hornblende, ilmenite, kyanite, magnetite, muscovite, pyrite, pyrrhotite, quartz, titanite, tourmaline

Special attraction: Tantiusques (Sturbridge graphite mine), Sturbridge, MA
Accommodations: Camping available in Tolland. Lodging available off of I-84, Manchester to Vernon.
Finding the site: From I-84, exit 68, take CT 195 north; in 0.6 mile CT 195 merges with CT 74 west. Continue for 2.1 miles and turn left onto Mountain Spring Road; proceed 0.6 mile to entrance on the left.
Rules and regulations: Safety gear is required: hard hat, reflective safety vest, steel-toed boots, safety goggles, and gloves.

Rockhounding

The discovery of garnet on Burgundy Hill is credited to Bruce Cramer (1884–1960), mining engineer and geologist, who stopped to examine an interesting rock on the roadside while on a trip from New York. Exploring further, he found indications of a sizable garnet (almandine) deposit, prompting him to lease and later purchase the land. Mining began in the 1930s; the almandine was extracted for use in industrial products such as garnet paper. The mine consisted of a 135-foot open cut and two tunnels that extended 145 feet into the rock. Much later, the garnet-studded stone at the site was quarried and marketed under trade names such as Jewel Building Stone and Burgundy Hill Wall Stone for decorative use in homes, commercial buildings, churches, landscaping, and memorials. President Eisenhower's home in Gettysburg, Pennsylvania, has a fireplace made of stone from Burgundy Hill. Today the quarry (also known as the Midwood quarry) produces crushed stone for construction purposes.

For collectors, the most interesting mineral at the site is deep red to reddish-purple almandine. Abundant crystals can be found in schist, some as large as 1½ inches in diameter. Large almandine crystals are generally flawed, but small ones embedded in quartz can be quite good. The schist also contains crystals of brown tourmaline (probably dravite) and rarely kyanite in small aquamarine-blue crystals.

One of the oldest mines in New England is located about 23 miles northeast of Burgundy Hill in Sturbridge, Massachusetts. The Tantiusques, or Sturbridge, graphite mine is owned by the Trustees of Reservations and is open to the public (however, collecting is not allowed). The abundant graphite at the site was originally mined by the local Nipmuc people to make ceremonial paints. John Winthrop the Younger (1606–1676) purchased the site from the Nipmucs in 1644; graphite was produced periodically from those early colonial times until the mine closed for good about 1911.

RHODE ISLAND

The old Harris quarry, Lincoln, Rhode Island

11. Cory's Lane Fossil Locality

This fossil was formed by the frond of an ancient tree fern and is known by the form genus name *Pecopteris*. (John Chipman collection)

Status: Open
Land manager: Public
Land type: Seashore
Type of deposit: Sedimentary (weakly metamorphosed shale, meta-anthracite)
Location: Portsmouth, Newport County
GPS: N41.6025 / W71.2758

Elevation: Sea level to high-water mark
Vehicle: Any
Best season: Apr through Oct, but year-round collecting is possible.
Tools: Crack hammer, chisels, scraper or putty knife, safety goggles
Minerals: Chlorite, hematite, muscovite, pyrite, quartz
Fossils: Pennsylvanian-age plant fossils: *Annularia, Alethopteris, Asterophyllites, Lepidodendron, Neuropteris, Pecopteris,* and many others
Special attraction: Purgatory Chasm, Middletown
Accommodations: Camping at Melville Ponds Campground, Portsmouth. Lodging available in Middletown and Newport.
Finding the site: From the junction of RI 24 and RI 114, follow RI 114 south for 0.7 mile. Turn right onto Cory's Lane; continue to the end. Walk to the right along the beach for a couple hundred feet to bedrock exposures (accessible only at low tide).
Rules and regulations: Collect below the high-water mark. No pets.

Rockhounding

The salt-laden breezes blowing off the cool waters of Narragansett Bay make this a delightful, refreshing place to collect in the warmer months. Even in the winter, when other New England collecting sites are likely to be buried in snow, it's possible to bundle up and collect. These shoreline outcrops with their abundant plant fossils have attracted interest from scientists and the public alike since the nineteenth century. You'll find leaf and stem impressions formed over 300 million years ago during Pennsylvanian time, in the low sea cliffs and in loose rocks on the beach. Scale trees (*Lepidodendron*)—extinct plants related to club mosses—grew in the widespread tropical rain forests of the Pennsylvanian epoch and sometimes reached heights of more than 100 feet; their fossilized impressions resemble tire tracks or snakeskin. *Annularia,* small groups of leaves arranged in a radial pattern, are the foliage of extinct treelike horsetails. These and many other fossils can be collected by splitting the shale so that it cleaves into slabs to reveal the fossil impressions.

Minerals at the site are few in number, but occasionally quartz can be found as small colorless crystals, often coated with reddish hematite. Narrow veins of a silky greenish-white fibrous material that closely resembles cross-fiber asbestos can be seen cutting across the shale. However, this material is not asbestos—it's actually an unusual threadlike intergrowth of muscovite and chlorite.

While the ledges along the beach do provide some shade at times, you're still likely to get a lot of sun here, so be sure to use sunscreen and wear a hat.

Sites 11–14

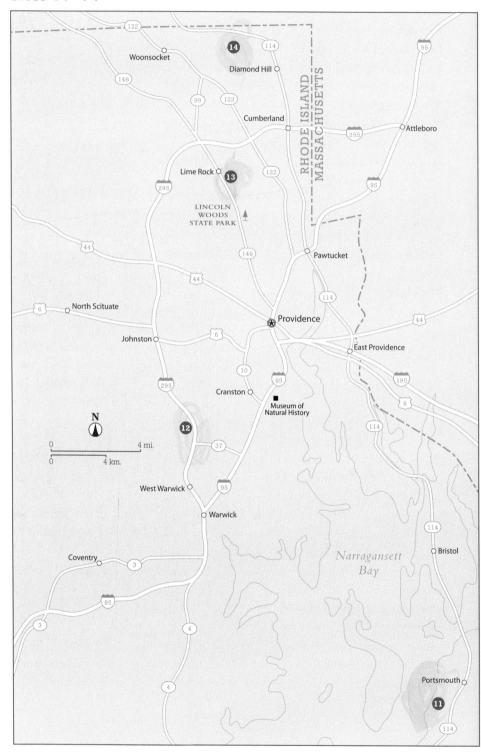

Tiny fibers of muscovite and chlorite can be seen in this close-up view.

Also, be forewarned: The shale has an oily consistency and you are probably going to get dirty sitting in it, splitting it, and handling it, so don't wear your good clothes.

If you have time for a side trip, visit Purgatory Chasm, 9.6 miles away in Middletown. It's a narrow, 50-foot-deep cleft in Pennsylvanian-age rock on the shore of Sachuset Bay. Thundering waves continuously crash onto the rocks at the bottom of the chasm, as the blue ocean water glistens in the distance. The cliffs are composed of conglomerate containing strangely elongated pebbles, cobbles, and boulders. Individual stones in the conglomerate, called clasts, consist primarily of quartzite; some of them are as large as a watermelon.

Annularia are the foliage of an extinct horsetail. (John Chipman collection)

12. Cranston Quarry

This early-morning view greeted rockhounds on a spring field trip to the Cranston quarry.

See map page 56.

Status: Restricted; no access, unless on an authorized field trip

Land manager: Private—P. J. Keating Company

Land type: Active crushed stone quarry

Type of deposit: Igneous (granite), metamorphic (calc-silicate rock), quartz and calcite veins

Location: Cranston, Providence County

GPS: Parking, N41.7633 / W71.4846

Elevation: Parking, 85 feet; quarry, 195 to 260 feet

Vehicle: Any

Best season: May through Oct

Tools: Crack hammer, chisels, digging tools, 10-power loupe

Minerals: Actinolite, adularia, albite, axinite, biotite, calcite, chlorite, clinozoisite, epidote, fluorapatite, fluorite, galena, grossular, hematite, ilmenite, magnetite, microcline, muscovite, pyrite, quartz (smoky), scheelite, sphalerite, titanite

Special attractions: Museum of Natural History, Providence; George B. Parker Woodland (mysterious rock cairns), Coventry

Accommodations: Camping at Holiday Acres, North Scituate. Lodging available in Warwick.

Finding the site: From I-95, exit 14, take RI 37 west for 5.3 miles. Turn right onto Natick Avenue; in 0.3 mile, merge onto RI 51 north and continue 0.4 mile.

Rules and regulations: Safety gear is required: hard hat, reflective safety vest, steel-toed boots, safety goggles, and gloves.

Rockhounding

Without a doubt, there are more minerals in this large quarry than are listed above, as reports from collectors have been spotty. Field trip participants have been hoping to turn up interesting material like the colorful lead and copper species found many years ago at a nearby I-295 road cut. When you visit the Cranston quarry, walk around to survey the entire site, paying special attention to any recently worked areas.

The major rock type here is the roughly 620-million-year-old granite of the Esmond Igneous Suite. Metamorphic rocks, quartz veins, and calcite-filled seams occur as well. Large cleavable masses of white calcite, several inches across, are conspicuous in certain parts of the quarry. The calcite exhibits bright orange-red fluorescence under shortwave ultraviolet light. An unusual peach-colored, opaque calcite also occurs in veins. Smoky quartz is fairly common, but good crystals are rare. Some of the clear smoky quartz is probably of sufficient quality to be faceted into gemstones. Pyrite is not too difficult to find,

Calcite from the Cranston quarry fluoresces orange-red under shortwave ultraviolet light.

though generally only in small crystals. Brassy pyrite crystals embedded in light green massive epidote make a particularly attractive combination. Pyrite is also found as cubic crystals scattered across "carpets" of forest-green chlorite or embedded in massive quartz.

Micromineral collectors will want to look for well-formed epidote, clinozoisite, and magnetite crystals—all have recently been found and make attractive additions to a collection. The magnetite occurs in sharp, lustrous black octahedrons and is associated with pyrite and epidote. Orange-red to pale brown grossular has been found in the quarry, mostly in massive form in calc-silicate rock; fluorescent scheelite can be associated. Ilmenite occurs as flat, steel-gray crystals with a dull luster embedded in quartz.

Epidote often occurs as crystals embedded in quartz.

One of the most interesting museums in New England is the Museum of Natural History at Roger Williams Park in nearby Providence. Founded in 1896, the museum contains a large number of minerals and fossils, many from Rhode Island and elsewhere in New England and frequently quite old. There are also collections of preserved plants, insects, shells, birds, and mammals. Archaeological and ethnographic artifacts, many from North America, are also on display.

13. Conklin Quarry

Bowenite is the state mineral of Rhode Island.

See map page 56.

Status: Restricted; no access, unless on an authorized field trip

Land manager: Private—Conklin Limestone Company

Land type: Rock dumps adjacent to a flooded quarry

Type of deposit: Metamorphic (marble, schist) and igneous (mafic dikes)

Location: Lime Rock, Lincoln, Providence County

GPS: N41.9264 / W71.4570

Elevation: 171 to 185 feet

Vehicle: Any

Best season: Apr through Oct

Tools: Crack hammer, chisels, safety goggles, garden trowel

Minerals: Actinolite, adularia, albite, almandine, anatase, andradite, antigorite (bowenite), apophyllite-(KF), aragonite, aurichalcite, axinite-(Fe), braunite, calcite, chalcopyrite, chlorite, chrysocolla, datolite, diopside, dolomite, dravite, epidote, ferrimolybdite, forsterite, galena, goethite, graphite, grossular, gypsum, hematite, heulandite, hydromagnesite, ilmenite, jarosite, kaolinite, lepidocrocite, magnesiohornblende, magnesite, magnetite, malachite, manganite, molybdenite, montmorillonite, muscovite, prehnite, pyrite, pyrolusite, pyromorphite, quartz (agate, chalcedony, citrine, smoky), rhodochrosite, rhodonite, rutile, scheelite, schorl, scolecite, siderite, talc, tremolite, zircon, zoisite

Special attraction: Lincoln Woods State Park, Lincoln

Accommodations: Camping at Holiday Acres Campground, North Scituate. Lodging available in Smithfield.

Finding the site: From I-295, exit 19, follow RI 146 south for 1.5 miles. Exit onto RI 246 north. Turn right onto Wilbur Road; quarry is on the right.

Rules and regulations: Rules to be provided by field trip leaders.

Rockhounding

One of Rhode Island's most famous mineral localities, the Conklin quarry ceased operating in 2004 and the huge pit was flooded. All that remains for collectors to rummage through are the rock dumps on the north side. Good specimens can still be found, albeit not like those that came out in the glory days.

Marble was extracted at the site for more than 300 years, originally to produce lime for making mortar and plaster, and later for use in agriculture. More recently, crushed snow-white marble was sold as decorative stone for landscaping. The marble is part of the ancient Blackstone group of metamorphic rocks, believed to be Precambrian in age. Another flooded old marble quarry, the Harris quarry, can be seen across the street from the Conklin quarry.

The quarry dumps mostly contain white marble.

Bowenite, a semiprecious gemstone discovered in Rhode Island, is common at the Conklin quarry. It was originally described from the nearby Dexter lime quarry and was named for George T. Bowen (1803–1828), a Rhode Island–born scientist who analyzed it in 1822. Bowenite was designated the official state mineral in 1966; however, it is not a valid mineral species, but a compact variety of the serpentine-group mineral antigorite. Bowenite is massive, translucent, and usually apple green or yellow-green, but can also be colorless, gray, brown, pink, or blue. It frequently contains flakes of talc or magnesite. Bowenite has long been used by stone carvers as a substitute for jade; in fact, it was once considered to be a variety of nephrite, one of the two true types of jade. It is unusually hard for a variety of serpentine and so is well-suited to be cut and polished, made into cabochons, or carved into figurines.

Calcite occurs in a variety of habits at the site: Rhombohedral, scalenohedral, and nail-head crystals are known; massive pieces exhibit brilliant red fluorescence under shortwave ultraviolet light. Black or brown botryoidal aggregates of goethite are common, often with a multicolored, iridescent metallic tarnish. Quartz crystals are usually colorless, but smoky quartz and rarely citrine have been found, too. Handsome masses of chalcedony with blue or yellow drusy quartz are treasured finds. Chert, a fine-grained sedimentary rock composed largely of quartz, is sometimes found with branchlike dendrites that resemble plant fossils but were actually formed by oxides of manganese.

The Conklin quarry has produced many interesting minerals, including (clockwise from top left): blue drusy quartz, diopside, iridescent goethite, and manganese oxides on chert.

14. Iron Mine Hill

Cumberlandite, the state rock of Rhode Island, is strongly magnetic.

See map page 56.

Status: Open

Land manager: Town of Cumberland

Land type: Abandoned iron mine/stone quarry

Type of deposit: Igneous (cumberlandite, gabbro)

Location: Cumberland, Providence County

GPS: Parking, N42.0064 / W71.4570; site, N42.0050 / W71.4569

Elevation: Parking, 368 feet; site, 385 to 410 feet

Vehicle: Any

Best season: Apr through Oct

Tools: None necessary

Minerals: Cumberlandite (a rock); actinolite, clinochlore, epidote, forsterite, hercynite, ilmenite, ilvaite, labradorite, magnetite, molybdenite, serpentine, talc

Special attraction: Museum of Natural History, Providence

Iron Mine Hill was a source of iron ore as early as 1703.

Accommodations: Camping at Holiday Acres, North Scituate. Lodging available in Woonsocket, North Smithfield, and Lincoln.

Finding the site: From I-295, exit 10, in Cumberland, follow RI 122 north for 2.7 miles. Turn right onto West Wrentham Road; proceed 2 miles. Turn left onto Elder Ballou Meeting House Road; park across from the cemetery. Walk along the path in the cemetery (west side) for 275 feet. Cross the rear stone wall and follow the path to the left for 150 feet.

Rules and regulations: No vehicles. Keep out of adjacent private property.

Rockhounding

Iron Mine Hill is the bedrock source of cumberlandite, the official state rock of Rhode Island. Cumberlandite is an unofficial name for a rare type of mafic intrusive rock known as titaniferous magnetite melatroctolite. The rock consists of approximately 49% forsterite (olivine), 32% titaniferous magnetite, 15% labradorite, and minor ilmenite and spinel; it is gray to black, heavy, and medium-grained with labradorite phenocrysts up to about 1 centimeter or so long. Due to its high magnetite content, it is strongly magnetic. In much of the deposit, the forsterite and labradorite have been altered to serpentine, chlorite, and actinolite, adding greenish tones to the rock. The precise age of the cumberlandite deposit is not known; it is estimated to be anywhere from 370 to 620 million years old. Cumberlandite is sometimes fashioned into spheres and polished for decorative use. Small pieces have been polished for use in jewelry as well. Pieces of cumberlandite have been mistaken for meteorites because of their dark color, heft, and magnetism.

During the last ice age, glaciers carried chunks of cumberlandite from Iron Mine Hill and dropped them over a large area extending many miles to the south, as far as Newport and even Block Island. The easily recognizable cumberlandite is found throughout this boulder train. It's a convenient marker for studying the extent and direction of the glacial advances.

The history of mining at Iron Mine Hill began as early as 1703, when the site was worked for iron ore. The ore was mixed with hematite from Cranston and likely taken to a foundry in Cumberland to be processed. Because of its high titanium content, the Iron Mine Hill ore was never economical to work. In later years the rock was quarried for road metal.

You don't really need any tools here—small, loose pieces of cumberlandite are abundant, and one or two samples should suffice. If the surface of a stone is weathered, you could use a heavy hammer to break it open to see the fresh rock inside.

MASSACHUSETTS

The rocks and minerals of Massachusetts have intrigued scientists and collectors alike since the early days of geology and mineralogy in America.

15. Wrentham Quarry

The Wrentham quarry is a popular field trip destination for mineral clubs.

Status: Restricted; no access, unless on an authorized field trip
Land manager: Private—Aggregate Industries Northeast Region. The quarry is often called Simeone quarry, after Simeone Corp., a former operator.
Land type: Active crushed stone quarry
Type of deposit: Igneous (granodiorite)
Location: Wrentham, Norfolk County
GPS: N42.0284 / W71.3525
Elevation: Entrance, 248 feet; quarry, 79 to 320 feet
Vehicle: Any
Best season: May through Oct
Tools: Crack hammer, chisels, digging tools, rake
Minerals: Ankerite, aragonite, calcite, marcasite, pyrite, quartz (colorless, amethyst, chalcedony)
Special attraction: Stony Brook Wildlife Sanctuary, Norfolk
Accommodations: Campgrounds located in Bellingham and Foxboro. Lodging available along US 1, Wrentham and Plainville.

Sites 15–20

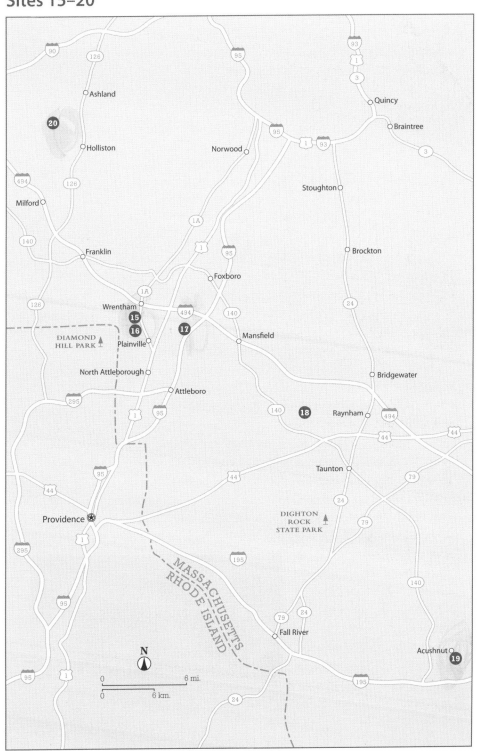

Finding the site: From I-495, exit 15, turn onto MA 1A south and continue for 0.9 mile. Turn right onto High Street; proceed 0.3 mile, turn right, and park.

Rules and regulations: Safety gear is required: hard hat, reflective safety vest, steel-toed boots, safety goggles, and gloves.

Rockhounding

At the start of a recent mineral club field trip, the Wrentham quarry manager made the following declaration to the thirty or so eager collectors standing in the parking lot: "There's amethyst here and lots of it. But it's not something we're concerned with—it all goes to the crusher." Heartbreaking but true— this is a crushed stone quarry after all. "You're welcome to keep what you find. Good luck."

Amethyst, once considered one of the "cardinal" gemstones along with ruby, sapphire, emerald, and diamond, lost much of its value after extensive deposits were discovered in Brazil. But New England amethyst is still treasured by mineral collectors, who value it for its relative scarcity—and Wrentham is the best place in the region to find it. The host rock here is coarse-grained granodiorite, an igneous rock consisting primarily of quartz and feldspar. In places the rock contains cavities or seams filled with secondary minerals such as calcite, ankerite, and pyrite—often in very attractive crystals. The feldspar has frequently been altered to white clay, and it's in this clay that you might find amethyst crystals. Sometimes only one point of a crystal will be visible, and you'll have to chip off the clay surrounding the rest of it. Not all the quartz crystals are purple; many are clear and colorless, a variety known as "rock crystal." Much rarer are scepters, where a crystal is situated on top of a narrower stem. Scepters at Wrentham can be colorless or purple; a purple crystal on top of a colorless stem is an especially valuable find.

A major advantage to collecting in the Wrentham quarry is that you're usually allowed to drive right down to the collecting area. This means you can load up your vehicle with your finds, without having to break your back carrying them any great distance. Be sure to bring some lunch and plenty of water. And there are no trees for shade, so sunscreen is highly recommended.

These amethyst crystals are associated with greenish-brown ankerite.

16. Masslite Quarry

This tiny footprint was left by an ancient amphibian, one of the first creatures to walk on land. (Sam Pavadore collection)

See map page 69.

Status: Restricted; no access, unless on an authorized field trip

Land manager: Private—Lorusso Corp

Land type: Active crushed stone quarry

Type of deposit: Sedimentary (weakly metamorphosed argillite, shale, sandstone, greywacke, conglomerate; meta-anthracite)

Location: Plainville, Norfolk County

GPS: N42.0155 / W71.3541

Elevation: Entrance, 235 feet; quarry, 145 to 390 feet

Vehicle: Any

Best season: May through Oct

Tools: Crack hammer, chisels

Minerals: Calcite, chlorite, gypsum, pyrite, quartz

Fossils: Mid-Pennsylvanian plant fossils—*Annularia, Alethopteris, Calamites, Cordaites, Lepidodendron, Mariopteris, Neuropteris, Palmatopteris, Sphenophyllium, Sphenopteris, Stigmaria,* and more; tracks/swimming traces of reptiles, amphibians, and temnospondyls; raindrop impressions; insect impressions and tracks

Special attraction: Diamond Hill Park, Cumberland, RI

Accommodations: Campgrounds located in Bellingham and Foxboro. Lodging available along US 1, Wrentham and Plainville.

Finding the site: From I-495, exit 15, follow MA 1A south for 1.2 miles. Turn right onto Cross Street; proceed 0.4 mile and turn left to enter the quarry.

Rules and regulations: Safety gear is required: hard hat, reflective safety vest, steel-toed boots, safety goggles, and gloves.

Rockhounding

Imagine for a moment standing at this site and suddenly being transported 315 million years back in time—what would you see? You'd see a lush tropical rain forest thick with ferns and club mosses growing under tall horsetail-like trees. Small amphibians and reptiles would be ambling through shallow muddy water; insects resembling giant dragonflies would be flying overhead. This ancient environment existed more than 80 million years before the dinosaurs first walked the earth. Time travel may be impossible, but we do have a "window" into that lost world—the fossilized impressions left by the plants and animals that inhabited it.

The rocks hosting these fossilized impressions are part of the Pennsylvanian-age Rhode Island Formation, part of the Narragansett structural basin; they were formed from sediments laid down in what are known as coal swamps. The most abundant plant fossils you'll find in the quarry are *Calamites, Cordaites,* and *Annularia,* and those of various ferns and seed ferns. *Calamites* are the treelike stem casts of an extinct genus of horsetails that grew as tall as 65 feet. Often the plant impressions are light gray on a dark gray matrix and make attractive specimens.

The top level of the quarry is the best area to search for rocks containing amphibian and reptile footprints; trackways up to 2 feet long have been collected. Fossilized footprints of *Bactrachicthys plainvillensis,* a tiny salamander-like amphibian (named after the town of Plainville), show that it had four feet, each about ½ inch long—its front feet had four toes, and its back feet five. *B. plainvillensis* is believed to have been among the first animals to walk on land.

A few minerals occur at this site, including pyrite; generous helpings of little brassy pyrite cubes can be found sprinkled across large slabs of weakly metamorphosed shale. Quartz crystals are also common, some with green inclusions of chlorite.

17. North Attleborough Fossil Site

Impressions of *Sphenophyllum* leaves are among the many types of fossils found at the site.

See map page 69.

Status: Open

Land manager: Town of North Attleborough

Land type: Rocky knoll

Type of deposit: Sedimentary (weakly metamorphosed shale)

Location: North Attleborough, Bristol County

GPS: Entrance, N42.0065 / W71.2870; site, N42.0108 / W71.2858

Elevation: Entrance, 160 feet; site, 155 to 160 feet

Vehicle: Any

Best season: Apr through Oct

Tools: Crack hammer, chisels, scraper or putty knife, pry bar, safety goggles

Minerals: Calcite, goethite, hematite, pyrite, quartz

Fossils: Mid-Pennsylvanian plant fossils—*Annularia, Calamites, Cordaites, Lepidodendron, Neuropteris, Sphenophyllium,* and many others

Special attraction: WWI Memorial Park and Zoo, North Attleborough

Accommodations: Campgrounds located in Foxboro and Mansfield. Lodging available along US 1 between I-495 and I-295.

Finding the site: From the junction of MA 152 and MA 106 in North Attleborough, follow MA 152 south for 0.2 mile. Turn left onto Plain Street; continue for 0.9 mile to the entrance of the North Attleborough Compost Site. Park across the street, and walk into the compost site; continue past the parking area, keeping to the right of the compost piles. The collecting site is about 300 feet NNW of the first pile, beyond a small grove of trees. The outcrop is low; it's best to use GPS to find it.

Rules and regulations: Park on the street, not on the compost site.

Rockhounding

About 310 million years ago, a large flying insect—an ancient relative of mayflies—touched down in some mud, left an impression of its entire body, and then up and flew away. The resulting 3-inch trace fossil is believed to be the oldest whole-body impression of a flying insect ever found. Its discovery and collection in 2008 behind a North Attleborough strip mall made scientific news around the world.

The present collecting site is just a few miles away from where that sensational fossil was found, and new discoveries are certainly possible here, too. Most of the fossils you'll find are the impressions of tropical plants that lived in a humid, swampy valley when this area was part of the ancient microcontinent of Avalonia. The rock consists of weakly metamorphosed shale belonging to the Pennsylvanian-age Rhode Island Formation. You shouldn't have any trouble finding plant fossils—they are abundant at this site—but look for insects, too.

To collect fossil specimens, use hammers and chisels to break up rock on the ledge, and a heavy-duty putty knife or similar tool to work your way in between the layers of shale in order to split them apart. The fossils will be found oriented flat against these layers. It's also possible to find specimens lying on the ground in the rubble left by other collectors. But the best and largest fossils will be found by working the ledge. Plant fossils are plentiful enough that you can afford to be picky. Bring home your best, and leave the rest for others to enjoy.

Though not noted as a mineral-collecting locality, calcite is abundant. The calcite is generally massive and is quite fluorescent (red) under shortwave ultraviolet light. A few crystals have also been found. Microcrystals of pyrite and quartz are readily available in seams in the shale.

18. Taunton Quarry

Pecopteris, a fossil fern, has a characteristic comb-like arrangement of leaflets. (Dana M. Jewell collection)

See map page 69.

Status: Restricted; no access, unless on an authorized field trip

Land manager: Private—Aggregate Industries Northeast Region

Land type: Active crushed stone quarry

Type of deposit: Sedimentary (weakly metamorphosed shale, sandstone, greywacke, conglomerate; meta-anthracite)

Location: Taunton, Bristol County

GPS: Entrance, N41.9276 / W71.1228

Elevation: Entrance, 88 feet; quarry, −85 to 70 feet

Vehicle: 4WD

Best season: May through Oct

Tools: Crack hammer, chisels, scraper or putty knife, pry bar

Minerals: Calcite, chlorite, epidote, goethite, pyrite, quartz

Fossils: Mid-Pennsylvanian plant fossils

Special attraction: South Shore Natural Science Center, Norwell

Accommodations: Camping at Boston/Cape Cod KOA, Middleboro. Lodging available in Raynham and Middleboro.

Finding the site: From I-495, exit 9, follow Bay Street south for 1.7 miles. Turn right onto Bassett Street; continue for 1.3 miles.

Rules and regulations: Safety gear is required: hard hat, reflective safety vest, steel-toed boots, safety goggles, and gloves.

Rockhounding

On each new field trip to the Taunton quarry, fossil collectors arrive excited by the possibility of making a new and wonderful discovery. Not much bedrock is exposed at the surface in southeastern Massachusetts, so sites like this one are important windows into the geologic past. The rock in the quarry belongs to the Pennsylvanian-age Rhode Island Formation and consists largely of dark gray, medium- to coarse-grained sandstone; conglomerate containing relatively large pebbles; and layers of dark gray shale containing abundant plant fossils.

There is little published about the fossils from this quarry, but collectors are finding that they are similar to those at other Pennsylvanian-age sites in the region.

Stone has been quarried at this site for over a hundred years. At first the operations were sporadic and small-scale; the rock was crushed for use as railroad ballast and possibly cut as dimension stone as well. Since about 1955 the rock has been extracted and crushed for use as construction aggregate, and the quarry has greatly expanded. The pit is now very deep, the lowest level lying well below sea level.

Quartz crystals occur in seams in the metamorphosed shale.

The list of minerals found in the quarry is short. Quartz is common, usually occurring as drusy crystals in thin veins but occasionally as larger individual crystals. Most crystals are colorless, but many have a yellow or orange iron oxide coating. Calcite occurs in veins and is generally massive; however, small disc-shaped crystals of ferroan calcite (or perhaps ankerite) are found associated with quartz crystals. Massive, pistachio-green epidote is also common in veins. Because most collectors come to the site in search of fossils, the list of mineral species is almost certainly not complete.

19. Acushnet Quarry

Pale greenish-blue fluorapatite, white albite, and dark green chlorite are classic alpine vein minerals.

See map page 69.

Status: Restricted; no access, unless on an authorized field trip

Land manager: Private—P. J. Keating Company

Land type: Active crushed stone quarry

Type of deposit: Metamorphic (gneiss with alpine-type fissure veins) and igneous (diorite, granite, aplite, pegmatite, mafic dikes)

Location: Acushnet, Bristol County

GPS: N41.6736 / W70.9081

Elevation: Entrance, 29 feet; lowest level, −250 feet (Death Valley, CA, the lowest point in North America, is −282 feet.)

Vehicle: 4WD

Best season: May through Oct

Tools: Crack hammer, chisels, digging tools, 10-power loupe

Minerals: Actinolite-tremolite (byssolite), adularia, albite (pericline), analcime, calcite, chabazite, chalcopyrite, chlorite, epidote, fluorapatite, fluorite, hematite, heulandite, hornblende, ilmenite, malachite, muscovite, prehnite, pyrite, quartz, rutile, stilbite, titanite

Special attraction: Dighton Rock State Park, Berkley
Accommodations: Camping at Myles Standish State Forest, Plymouth and Carver Lodging available in New Bedford, Fairhaven, and Dartmouth.
Finding the site: From MA 24, exit 12, in Taunton, follow MA 140 south for 13.7 miles. Take exit 6 to MA 18 south; continue for 2.3 miles. Turn left onto Tarkiln Hill Road; proceed 1.3 miles. Turn right onto South Main Street; continue for 0.7 mile.
Rules and regulations: Safety gear is required: hard hat, reflective safety vest, steel-toed boots, safety goggles, and gloves.

Rockhounding

The Acushnet quarry is an outstanding North American locality for mineralization in alpine-type fissure veins, named for the Swiss Alps, where they were first studied and described. Cavities in the veins often contain good crystals of several minerals, frequently sprinkled or coated with dark green flakes of chlorite. In fact, if you find chlorite, examine the specimen and surrounding rocks closely, as this mineral is a good indicator of alpine-type veins. Yellow or pale blue fluorapatite, green or brown titanite, and dark green chlorite-dusted crystals of adularia and pericline are all typical of this environment.

What you find on a particular day will depend on what area of the quarry is being worked—rocks are continually being blasted and moved around. A keen eye and a little luck will help you zero in on a promising area to begin your search. You may have seen sensational specimens from Acushnet on display in a museum or featured in a magazine or on a website. Don't expect to just stumble across one of these beauties—it's (usually) not that easy. Be patient. Take time to survey the various rock types first.

Quartz crystals are abundant at Acushnet, usually colorless or milky and lining cavities; individual crystals up to 8 inches long have been found. Pyrite can occur as fist-size chunks of massive "fool's gold," but is more common as scatterings of little brassy cubes. Rarely, wirelike microcrystals can be found. If you're interested in micro and thumbnail-size specimens, look for well-formed crystals of zeolite species like chabazite, heulandite, and stilbite. Tiny vugs filled with green crystals of epidote and white fibers of byssolite are also attractive under the 'scope.

The bottom level of the Acushnet quarry is well below sea level, and shade is hard to come by most of the time; the sun can feel relentless beating down on your hard hat in hot weather. If you visit during the summer, be sure to drink plenty of water and try to collect early in the morning, while it's relatively cool. Fortunately insects are not really a problem here any time of year.

20. Ashland Quarry

The quarry partially fills with water when not in operation.

See map page 69.

Status: Restricted; no access, unless on an authorized field trip

Land manager: Private—Aggregate Industries Northeast Region

Land type: Active crushed stone quarry

Type of deposit: Metamorphic (schist, amphibolite, gneiss, quartzite; alpine-type fissure veins) and igneous dikes

Location: Ashland, Middlesex County

GPS: N42.2314 / W71.4768

Elevation: Parking, 264 feet; lowest level, 164 feet

Vehicle: 4WD

Best season: May through Oct

Tools: Crack hammer, chisels, digging tools, 10-power loupe

Minerals: Actinolite, albite, almandine, anthophyllite, aurichalcite, axinite-(Fe), biotite, bornite, calcite, chabazite, chalcopyrite, chamosite, chrysocolla, clinozoisite, epidote, ferro-hornblende, fluorapatite, goethite, hematite, heulandite, ilmenite, kamphaugite-(Y), laumontite, magnetite, malachite, microcline, montmorillonite, muscovite, natrolite, oligoclase, opal (hyalite), prehnite, pyrite, pyrrhotite, quartz, sphalerite, stellerite, stilbite, titanite

Special attraction: Purgatory Chasm, Sutton

Accommodations: Camping at Sutton Falls Camping Area, Sutton. Lodging available in Framingham.

Finding the site: From the junction of MA 135 and MA 126 in Framingham, follow MA 135 west for 4.1 miles. Turn left onto Olive Street; continue for 0.9 mile. Turn left onto Spring Street; proceed 0.3 mile.

Rules and regulations: Safety gear is required: hard hat, reflective safety vest, steel-toed boots, safety goggles, and gloves.

Rockhounding

Opened in 1948, the Ashland quarry has long been a favorite destination for mineral clubs because of its varied geology and the relative ease of collecting attractive specimens. Bayer-Mingolla and Trimount, former names of the quarry, are often seen on old mineral labels.

Among the many interesting rocks in the quarry is amphibolite, which contains long, shiny black crystals of ferro-hornblende that seemingly float on a fine-grained greenish matrix. Bronzy pyrite cubes frequently occur in the

Orange "balls" of kamphaugite-(Y) are associated with white laumontite.

amphibolite, some reaching ½ inch across. Alpine-type fissure veins in metamorphic rock host crystals of gemmy, greenish-yellow titanite nestled in beds of sparkly dark green chamosite. Fluorapatite also occurs in these veins as colorless or yellow crystals, up to ½ inch long. Dark metallic-gray, octahedral magnetite crystals are not uncom-

These pale yellow stilbite crystals were discovered in a tiny pocket.

mon at Ashland and can be up to 3 millimeters long. Zeolite minerals occur in small but good crystals; white to yellow aggregates of stilbite, resembling wheat sheaves, are among the most frequently found. Superb specimens of pistachio-green epidote, in crystals up to 5 inches long, have been collected as well. Blue and green splotches of secondary copper minerals such as malachite and chrysocolla can be found as the result of the alteration of chalcopyrite.

In 2006 specimens containing tiny cream- to orange-colored "balls" of an unidentified mineral associated with calcite, stilbite, and laumontite were found on a mineral club field trip. The club "experts" were stumped, so a sample was given to a petrologist for analysis at a local university laboratory. Test results showed the mineral to be kamphaugite-(Y), a rare-earth carbonate mineral first discovered in Norway in 1993. Ashland is the second known locality for kamphaugite-(Y) in the United States. This is one of many examples in New England of amateur rockhounds making significant contributions as "citizen scientists" by partnering with professionals to help make discoveries.

Octahedral magnetite crystals are common at this site.

21. Swampscott Quarry

Allanite-(Ce) is a rare-earth mineral in the epidote group.

Status: Restricted; no access, unless on an authorized field trip
Land manager: Private—Aggregate Industries Northeast Region
Land type: Active crushed stone quarry
Type of deposit: Igneous (gabbro-diorite, granite, granitic pegmatite, syenite, basalt, felsite)
Location: Swampscott and Salem, Essex County
GPS: Office, N42.4834 / W70.9150
Elevation: Office, 60 feet; quarry, −103 to 104 feet
Vehicle: 4WD
Best season: May through Oct
Tools: Crack hammer, chisels, digging tools
Minerals: Allanite-(Ce), augite, biotite, calcite, chalcopyrite, chlorite, epidote, fluorite, galena, hematite, heulandite, hornblende, labradorite, laumontite, magnetite, microcline, molybdenite, prehnite, pyrite, quartz, siderite, sphalerite, zircon

Special attractions: Saugus Iron Works National Historic Site, Saugus; Babson Farm Quarry at Halibut Point State Park, Rockport

Accommodations: Camping at Harold Parker State Forest, Andover. Lodging available in Salem, Peabody, and Saugus.

Finding the site: From MA 128, exit 25A, follow MA 114 south for 2.5 miles towards Salem. Turn right onto MA 107 south; continue for 1.6 miles. Turn left onto Swampscott Road; proceed 1.4 miles to quarry office.

Rules and regulations: Safety gear is required: hard hat, reflective safety vest, steel-toed boots, safety goggles, and gloves.

Rockhounding

The Swampscott quarry began operating more than a century ago and has grown to a whopping 160 acres. Stone from the site was formerly used for stone walls and building foundations; you can still see Swampscott stone in old homes and walls throughout northeastern Massachusetts. Today the stone is crushed for use in asphalt and concrete and for a variety of other uses in the construction industry.

The quarry is located in a 6-square-mile pluton composed chiefly of gabbro, part of the Salem gabbro–diorite, a formation named in 1910 by the geologist C. H. Clapp. Quartz crystals occur in seams in the rock, some of them with dark green inclusions of chlorite. Shiny dark gray metallic hematite crystals are sometimes associated with the crystals. Black allanite-(Ce) and bright metallic-gray molybdenite can be found in pink microcline feldspar in pegmatite veins. Smooth pistachio-green specimens of epidote can be collected from slickensides—naturally polished rock surfaces formed along faults in the rock. Slickensides are common in the quarry, and some large decorative specimens of epidote can be collected. There is much to explore at this site; the mineral-collecting potential of the quarry has not been thoroughly investigated, and the list above is almost certainly incomplete.

Saugus Iron Works National Historic Site in nearby Saugus is a 9-acre park with a reconstructed colonial ironworks complex. The original ironworks operated from 1646 to ca. 1670. The iron ore came from bog ore deposits in Saugus and neighboring towns, and gabbro mined on the coast of Nahant (similar to Salem gabbro–diorite, but a different formation) was used as a fluxing agent. The park has guided tours, a museum, and a nature trail.

Sites 21–24

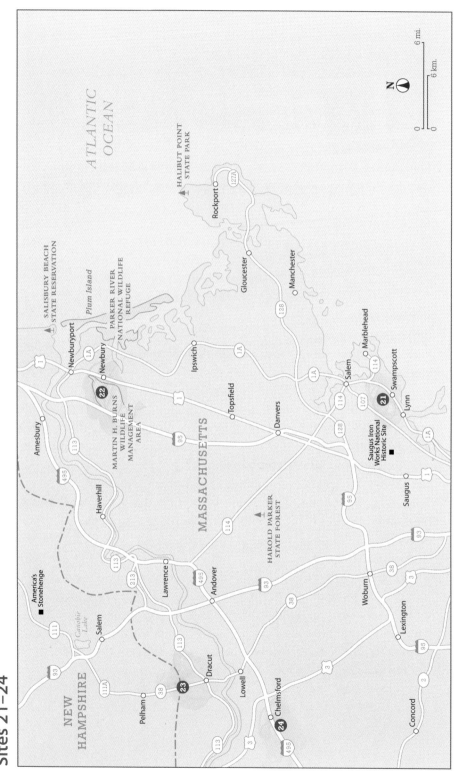

22. Chipman Mine

Glacial boulders are common in the Burns Wildlife Management Area.

See map page 84.

Status: Open to the public, but mineral collecting is allowed only with a state permit.

Land manager: Massachusetts Division of Fisheries & Wildlife, Northeastern District

Land type: Dumps of an abandoned mine in a forest

Type of deposit: Hydrothermal lead-silver-copper-zinc ore deposit

Location: Martin H. Burns Wildlife Management Area, Newbury, Essex County

GPS: Parking, N42.7813 / W70.9228 or N42.7898 / W70.8876; mine site, N42.7846 / W70.9059

Elevation: 61 to 66 feet

Vehicle: Any

Best season: Apr through Oct

Tools: Crack hammer, chisels, safety goggles, garden trowel

Minerals: Ankerite, arsenopyrite, azurite, bornite, chalcopyrite, covellite, galena, hematite, malachite, muscovite, pyrite, quartz, siderite, sphalerite, tetrahedrite

Special attraction: Parker River National Wildlife Refuge, Newburyport

Accommodations: Camping at Salisbury Beach State Reservation, Salisbury. Lodging available in Newburyport.

Finding the site: From I-95, exit 56, take Scotland Road east for 400 feet to Burns WMA parking area on right. From there, you'll need to use GPS to bushwhack about a mile to the site. Alternatively, continue east on Scotland Road for 1.9 miles; turn right onto Highfield Road; proceed 0.3 mile and park near the power substation. Walk west along rail trail for 0.75 mile. Using GPS, leave rail trail and bushwhack 0.3 mile to the site.

Rules and regulations: The permit allows for the collection of small amounts of loose rocks and minerals, using hand tools only. Hunting is allowed (except Sun), so a hunter-orange cap is required for safety.

Silver-bearing galena was the primary ore of the Chipman mine.

Rockhounding

The silver rush of Essex County began, according to a 1901 *Scientific American* article, when a man named Edward Rogers discovered "float ore" in a Newbury pasture in 1868. Rogers and a partner traced these surface fragments to land belonging to a Mrs. Jaques and purchased 8 acres from her for $350 ($5,700 in 2013 dollars). After mining 6 tons of galena, the partners sold the land in 1874 for $100,000 ($2 million in 2013 dollars). The hopeful new owners, two gentlemen named Chipman and Kelley, started mining immediately. The ore they were after was silver-bearing galena associated with the copper mineral tetrahedrite. The galena was said to contain an average of 60 to 70 ounces of silver per ton, while the tetrahedrite contained both silver and gold. The excitement sparked by the new mining venture spread rapidly—prospecting began in large parts of Newbury and in neighboring towns

Chalcopyrite with a colorful tarnish is sometimes called "peacock ore." (John Chipman collection)

as well. Land prices and sales boomed as the silver rush swept the region. Though some individuals made a great deal of money selling land, the mining ventures themselves turned out not to be profitable. The silver rush fizzled, and by 1880 the mines were all but abandoned.

In the twentieth century the Chipman mine was a favorite destination for mineral club–sponsored field trips. However, like so much land in the region, the mine area became a tempting target for residential development. Fortunately, conservation-minded individuals worked to annex 103 acres of forest, including the mine, to the state's Martin H. Burns Wildlife Management Area. Public access has been maintained; however, a state permit is now required to collect minerals.

Aside from quartz, the most common mineral in the dumps is siderite, weathered on its surface to a reddish-brown color. Break open a piece and you'll see that the fresh material is actually tan or brown; you might also find silvery galena, brassy pyrite, golden-yellow chalcopyrite, or resinous red-brown sphalerite. The stones containing these metallic minerals are noticeably heavier than those without them. Some of the chalcopyrite has been altered to green malachite and very rarely, blue azurite.

A word of caution: Ticks are a significant hazard here—they thrive in the wildlife management area because of its abundant deer population. Be sure to use sufficient insect repellent and check yourself for ticks when you leave.

The Chipman and other area mines were worked for silver in the 1870s. Silver from the region was used to produce this ingot in 1878. (Sam Pavadore collection)

23. Dracut Quarry

Calcite crystals from the Dracut quarry can make outstanding specimens. (Dana M. Jewell collection)

See map page 84.
Status: Restricted; no access, unless on an authorized field trip
Land manager: Private—P. J. Keating Company
Land type: Active crushed stone quarry
Type of deposit: Igneous (diorite, gabbro, norite, granitic pegmatite) and metamorphic (schist, phyllite, quartzite, granofels)
Location: Dracut, Middlesex County (a small portion is in Pelham, NH)
GPS: N42.6963 / W71.3137
Elevation: Entrance, 144 feet; quarry, 39 to 210 feet
Vehicle: Any
Best season: May through Oct
Tools: Crack hammer, chisels, digging tools, 10-power loupe
Minerals: Actinolite, adularia, albite, almandine, apophyllite, augite, biotite, calcite, chabazite, chalcopyrite, chlorite, clinozoisite, diopside, epidote, enstatite, fluorapatite, fluorite, goethite, grossular, hematite, heulandite, hornblende, ilmenite, labradorite, laumontite, magnetite, microcline, muscovite, olivine, opal (hyalite), prehnite, pyrite, pyrrhotite, quartz, scheelite, schorl, stilbite, titanite

Special attraction: America's Stonehenge, Salem, NH

Accommodations: Camping at Harold Parker State Forest, Andover. Lodging available along I-93 from Andover, MA, to Salem, NH.

Finding the site: From I-495, exit 38, in Tewksbury, follow MA 38 north for 5.5 miles.

Rules and regulations: Safety gear is required: hard hat, reflective safety vest, steel-toed boots, safety goggles, and gloves.

Stilbite is often found in fan-shaped crystal aggregates associated with calcite.

Rockhounding

Exceptional mineral specimens have been collected from veins of calcite and prehnite in the Dracut quarry, but it takes patience and luck to find them. Fine calcite specimens consisting of large white to tan crystals on matrix have made calcite the biggest attraction for most collectors. Massive, pale golden-yellow calcite is common and exhibits strong white fluorescence under shortwave ultraviolet light, and long-lasting phosphorescence as well. The prehnite at the Dracut quarry is unusual—worldwide, this mineral typically occurs as greenish botryoidal aggregates. But here prehnite is more commonly found as individual pale green or colorless crystals or as clusters of thick, well-formed crystals.

This is probably the best site in eastern New England to collect specimens of zeolite minerals such as stilbite, heulandite, and chabazite. Stilbite is the most common, occurring as water-clear or pale orange-brown crystals often in large radial, fan-shaped aggregates. Massive purple fluorite, pale green or pink clinozoisite, black schorl, and green drusy epidote have also been found. Hyalite in thin coatings produces intense green fluorescence. Check out rocks in the most recently blasted areas to see what might turn up. No doubt, the list of minerals for this locality should be much longer, and in time inquisitive collectors will be making new discoveries.

The igneous rocks in the quarry consist primarily of diorite and norite of the Dracut Pluton; the metamorphic rocks include schist and related rocks of the Berwick Formation. Norite, a variety of gabbro, contains enstatite and labradorite. Worldwide, nickel ores are often associated with norite, and in fact there once was a nickel mine a few miles southeast of the Dracut quarry. The mine began operating for nickel in 1876, but long before then—as early as the mid-1600s—the deposit was mined for iron. Miners at the time did not know what nickel was, because the element would not be discovered until 1751.

24. Chelmsford Lime Quarries

The old lime quarries in Chelmsford date to the 1700s.

See map page 84.
Status: Open
Land manager: Town of Chelmsford
Land type: Abandoned quarries in a wooded area
Type of deposit: Metamorphic (dolomitic marble, calc-silicate granulite, skarn, amphibolite, gneiss, schist, quartzite)
Location: Lime Quarry Reservation, Chelmsford, Middlesex County
GPS: Parking, N42.5919 / W71.3690
Elevation: Parking, 167 feet; quarries, 170 to 220 feet
Vehicle: Any
Best season: Apr through Oct
Tools: Crack hammer, chisels, safety goggles
Minerals: Actinolite, brookite, calcite, clinozoisite, diopside, dolomite, fluorapatite, forsterite, geikielite, humite group, phlogopite, pyrite, pyrrhotite, quartz, rutile, scapolite, scheelite, serpentine, spinel, titanite, tremolite

Special attraction: Minute Man National Historical Park, Concord
Accommodations: Camping at Minuteman Campground, Littleton. Lodging available along I-495 in Westford, Chelmsford, and Tewksbury.
Finding the site: From I-495, exit 33, in Chelmsford, take MA 4 south for 0.4 mile. Turn right onto MA 110 west and proceed 1 mile.
Rules and regulations: Hobby collecting only. Do not damage vegetation.

Rockhounding

A handful of marble quarries in Chelmsford were worked to produce lime from about 1736 to 1830. The town acquired some of the old quarry land in 1967 and established Lime Quarry Reservation, which was expanded in 1976 to its present 40 acres. Trails through the woods are used by local residents for hiking, dog walking, and nature study. Recently loose rocks and debris were removed from the base of one of the quarry walls to make it more accessible to climbers.

Actinolite is commonly found on the quarry dumps.

There are two main pits and several smaller excavations on the reservation. The quarry dumps contain a variety of rocks and minerals of interest to collectors. Gray coarse-grained dolomitic marble is common in the first quarry, the one closest to the parking area. Green amphibole (actinolite) is found in large groups of elongated, bladed crystals in both of the main pits; white or gray amphibole (tremolite), often fibrous, is less common. Fluorapatite occurs in attractive light teal-blue, hexagonal crystals. Brown titanite crystals up to an inch long have been found, especially near the first quarry. Scapolite is usually massive but sometimes occurs in good-quality crystals. Diopside is common in fine groups of light green crystals. Scheelite, which has brilliant bluish-white fluorescence, occurs near the second quarry.

An unusual dike that looks something like an old cement wall traverses the first quarry. It was left standing by the workers as they extracted the softer carbonate rocks on either side of it. The dike consists of massive quartz, feldspar, and scapolite. Don't hammer at this dike (there is nothing worthwhile to collect in it anyway) or any of the quarry walls, so that others may enjoy viewing the fascinating geological features. Collect only from the rock dumps, which are plentiful and contain the best material.

25. Littleton Quarry

The muscovite variety fuchsite is colored green by chromium.

Status: Restricted; no access, unless on an authorized field trip
Land manager: Private—Aggregate Industries Northeast Region
Land type: Active crushed stone quarry
Type of deposit: Igneous (granite) and metamorphic (quartzite, phyllite, schist)
Location: Littleton, Middlesex County
GPS: Entrance, N42.5506 / W71.5257
Elevation: Entrance, 250 feet; quarry, 119 to 254 feet
Vehicle: 4WD
Best season: May through Oct
Tools: Crack hammer, chisels, digging tools, 10-power loupe
Minerals: Adularia, anatase, arsenopyrite, biotite, calcite, chalcopyrite, chlorite, chrysocolla, epidote, galena, hornblende, malachite, microcline, millerite, muscovite (fuchsite), pyrite, quartz, rutile, titanite
Special attraction: Minuteman National Historical Park, Concord
Accommodations: Camping at Boston Minuteman Campground, Littleton. Lodging available off of I-495 in Westford and Chelmsford.
Finding the site: From I-495, exit 30, follow MA 2A/110 west for 1.9 miles.
Rules and regulations: Safety gear is required: hard hat, reflective safety vest, steel-toed boots, safety goggles, and gloves.

Sites 25–29

Rockhounding

The Littleton quarry is a big site with a lot of potential for collectors, but so far finding worthwhile specimens has not been easy. Rockhounds with an open mind and a sense of adventure might want to try their luck here. For those up to the challenge, sulfide minerals like pyrite, arsenopyrite, and galena are the easiest to spot and can be well crystallized. Small amounts of colorful secondary copper minerals like green malachite and blue-green chrysocolla have also been found.

Micromineral collectors should search for small cavities containing quartz crystals—these can be associated with well-crystallized titanium minerals such as anatase, rutile, and titanite. Anatase forms lustrous blue-gray bipyramidal crystals, always a collector favorite. Rutile occurs in brilliant golden-brown needles, and titanite is found as vitreous brown crystals emplaced on colorless crystals of quartz. On a 2010 field trip, one collector discovered a large amount of bright green chromian muscovite (known as fuchsite), and it turned out to be some of the finest found in New England. (The best-known fuchsite locality in the region is in Freeport, Maine; however, that site is now off-limits to collectors.)

Walk around and survey the quarry first, looking for telltale signs of sulfide mineralization and for veins of quartz or calcite. The sulfides, when fresh, have a bright metallic luster. Dark green chlorite associated with quartz can be a sign of alpine-type vein mineralization and should be closely examined.

One of the rocks quarried at the site is Ayer granite, which is easily recognized by its large white, rectangular phenocrysts of microcline feldspar. This distinctive rock formed during the Silurian period about 433 million years ago. Look for loose pieces along the quarry road leading into the pit. Be sure to collect a sample—a big chunk of Ayer granite makes an attractive "yard rock" as well as a geological conversation piece.

A few of the minerals found at this site are (clockwise from top left): rutile, microcline, titanite, and galena.

26. Lancaster Chiastolite Locality

Chiastolite can be found in the ledges and boulders of Blood Town Forest.

See map page 93.
Status: Open
Land manager: Town of Lancaster
Land type: Outcrops and boulders in a forest
Type of deposit: Metamorphic (schist)
Location: Blood Town Forest, Lancaster, Worcester County
GPS: Parking, N42.4725 / W71.7110
Elevation: 370 to 390 feet
Vehicle: Any
Best season: Apr through Oct
Tools: Crack hammer, chisels, safety goggles, garden trowel, rake
Minerals: Andalusite, chiastolite, muscovite, quartz
Special attraction: Wachusett Mountain State Reservation, Princeton
Accommodations: Camping at Willard Brook State Forest, Ashby, and Pearl Hill State Park, Townsend. Lodging available in Leominster.
Finding the site: From I-190, exit 7, follow MA 117 east for 1 mile. Turn right onto Brockelman Road; proceed 1.1 miles to the town forest parking area. Walk along the trail on the right for about 600 feet. Look for boulders and outcrops on the ridge.
Rules and regulations: Do not damage trees or other vegetation. Fill in holes. Do not leave any trash. Hobby collecting only, using hand tools.

Rockhounding

The Lancaster-Sterling area is world famous for specimens of chiastolite, also known as cross stone; these stones have been collected, studied, and written about since at least as early as 1816, when the American mineralogist Parker Cleaveland (1780–1858), described *macle,* an old name for chiastolite, from Sterling. Today the best known and most accessible place to collect this fascinating stone is in Lancaster's town forest—Blood Town Forest.

Chiastolite is usually described as a variety of the mineral andalusite. However, most if not all of the chiastolite from Lancaster is actually pseudomorphic after andalusite; in other words, what was originally andalusite has been replaced by other minerals. When Professor Benjamin Shaub (1893–1993) of Smith College studied Lancaster chiastolite in the 1950s, he observed that a typical specimen consisted of a cyclic-twin group of four completely altered andalusite crystals. The white part of the chiastolite pattern was found to be made primarily of muscovite; the inner dark section, or core, consisted of fine-grained muscovite and chlorite, along with a minor amount of quartz and iron and titanium minerals.

The best approach here is to look for low-lying outcrops and boulders of schist, many of which will be covered with leaves or pine needles. Try using a rake to remove some of the forest debris when searching for potential rock to break. Look for diggings and tailings left by previous collectors. The schist you are seeking will contain elongated, cigar-shaped crystals of chiastolite that look like cylinders with tapered ends. The crystals are up to 6 inches long and 1 inch across. Break the schist with a hammer and chisel, perpendicular to the chiastolite crystal axis. You might see a cross pattern if the rock breaks the right way, but to get the best chiastolite specimens, you'll need to take some home and use a rock saw to cut across the crystals. The pattern of the chiastolite changes incrementally as you cut across different sections.

Despite the many campfire stories circulating for decades about gruesome murders and haunted woods, Blood Town Forest was actually named after Arthur W. Blood, who donated 125 acres of land to the town in 1946.

This polished cross section shows the characteristic cross-like pattern of chiastolite. (Linda Frahm collection)

27. Lunenburg Quarry

The west wall of the Lunenburg quarry stands starkly against the summer sky.

See map page 93.

Status: Restricted; no access, unless on an authorized field trip

Land manager: Private—P. J. Keating Company

Land type: Active crushed stone quarry

Type of deposit: Metamorphic (granofels, phyllite, schist), fault-related rocks, minor igneous dikes

Location: Lunenburg and Lancaster, Worcester County

GPS: Office, N42.5402 / W71.6883; quarry, N42.5339 / W71.6966

Elevation: 279 to 430 feet

Vehicle: 4WD

Best season: May through Oct

Tools: Crack hammer, chisels, digging tools, 10-power loupe

Minerals: Adularia, almandine, ankerite, biotite, calcite, chalcopyrite, chlorite, diopside, fluorapatite, fluorite, hornblende, kyanite, malachite, muscovite (fuchsite), pyrite, pyrrhotite, quartz, sphalerite, titanite

Special attraction: Lime Kiln & Quarries Conservation Area, Bolton

Accommodations: Camping at Willard Brook State Forest, Ashby, and Pearl Hill State Park, Townsend. Lodging available in Leominster.

Finding the site: From MA 2 west, take exit 35 to Fort Pond Road and turn left. Turn right onto Lunenburg Road; continue for 1 mile. Turn right onto Leominster-Shirley Road; proceed 0.3 mile to the office.

Rules and regulations: Safety gear is required: hard hat, reflective safety vest, steel-toed boots, safety goggles, and gloves.

Rockhounding

Impressive quartz crystals up to several inches long have been collected from fault-related quartz veins at this site. The crystals occur in pockets in the silicified zone of the Wekepeke Fault, an ancient, inactive earthquake fault that runs from southern New Hampshire into central Massachusetts. Some of the quartz crystals are doubly terminated and glass clear, resembling so-called Herkimer "diamonds" from New York State. On a recent field trip, collectors searched for crystals in a large pile of broken-up rock and dirt left as a favor by quarry personnel, who had used an excavator to extract material from a pocket area in the wall. Loose crystals were found by digging and sifting through the pile with a garden trowel—the same way crystals are collected at the famous quartz crystal mines in Arkansas. Quartz enthusiasts happily spent the entire day getting down and dirty searching for the crystals, which ranged from thumbnail-size to a few inches long. Matrix pieces consisting of clear quartz crystals and tan wafer-shaped ankerite or small white crystals of calcite were also collected in slabs up to a foot across.

After quartz, the next most popular mineral at the site is kyanite, an uncommon species in eastern Massachusetts. Bladed crystals ranging in color from light to deep royal blue and up to several inches long occur embedded in massive quartz; when altered the kyanite is often pale green. Brilliant green fuchsite, a chromian variety of muscovite, is occasionally found; the best place to look for it is in the southeast part of the quarry. On the northwest upper level, there is attractive banded calc-silicate schist that makes a good-looking landscaping stone, or "yard rock."

Deep blue kyanite is rare in eastern Massachusetts.

Sulfide minerals can be collected in the quarry, but good crystals are usually only suitable as micromount specimens. Crystals of pyrite are often seen sprinkled across calcite or ankerite; these are particularly attractive when found with a multicolored tarnish. Less commonly, well-formed red-brown crystals of sphalerite have been found nestled in clusters of white calcite crystals. Sparse copper mineralization is also present—golden chalcopyrite and its green alteration product, malachite, are occasionally found.

28. Rollstone Hill Quarry

Black tourmaline (schorl) is very common throughout the quarry.

See map page 93.

Status: Open

Land manager: City of Fitchburg

Land type: Abandoned granite quarry

Type of deposit: Igneous (granite with pegmatite veins)

Location: Fitchburg, Worcester County

GPS: Access road, N42.5744 / W71.8089; quarry, N42.5795 / W71.8106

Elevation: Access road, 715 feet; quarry, 675 to 830 feet

Vehicle: Any

Best season: Apr through Oct

Tools: Crack hammer, chisels, safety goggles, 10-power loupe

Minerals: Allanite-(Ce), almandine, arsenopyrite, beryl, biotite, calcite, chalcopyrite, chamosite, fluorapatite, fluorite, ilmenite, microcline, molybdenite, muscovite, opal (hyalite), pyrrhotite, quartz, schorl, titanite, uraninite, zircon

Special attraction: Wachusett Mountain State Reservation, Princeton

Accommodations: Camping at Willard Brook State Forest, Ashby. Lodging available along MA 2, Westminster to Leominster.

Finding the site: From MA 2, exit 31B, follow MA 12 north for 1.7 miles. Turn left onto Wonoosnoc Road; proceed 0.6 mile. Turn right onto South Street; continue for 1.4 miles. Turn left onto Pine Street; proceed 0.4 mile. Turn left onto Rollstone Street and then right onto Pratt Road and continue 475 feet. Walk along the access road on the right 0.25 mile to the cell tower. The quarry extends NNW for 700 to 800 feet.

Rules and regulations: Do not block access road.

Rockhounding

Granite was quarried on Rollstone Hill for more than a century, from before 1830 until the 1940s. The city of Fitchburg now owns 75 acres of land on the hill, including old quarries and adjacent woodland. For generations, collectors have visited the site to search for minerals in the many pegmatite veins that traverse the granite in exposed ledges and in rock piles left behind by quarry workers.

Five types of pegmatite veins occur in the quarry, each named for a characteristic mineral: biotite, tourmaline, beryl, titanite, and allanite. Most

Large piles of granite rise above the floor of the overgrown, abandoned quarry.

collectors focus on tourmaline pegmatites, the most common type, because of their well-formed and often large crystals of black tourmaline (schorl) embedded in massive smoky quartz or white microcline. World-class specimens have been collected, including some consisting of groups of crystals arranged in a radial or "sunburst" pattern. Be careful when attempting to trim specimens down to a manageable

Almandine is not common at the site, but when found can be quite attractive.

size—schorl is quite brittle and will shatter easily if sufficient care is not used.

Gem-quality golden beryl and aquamarine were found while the quarry was still in operation, as is evidenced by the fine specimens in the collection at Harvard University. However, it seems very little beryl remains on Rollstone Hill, though it's possible to find small colorless or pale green crystals if you're lucky. Allanite-(Ce), a black, slightly radioactive rare-earth mineral in the epidote group, is the namesake of the allanite-type pegmatites, where it is the most common mineral. The crystals are usually superficially altered to a brown color. Orange-red almandine garnet, brown titanite, and very pale green fluorapatite are uncommon, but when found make attractive thumbnail specimens. The fluorapatite exhibits bright yellow fluorescence under shortwave ultraviolet light, which easily distinguishes it from beryl.

Rollstone Boulder, an enormous glacial erratic weighing more than 100 tons, once rested on the summit of the hill. It was something of a tourist attraction and frequently depicted on postcards. In the 1920s, when quarrying operations threatened the boulder, the city saved it by blasting it apart and reassembling it on the upper common, where it can still be seen today. Rollstone Boulder isn't made of local granite, as you might expect; it consists of Kinsman granodiorite, a rock that occurs far to the north-northwest in New Hampshire and was left behind by the last receding glacier of the ice age.

Rollstone Hill literally overlooks downtown Fitchburg and has been frequented for generations by residents of the city. Some of them have left spray-painted messages on rock walls and slabs, along with broken glass and other debris. Please be careful when visiting.

29. Beryl Hill

The association of beryl with light-smoky quartz is a Beryl Hill classic. (Paul Young collection)

See map page 93.

Status: Restricted; no access, unless on an authorized field trip

Land manager: Private

Land type: Small excavations on a wooded hillside

Type of deposit: Igneous (granitic pegmatite)

Location: Royalston, Worcester County

GPS: Parking, N42.6912 / W72.1447

Elevation: Parking, 1,046 feet

Vehicle: Any

Best season: May through Oct

Tools: Crack hammer, chisels, safety goggles, digging tools, screen, rake

Minerals: Albite, almandine, beryl (aquamarine), biotite, muscovite, quartz, schorl

Special attraction: Doane's Falls Reservation, Royalston

Accommodations: Camping at Tully Lake Campground, Royalston. Lodging available along MA 2, Gardner to Orange.

Finding the site: From the junction of US 202 and MA 12 in Winchendon, proceed west on US 202 for 0.9 mile. Turn right onto River Street; continue for 1.5 miles. Turn right onto Brooks Road; proceed 1.1 miles. Turn left onto Deland Road; continue for 2.4 miles. Turn left onto Beryl Hill Road; proceed 0.4 mile to the end. Field trip participants will be guided to the site, a 0.5-mile hike.

Rules and regulations: Hand tools only. Safety goggles and sturdy footwear required.

Rockhounding

The granitic pegmatites on Beryl Hill were mined for gem beryl, particularly pale to deep blue aquamarine, at least as early as the 1870s. In the early part of the twentieth century, the mine was operated by F. H. Reynolds of Boston, and so is also known as the Reynolds mine. Most specimens from Beryl Hill are not true aquamarine, as they tend to be a pale shade of yellow-green or blue-green. Interesting dark orange crystals were also found during early mining operations.

Modern-day collectors continue to unearth fine beryl specimens, though not like the big, showy crystals of years past. Most collecting is done on the dumps by breaking up large rocks or sifting through the tailings. You can also use a screen to search for hidden beauties in the soil. The best crystals are usually embedded in a somewhat granular light-smoky quartz matrix, which you can carefully chip away at with tile nippers to expose more of the crystal. Resist the temptation to use a hammer and chisel to trim your specimens—beryl is cleavable and can break very easily. As for other minerals, dark red almandine is fairly common, as are large silvery plates of muscovite and black schorl.

Royalston is a sparsely populated town with a rural feel more typical of northern New Hampshire or Maine than Massachusetts. It has only one small store (a convenience store and deli) and one restaurant, and those are on the other side of town. Pack a lunch and plenty of water before heading out to collect. The walk up to the mine is through a mixed hardwood and pine forest along a well-defined logging road and not too difficult. Be sure to use bug spray, especially in the late spring and early summer when the biting insects are fiercest. Look for wild blueberries in clearings from mid-July to September.

Beryl at this site is usually found embedded in quartz; this light green crystal is 15 millimeters long.

30. Manhan Lead-Silver Mine

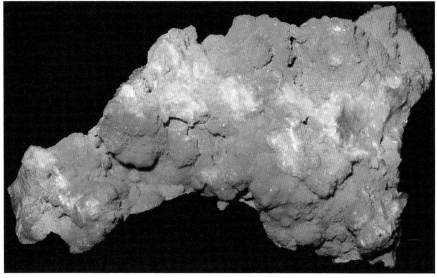

Beds of drusy green pyromorphite are commonly found carpeting quartz.

Status: Open
Land manager: Private—New England Forestry Foundation (NEFF)
Land type: Dumps of an abandoned lead-silver mine
Type of deposit: Hydrothermal vein deposit
Location: Hartnet-Manhan Memorial Forest, Easthampton, Hampshire County
GPS: Parking, N42.2818 / W72.7318; collecting area, N42.2812 / W72.7322
Elevation: Parking, 310 feet; site, 245 to 250 feet
Vehicle: Any
Best season: Apr through Oct
Tools: Crack hammer, chisels, safety goggles, digging tools, 10-power loupe
Minerals: Anglesite, aurichalcite, azurite, barite, brochantite, calcite, caledonite, cerussite, chalcanthite, chalcocite, chalcopyrite, chrysocolla, covellite, cuprite, fluorite, galena, goethite, hemimorphite, hydrozincite, langite, leadhillite, linarite, malachite, plumbogummite, pyrite, pyromorphite, quartz (chalcedony, colorless, citrine), silver, smithsonite, sphalerite, wroewolfeite, wulfenite
Special attractions: Dinosaur Footprints Reservation, Holyoke; Springfield Science Museum, Springfield; Beneski Museum of Natural History, Amherst

Accommodations: Camping at Tolland State Forest, Otis. Lodging available off of I-91, Northampton to Holyoke.

Finding the site: From MassPike, exit 3, follow MA 10 north 6.8 miles. Turn left onto Pomeroy Meadow Road; continue for 3 miles. Turn left onto Loudville Road; proceed 2.4 miles to parking area on left. Walk east along Loudville Road; follow logging road downhill to where it curves. Walk straight ahead 20 feet to the collecting area.

Rules and regulations: No commercial collecting. Hand tools only. Dig only in area marked by NEFF signs. Holes deeper than 1 foot must be filled in. Do not cut trees.

Rockhounding

The history of the Manhan mine, the largest of several old area mines, reaches far back into colonial days to when Robert Lyman of Hartford, Connecticut, discovered a deposit of lead ore (galena) sometime around 1678. Beginning in 1680, the mine was worked for about ten years or so, and then abandoned for more than seventy years. In 1765 Ethan Allen—future hero of the American Revolution—and nine other men began mining the deposit, but work stopped in 1775 during the war. The mine was active again from 1809 to 1828 and for a final stretch beginning in 1852 before being closed permanently in 1865. Today mineral collectors are still finding good specimens in old mine dumps on the banks of the North Branch of the Manhan River. The collecting site is in the Hartnet-Manhan Memorial Forest, a 148-acre tract near the village of Loudville. The river is shallow and rocky, perfect for rinsing off mud-caked specimens. Abundant shade and cool water make this a refreshing place to collect on hot summer days.

Hand-size specimens of drusy quartz, chalcedony, and massive galena can be obtained at the site, but most collectors search for small, vividly colored crystals of pyromorphite and wulfenite. Pyromorphite is usually green and found as either tiny barrel-shaped or radiating needlelike crystals. Wulfenite is easily recognizable, occurring as bright orange, yellow, or red tabular crystals. The crystals can be square-shaped or pyramidal, and are frequently found perched on pyromorphite or drusy quartz.

Other minerals at the site include green sprays of malachite, deep blue linarite, blocky white barite, and highly lustrous cerussite and anglesite. Tiny wires of native silver are sometimes seen in casts left by galena. Be sure to bring a 10-power loupe with you to examine specimens closely. Dig in the dumps and search the surface tailings. Some collectors have had luck finding excellent specimens among the stones in the bottom of the river. Because wulfenite has a high specific gravity, loose crystals can even be panned from the river gravel as you would pan for gold.

Sites 30–33

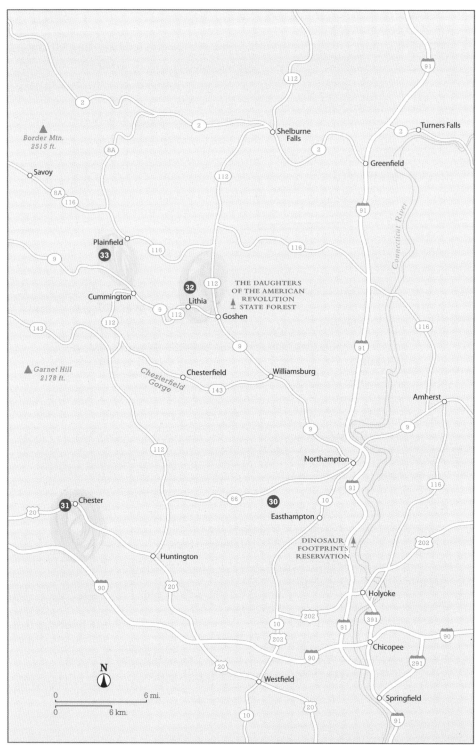

31. Chester Emery Mines

Margarite, a calcium-rich member of the mica group, is abundant at the Chester emery mines. (John Chipman collection)

See map page 106.

Status: Open to the public, but mineral collecting is allowed only with a state permit.

Land manager: Massachusetts Division of Fisheries & Wildlife, Western District

Land type: Mine dumps on a forested mountainside

Type of deposit: Metamorphic (emery vein, schist, amphibolite)

Location: J. J. Kelly Wildlife Management Area, Chester, Hampden County

GPS: Old mine: parking, N42.2795 / W72.9880; site (upper level), N42.2780 / W72.9885. Wright mine: parking, N42.2649 / W72.9787; site, N42.2644 / W72.9842.

Elevation: 655 to 1,275 feet

Vehicle: Any

Best season: May through Oct

Tools: Crack hammer, chisels, safety goggles

Minerals: Actinolite, almandine, amesite, aragonite, biotite, brookite, calcite, carbonatecyanotrichite, chalcopyrite, chamosite, chloritoid, chromite, clinochlore, clinozoisite, cordierite, corundum, cummingtonite, diaspore, dravite, epidote, ferro-hornblende, hematite, ilmenite, kyanite, magnesite, magnetite, malachite, margarite, molybdenite, pyrite, quartz, rutile, talc, titanite

Special attraction: Becket Land Trust Historic Quarry, Becket

Accommodations: Camping at Walker Island Campground, Chester. Lodging available along US 20 in Lee.

Finding the site: Old mine: From the junction of US 20 and MA 10 in Westfield, follow US 20 west for 18.9 miles. Turn left onto Hampden Street, cross the bridge, and turn immediately right into the parking area. Walk up the path closest to Hampden Street for about 100 feet; turn right and take the trail that leads straight ahead uphill, hugging the bank on the right, for about 400 feet to the upper-level dumps. **Wright mine:** From Old mine trailhead, follow US 20 east for 1.3 miles. Turn right onto Round Hill Road and proceed 0.8 mile; park and follow woods road (across from driveway) about 0.3 mile to dumps.

Rules and regulations: A small amount of loose rocks and minerals may be collected from dumps located a safe distance from mine adits and pits. Hand tools only. Entry into the adits is prohibited.

Rockhounding

In 1865 geologist Charles Jackson announced the discovery in Chester of "an inexhaustible bed of the best emery in the world in the middle of the State of Massachusetts." Mining for emery began in 1868, and six mines were eventually operated; all have been abandoned since about 1913. The three mines north of US 20—the Macia, Sackett, and Snow—are rarely visited. The mines south of US 20—the Old, Melvin, and Wright—are within the Kelly Wildlife Management Area. Directions above are given for the two most popular sites, the Old and Wright mines. Collectors are not permitted in underground portions of the mines for their own safety and because the tunnels are a protected bat habitat. The dumps are very productive; large areas have yet to be investigated

This sea-green talc specimen was collected in the upper dumps of the Old mine.

Autumn is a great time of year to collect in the old dumps of the Wright mine.

by collectors. The lower part of the Old mine is right next to the parking area; the upper-level dumps are reached by a short, steep trail. The Wright and Melvin mines are accessible by long uphill hikes.

Chester is a world-famous locality for margarite, an uncommon pink mica mineral. Attractive specimens can easily be found on the mine dumps, especially at the Wright mine. The margarite is usually associated with the fine-grained mixture of magnetite and corundum known as emery, the focus of the mining activity. Emery is easily identified by its greater "heft" and its strong magnetism. Good specimens of micaceous green talc occur associated with magnesite at the Old mine. Crystals of green chamosite and clinochlore, pale yellow clinozoisite, white or purple diaspore, and dark brown dravite are also popular with collectors. Chester is the type locality for the rare mineral amesite (1876), named for one of the mine owners, James T. Ames, who was also a mineral collector.

Slag minerals including sapphire-blue hoppered crystals of spinel and a yellow-green species known as diaoyudaoite can be found in the lower Old mine area. These minerals were formed during an ill-fated attempt to smelt emery at a time when the miners mistook the rock for iron ore before its true nature was known.

32. Barrus Farm Pegmatite Locality

Bull's-eye tourmaline is a prized find at this old locality. (Ken Gliesman collection) Photo by Ken Gliesman

See map page 106.

Status: Restricted; no access, unless on an authorized field trip
Land manager: Private
Land type: Rocky, wooded area
Type of deposit: Igneous (granitic pegmatite)
Location: Lithia, Goshen, Hampshire County
GPS: Parking, N42.4671 / W72.8400
Elevation: Parking, 1,360 feet; site, 1,325 to 1,350 feet
Vehicle: Any
Best season: May through Oct
Tools: Crack hammer, chisels, safety goggles, digging tools, screen
Minerals: Albite, almandine-spessartine, beryl (aquamarine, goshenite, morganite), cassiterite, columbite, cymatolite, elbaite, fluorapatite, microcline, montmorillonite, muscovite, pollucite, quartz, schorl, spodumene, zircon (cyrtolite)

Pink is an uncommon color for muscovite. (Ken Gliesman collection) Photo by Ken Gliesman

Special attraction: Chesterfield Gorge, Chesterfield
Accommodations: Camping at Daughters of the American Revolution State Forest, Goshen. Lodging available in Northampton.
Finding the site: From the junction of MA 9 and MA 143 in Williamsburg, follow MA 9 west for 7.1 miles. Turn right onto Spruce Corner Road; proceed 0.6 mile. Take driveway on right to the end. You will be guided to the site by the field trip leader.
Rules and regulations: Hand tools only.

Rockhounding

Tourmaline from the Barrus (formerly Weeks) farm attracted a great deal of interest from early American mineralogists, and surprisingly specimens can still be collected after more than 200 years. The site is located in the hamlet of Lithia on a densely forested hillside behind an old farm. You'll see llamas and horses grazing in the fields as you approach the farmhouse. A footpath behind the house leads slightly downhill to the collecting site, which is beside a small seasonal brook.

Tourmaline (elbaite and schorl) crystals measuring up to several inches long are found in boulders of pegmatite on the hillside. They occur in a number of colors, most with a varietal name: light to indigo blue (indicolite), pink (rubellite), green (verdelite), green rind with pink interior (watermelon tourmaline), green rind with blue interior (bull's-eye tourmaline), colorless (achroite), yellow-green, blue-green, bluish black, and black. Blue and black are the most common colors. With rare exceptions, the tourmaline crystals are not of sufficient quality to be cut into gems, but they make attractive specimens nonetheless. The bedrock origin of the boulders has not been located; it is probable that the ledge is concealed under soil and forest debris.

Mica with an attractive soft-pink color is sometimes associated with elbaite. It resembles lepidolite but is actually a rose-colored muscovite. Spodumene is abundant; it is usually colorless or gray, but occasionally has a yellow-green or pink tint. Translucent crystals up to 2 inches long and opaque crystals as long as 18 inches are known. The Barrus pegmatite is the type locality for the colorless variety of beryl known as goshenite. It was described by the mineralogist Charles U. Shepard in 1844 and named after the town of Goshen. It can be distinguished from quartz at the site by its greater transparency and glasslike appearance; quartz from Barrus is generally cloudier and smokier.

Because this site is not an operating mine, like so many of the tourmaline localities in Maine, fresh material can only be found by breaking up stones and boulders. Digging into the dumps can also be rewarding. Try screening the tailings or brook gravel to search for small loose crystals.

33. Betts Manganese Mine

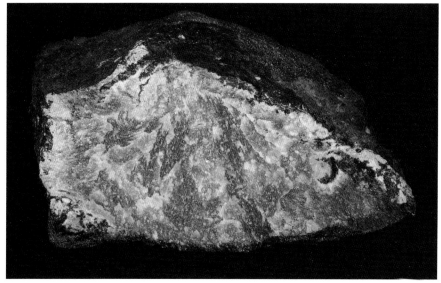

Rhodonite is the official state gemstone of Massachusetts. (John Chipman collection)

See map page 106.

Status: Open; fee and reservations required

Land manager: Private—Earthdance (www.earthdance.net)

Land type: Abandoned open-pit mine and dumps in a wooded area

Type of deposit: Hydrothermal ore deposit

Location: Plainfield, Hampshire County

GPS: Earthdance, N42.4966 / W72.9453; site, N42.4941 / W72.9463

Elevation: 1,400 to 1,450 feet

Vehicle: Any

Best season: May through Oct

Tools: Crack hammer, hand sledge, chisels, safety goggles, digging tools, rake

Minerals: Actinolite, alabandite, alleghanyite, ankerite, arsenopyrite, bafertisite, barite, bementite, biotite, calcite, caryopilite, chalcopyrite, chloritoid, clinochlore, cobaltite, cryptomelane, cummingtonite, epidote, ferro-hornblende, fluorapatite, fluorite, galena, hematite, ilmenite, jacobsite, kutnahorite, löllingite, magnetite, marcasite, molybdenite, muscovite, neotocite, pyrite, pyrolusite, pyrophanite, pyrrhotite, quartz, ranciéite, rhodochrosite, rhodonite, rutile, schallerite, scheelite, sonolite, spessartine, sphalerite, takanelite, tephroite

Special attractions: Berkshire Museum, Pittsfield; Wahconah Falls State Park, Dalton

Accommodations: Camping at Peppermint Park, Plainfield, and Mohawk Trail State Forest, Charlemont. Lodging available in Worthington and Pittsfield.

Finding the site: From the junction of MA 9 and MA 112 in Goshen, proceed west on MA 9 for 10.1 miles. Turn right onto Packard Road/Prospect Street; continue for 0.9 mile to Earthdance.

Rules and regulations: Hand tools only.

Rockhounding

Rhodonite was named the official state gemstone of Massachusetts in 1979, chosen because of its beautiful pinkish-red color and its abundance in Plainfield, especially at the Betts mine, and because of the state's reputation as one of the gem material's premier localities in the world. The Betts mine opened in 1848 and over the next century was worked periodically for

Orange spessartine is sometimes associated with metallic, striated rutile.

manganese ore as well as for rhodonite for decorative purposes and gem use. Today the mine is a popular destination for rockhounds, who collect on the dumps for a small fee.

The old dumps are conveniently located just a stone's throw from the road. Many of the rocks are hidden under leaves and forest debris, so you'll need to scrounge around a bit to find good material. The two common pink minerals you'll encounter are rhodochrosite—a bright pink, relatively soft carbonate mineral that occurs in veins—and rhodonite, a massive pinkish-red silicate mineral that is much harder. When found on the dumps, rhodonite usually has a black weathered exterior, so you'll need to crack it open to reveal the mineral's pink color. Ornaments carved from Betts rhodonite are pink streaked with black or gray due to inclusions of manganese oxides.

Ankerite is another carbonate mineral found at the site; it is pale pinkish gray but weathers to dark brown. Clusters of lustrous orange spessartine garnet crystals are abundant and are occasionally associated with brown radial aggregates of fibrous cummingtonite, a mineral first discovered in the neighboring town of Cummington. Good specimens of pyrite and rutile can sometimes be found by breaking up the weathered black rocks on the dumps. Many rare manganese minerals have been reported from the site; some like bafertisite, schallerite, and takenelite are only known from a handful of other localities in the world.

VERMONT

Prehistoric Native American petroglyphs, Bellows Falls, Vermont

34. Hatch Limestone Quarry

Limestone is quarried at this site in Ferrisburgh near the Panton town line.

Status: Restricted; no access, unless on an authorized field trip
Land manager: Private
Land type: Open pit
Type of deposit: Sedimentary (limestone)
Location: Ferrisburgh, Addison County
GPS: N44.1721 / W73.3304
Elevation: Entrance, 181 feet; site, 197 to 238 feet
Vehicle: Any
Best season: May through Oct
Tools: Crack hammers, hand sledge, chisels, pry bar
Minerals: Aragonite, calcite, fluorite, pyrite, quartz
Fossils: Marine fossils including brachiopods, cephalopods, coral, crinoid stems, gastropods *(Maclurites)*, "sunflower coral," trilobites, and worm burrows
Special attractions: Button Bay Sate Park and Lake Champlain Maritime Museum, Ferrisburgh; Chimney Point Historic Museum, Addison
Accommodations: Camping at Button Bay Sate Park, Ferrisburgh, and D.A.R. State Park, Addison. Lodging available along US 7, Shelburne.
Finding the site: From the junction of US 7 and VT 22A in Ferrisburgh, follow VT 22A south for 1.8 miles. Turn right onto Panton Road; continue for 4.2 miles. Turn right onto Jersey Street and proceed 0.4 mile to a fork. Bear right and continue for 1.3 miles.
Rules and regulations: Steel-toed boots, leather gloves, and safety goggles required.

Sites 34-36

Rockhounding

Limestone at the Hatch quarry contains a variety of marine fossils, remnants of a reef habitat that existed more than 440 million years ago. This gray limestone, part of the Ordovician Crown Point Formation, is known locally as Panton stone and is used commercially for landscaping. The fossils include *Maclurites,* an extinct genus of gastropods (snails) with coiled shells; crinoids, members of a class of flowerlike marine animals, sometimes called "sea lilies," that were attached by a stem to the seafloor; nautiloids, members of a subclass of cephalopods (mollusks), marine predators that flourished during Ordovician time; and trilobites, a famous group of extinct marine arthropods. Fossils are so abundant that you can afford to be choosy. Be sure to wrap your finds carefully with newspaper or other soft wrapping material.

Ordovician marine fossils are abundant in the quarry.

A somewhat mysterious disc-shaped fossil occurs in Panton stone that can be up to 2 feet across. It has been called "sunflower coral," but is definitely neither a coral nor a sunflower (though it does resemble one). Discovered in the nineteenth century, *Fisherites reticulatus* (formerly *Receptaculites oweni*) was long thought to be a kind of porifera or sponge, but many scientists now believe the fossils originated as colonies of green sea algae. However, others still think an ancient sponge-like creature—albeit an unknown one—is responsible for the unusual discs.

Ferrisburgh is a quiet rural town with twenty-eight operating dairy farms and 21 miles of scenic shoreline along Lake Champlain with views of New York's Adirondack Mountains. Two attractions in the town worth visiting are Button Bay State Park, named for its button-like concretions found in clay banks and on beaches, and the Lake Champlain Maritime Museum, with exhibits covering local maritime history and nautical archeology.

35. Omya Middlebury Quarry

Marble is extracted from the quarry for the production of calcium carbonate.

See map page 117.

Status: Restricted; no public access, except during open-house events
Land manager: Omya, Inc.
Land type: Active crushed stone quarry/calcium carbonate mine
Type of deposit: Metamorphic (marble, metamorphosed dolostone)
Location: Middlebury, Addison County
GPS: N44.0000 / W73.1249
Elevation: 400 to 494 feet
Vehicle: Any
Best season: Oct
Tools: Knapsack, 10-power loupe
Minerals: Calcite, dolomite
Special attractions: Vermont Marble Museum, Proctor; Weybridge Cave Natural Area, Weybridge

Accommodations: Camping at Branbury State Park, Salisbury. Lodging available in Middlebury.

Finding the site: From the junction of US 7 and VT 125 in East Middlebury, follow US 7 north 1.1 miles. Turn right onto quarry road and proceed 1.5 miles.

Rules and regulations: Rules will be provided by quarry personnel.

Rockhounding

Each October during Earth Science Week, Omya holds a one-day open house at the company's huge open pit in Middlebury. Earth Science Week is an annual educational event sponsored by the American Geological Institute, Vermont Geological Survey, and Vermont Geological Society, as well as many other organizations, businesses, and individuals. Visitors to the Omya quarry learn about local geology and participate in various activities designed to appeal to rockhounds of all ages. Of course, rock and mineral collecting is one of those activities, but you can also learn about testing minerals, join a scavenger hunt, or help create an earth science mural. Younger kids enjoy playing on a big pile of marble sand.

The quarry rock primarily consists of pure snow-white to light gray marble of the Early Ordovician Shelburne Formation, though some of it is rather schistose and more grayish green. Unlike most quarries in Vermont, the marble is not extracted for use as dimension stone or aggregate. Instead, it is mined for its calcium carbonate content, which is extracted and ground, milled, and purified for use in food, pharmaceuticals, and various industrial applications. It is used, for example, in paint, plastics, vinyl siding, and acid-free paper, and in antacids, toothpaste, gum, and diapers. Dolostone, a rock consisting primarily of the mineral dolomite, also occurs in the quarry but is not mined as an ore.

Attractive salmon-colored calcite crystals have been found at the Omya quarry and are prized by collectors. Other collectible mineral species may be found in the future. Many visitors take home representative samples of pure-white or patterned marble as souvenirs or for decorative use.

A visit to the Vermont Marble Museum in Proctor, 27 miles away from the Omya Middlebury quarry, can be an informative side trip or a destination all its own. Extensive exhibits at the museum showcase the Vermont marble industry's more than 200-year history. Outside the museum building, an easy 0.25-mile trail leads to the water-filled Sutherland Falls quarry, the oldest marble quarry in Proctor, dating to 1836.

36. Rock of Ages

You won't need your bowling shoes at the outdoor granite bowling alley.

See map page 117.

Status: Open late May to mid-Oct. For schedule and fees, visit www.rockofages.com.

Land manager: Rock of Ages Corporation

Land type: Active dimension stone quarry

Type of deposit: Igneous (granodiorite)

Location: Graniteville, Barre, Washington County

GPS: Visitor center, N44.1558 / W72.4927

Elevation: Visitor center, 1,241 feet

Vehicle: Any

Best season: Late May to mid-Oct

Tools: None necessary

Rock: Granodiorite

Special attractions: Vermont Granite Museum and Barre Town Forest, Barre

Accommodations: Camping at Lazy Lions Campground, Graniteville, and Allis State Park, Brookfield. Lodging available in Barre and Berlin.

Finding the site: From I-89, exit 6, take VT 63 east for 4 miles to the junction of VT 14. Continue straight ahead on Middle Road for 1.5 miles.

Rules and regulations: Self-guided tours of the quarry are not allowed.

Rockhounding

Rock of Ages has been a major Vermont attraction since quarry tours began in 1924. A narrated tour begins at the visitor center and takes you to an overlook of the E. L. Smith quarry, with its sheer cliffs dropping hundreds of feet. This dramatic site was used as a filming location for the 2009 movie *Star Trek*. If you would like to see the quarry workers in action (and you should), take the tour on weekdays before 3:30 p.m.

You can also take a self-guided factory tour (weekdays only) to view artisans and sculptors working to turn blocks of stone into monuments, statues, and other works of art. Traditional stone-carving as well as modern methods using lasers and computer-aided diamond saws are used. Free samples of granodiorite are available from the grout bin. The visitor center features historical exhibits, an informative video presentation, and a well-stocked gift shop. An outdoor granite bowling lane, built in 1958, is free to use, too.

From mid-June to mid-October, you can actually sandblast a design into stone yourself and bring your creation home. First, decide whether you want a tile, trivet, or wall hanging and choose a stencil pattern. Stand at the booth containing the sandblasting machine and place your hands into the heavy-duty gloves. Using a special "gun" that fires a stream of air along with abrasives, carve your design into your stone. When you're finished, someone from Rock of Ages will place a "Made by Me" sticker on it and wrap it up for you to take home.

The rock in the quarry, though known commercially as Barre granite, is technically not granite but a related rock called granodiorite. It is Devonian in age—about 380 million years old. The individual minerals making up the granite occur in grains from 1 to 5 millimeters and consist of about 35% altered oligoclase, 27% quartz, 21% microcline, 9% biotite (partially altered to chlorite), and 6% muscovite. Minor accessories include zircon, titanite, apatite, and allanite. In addition to granodiorite, younger black dikes of Mesozoic-age lamprophyre are present in the quarry and can be seen from the observation platform.

The granite industry in Barre dates back to the late nineteenth century, and many old quarries dot the landscape. You can visit some of them and experience the local geology up close in Barre Town Forest, a 370-acre forest with miles of scenic hiking trails on Millstone Hill.

37. Camp Plymouth State Park—Gold Panning

Gold has been panned from Buffalo Brook for more than a century and a half. This nugget weighs 0.116 gram.

Status: Open. Day-use hours during park season (Memorial Day weekend through Columbus Day weekend) are 10 a.m. to official sunset; small fee applies. No charge for off-season day use.

Land manager: Vermont Department of Forests, Parks and Recreation

Land type: Rocky brook in a forest

Type of deposit: Alluvial placer deposit

Location: Plymouth, Windsor County

GPS: Park entrance, N43.4766 / W72.6950

Elevation: Park entrance, 1,093; site, 1,055 to 1,355 feet

Vehicle: Any

Best season: Late May to mid-Oct. Use caution in the off-season; hunting is allowed.

Tools: Plastic gold pan, shovel, trowel, small plastic bottle, tweezers

Minerals: Almandine, gold, magnetite

Special attraction: Vermont Marble Museum, Proctor

Accommodations: Camping available in the park. Lodging available in Ludlow.

Finding the site: From the junction of VT 103 and VT 100 in Ludlow, follow VT 100 north for 5.2 miles. Turn right onto Kingdom Road and proceed 0.7 mile; turn left onto Scout Camp Road and continue for 0.5 mile.

Rules and regulations: Hand panning only. The use of sluice boxes, suction dredges, or other mechanical means of mining is prohibited. Do not disturb stream banks. Children under 15 must be supervised by an adult. No pets.

Rockhounding

Visitors to Camp Plymouth State Park come to enjoy swimming, canoeing, and kayaking on Echo Lake as well as picnicking, hiking, and camping in the 295-acre park; but treasure seekers come to pan for gold along Buffalo Brook, just as they did over 150 years ago.

Gold was discovered in Vermont in the 1850s by a prospector who had recently returned home from the gold rush in California. While fishing in Reading Pound Brook, he spotted the glint of something gold-colored through the clear, cold water. He plucked it up from the bottom of the brook and immediately noticed how heavy it was for its size. There could be no mistake—it was a gold nugget, and from right here in Vermont! He kept his discovery secret for a time, but word inevitably got out, sparking Vermont's own gold rush. Prospectors gravitated to the area in droves and began panning in nearby Broad and Buffalo Brooks, too. Soon commercial mining began

This tranquil section of Buffalo Brook is near the park entrance.

Sites 37-40

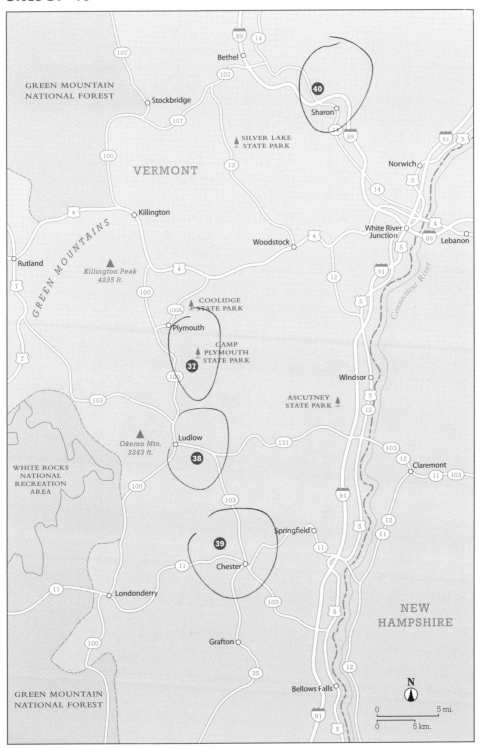

and a new town, complete with hotels and saloons, sprang up in a place called Plymouth Five Corners. Ultimately the gold-mining ventures were not profitable, and by the 1860s the former boom town was pretty much a ghost town.

But some diehards never gave up. In 1880 prospectors located a bedrock gold deposit—a sort of "mother lode'—in a quartz vein high on the banks of Buffalo Brook. The Rooks Mine (later called the Fox Mine) opened and became the largest of Vermont's gold mines. The mine operated for several years before closing near the end of the 1880s. Some of the mine ruins, including the processing mill along the brook, are located in Camp Plymouth State Park. Visitors are cautioned to avoid the mine area for their own safety due to the presence of abandoned shafts.

Buffalo Brook has produced flakes of gold and the occasional nugget for recreational prospectors ever since the mines closed. In fact, the chance of finding gold is said to have improved significantly after Hurricane Irene hit Vermont in August 2011, causing widespread flooding and erosion and thereby moving a lot of gold around. To find your own gold, survey the brook for a promising spot. Scoop up some dirt and gravel from the bottom of the middle of the brook, especially from bedrock crevices. Fill about three-quarters of your gold pan, but pick out and discard any large stones. Shake the pan back and forth just under the surface of the water so that the heavy minerals such as gold will settle to the bottom of the pan, while the lighter ones are carried away by the current. Repeat this procedure until only the heavy dark sand and any gold remain in the pan. The heavy sands will contain black magnetite, red almandine garnet, and other minerals. Pick out any gold with tweezers and place it into a container. Another option is to bring the concentrated black sands home for further processing.

38. Argonaut Mine

Talc is the softest mineral on the Mohs scale, with a hardness of 1.

See map page 125.

Status: Restricted; no access, unless on an authorized field trip

Land manager: Private—Imerys Talc Vermont, Inc.

Land type: Active talc mine

Type of deposit: Metamorphic (metamorphosed ultramafic rock: talc-carbonate rock and serpentinite; also amphibolite, schist, granofels)

Location: Ludlow, Windsor County

GPS: Office, N43.3847 / W72.6682; mine, N43.3667 / W72.6749

Elevation: Office, 1,032 feet; mine, 1,505 to 1,809 feet

Vehicle: Any

Best season: May through Oct

Tools: Crack hammer, chisels, digging tools

Minerals: Actinolite, albite, almandine, antigorite, apatite, biotite, chlorite, chromite, clinochlore (chromian), dolomite, forsterite, magnesite, magnetite, muscovite, quartz (milky, smoky), pyrite, talc

Special attraction: Vermont Museum of Mining and Minerals, Grafton
Accommodations: Camping at Camp Plymouth State Park, Plymouth. Lodging available along VT 103 in Ludlow.
Finding the site: From the junction of VT 131 and VT 103 in Proctorsville, follow VT 103 north for 1.2 miles. Turn left onto East Hill Road; proceed 0.2 mile to office.
Rules and regulations: Safety gear is required: hard hat, reflective safety vest, steel-toed boots, safety goggles, and gloves.

Rockhounding

After a day of handling talc at this mine, your hands will feel *really* soft. And well they should, because talc is the softest mineral—number 1 on Mohs scale of hardness—so soft you can scratch it with your fingernails. Talc is, of course, used in baby powder and talcum powder, but is also used in a wide variety of other products from dried foodstuffs to chewing gum,

This close-up view of an actinolite crystal from the Argonaut mine shows just how deep emerald-green the mineral can be.

pharmaceuticals to plastics, fertilizers, paint, floor and wall tiles, tires, and much, much more. Sea-green pieces of smooth talc up to several inches long can be collected at the Argonaut mine, and it's everywhere—you can pick up some choice pieces off the top of the ground or from rock piles, or if you'd like, hammer some out of a boulder. Transparent folia of talc look a little like mica, but they're much softer and not as flexible. The best specimens are usually small, but chunks as large as a coconut can be collected if you so choose.

The most common associate of talc is magnesite (magnesium carbonate), which looks a lot like calcite but is harder and a bit heavier. Magnesite occurs as white, tan, pale pink, or smoky masses with rhombohedral cleavage; occasionally it is associated with deep golden-yellow apatite. Other minerals may be found in the rocks that surround the talc-carbonate rock. Good crystals of grass-green to emerald-green actinolite can be collected from amphibolite. Massive green serpentine (antigorite) is abundant, commonly associated with magnetite. Recently, purple chromian clinochlore has been found associated with chromite.

The view of the Green Mountains from this hillside site is outstanding, and the frequent breezes feel good. But bring your sunglasses! On a sunny day, light reflecting off of the snow-white rocks can be blinding.

39. Gould Talc Mine

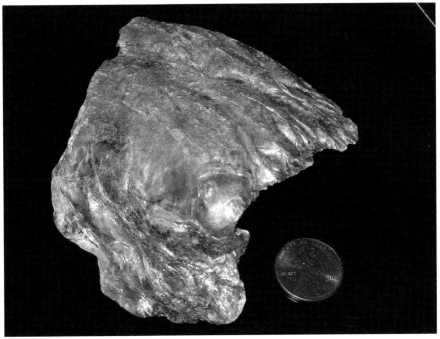

Foliated micaceous talc is abundant near the old mine.

See map page 125.

Status: Open

Land manager: Town of Chester

Land type: Abandoned talc mine

Type of deposit: Metamorphic (metamorphosed ultramafic rock: talc-carbonate rock and serpentinite)

Location: Chester Town Forest, Chester, Windsor County

GPS: Trailhead, N43.2844 / W72.6346; site, N43.2854 / W72.6298

Elevation: Trailhead, 1,275 feet; site 1,477 feet

Vehicle: Any

Best season: May through Oct

Tools: None necessary

Minerals: Actinolite, chlorite, magnetite, pyrite, serpentine, talc

Special attraction: Vermont Museum of Mining and Minerals, Grafton
Accommodations: Camping at Jamaica State Park, Jamaica. Lodging available in Chester.
Finding the site: From the junction of VT 35 and VT 11 in Chester, follow VT 11 west for 1.5 miles. Turn right onto Reservoir Road; proceed 1.1 miles. Turn right onto Water Farm Road; proceed 0.4 mile to the Lost Mine trailhead and parking area. Follow the trail uphill 0.3 mile to the Big Tree Loop side trail; take side trail about 100 feet to mine.
Rules and regulations: Park in designated area only.

Rockhounding

There is not much information available about this old talc mine, but according to a town pamphlet, it was part of the Carlton mine property, one of many talc mines in the Green Mountains of Vermont. The actual Carlton mine site is about 0.7 mile southwest of the Gould mine. The Carlton mine was a famous mineral-collecting locality for much of the twentieth century, well-known for large cubes of pyrite and other minerals. The mine was important to the science of mineralogy as well, as it was the type locality for three new minerals, including chesterite—named after the town.

Opened about 1894, the Carlton mine was at least 200 feet deep. It was abandoned after a serious cave-in in 1943, but it operated again for a time in the 1950s. Unfortunately it is now flooded, located in a backyard and off-limits. The Gould mine is also flooded and appears to have been abandoned long ago. Small rock dumps and rusty old mining artifacts are all that remain.

In the early years of mining, talc from the mines was loaded into wagons and transported by teams of oxen to a mill beside the railroad tracks in Chester Depot. There the talc was crushed to a fine powder for use in the production of plaster board, soapstone finish, dusting powder for tires, and in many other products.

At the Gould mine, talc is plentiful in loose pieces on the dumps. You'll recognize it by its greenish-gray color, micaceous habit, and most of all by its noticeable softness, which you can feel by rubbing it between your fingers. The country rock bordering the deposit consists of amphibolite on the east and mica schist on the west. You might notice small crystals of almandine, hornblende, or pyrite (often altered) in these rocks.

40. Sharon Concretion Locality

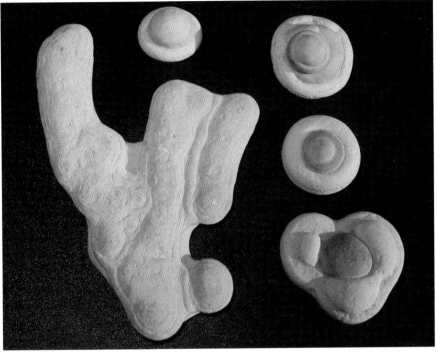

Concretions can be found in some pretty amazing shapes. (Linda Frahm collection)

See map page 125.
Status: Restricted; no access, unless on an authorized field trip
Land manager: Private
Land type: Sand and gravel bank
Type of deposit: Unconsolidated (varved sediments deposited in a glacial lake)
Location: Sharon, Windsor County
GPS: Parking, N43.7900 / W72.4890
Elevation: 510 to 525 feet
Vehicle: Any
Best season: May through Oct
Tools: Small digging tools, cardboard flats
Material: Concretions

Special attraction: Montshire Museum of Science, Norwich

Accommodations: Camping at Silver Lake State Park, Barnard, and Allis State Park, Brookfield. Lodging available in White River Junction.

Finding the site: From the junction of VT 132 and VT 14 in Sharon, follow VT 14 west for 1.9 miles to a parking area on the left. Carefully cross the highway to enter the site.

Rules and regulations: Rules to be provided by trip leaders.

Rockhounding

Concretions, also known as claystones or mud-babies, come in a variety of shapes including ovals, spheres, and flattened forms resembling puzzle pieces; some even look like animals or other familiar figures and are prized as natural "art." They are easy to find at this site and fun to collect. The concretions formed in annual layers of sediment (called varves) deposited in Glacial Lake Hitchcock, a large lake that extended from northern Vermont all the way down to Connecticut 10,000 to 15,000 years ago, during the Pleistocene age. The concretions are found in layers of varved clays composed of fine-grained silt or sand; they were cemented into their present forms by calcium carbonate and/or iron oxide.

The collecting site is at a sand and gravel bank just a couple hundred feet from the White River. Horizontal layers of sediment deposited by Glacial Lake Hitchcock are plainly visible in the bank. Concretions are found in layers of fine-grained sediment. If you visit after a rainstorm, it'll be easy to spot concretions on the surface. Otherwise, look along the base of the sand bank, where they may have tumbled down, or dig into the fine-grained layers. You'll probably have to rinse your concretions off to see their true shapes, which can range from simple "buttons" to very intricate natural sculptures.

Concretions at this site are so abundant that collectors can afford to be very picky about what they choose to bring home. Kids love this place because it's like a big sandbox filled with treasure, but keep an eye on them because it is close to the highway. You're likely to get dirty, so bring a change of clothes. There is little shade, so sunscreen is advised. Cool off afterwards by the White River adjacent to the parking area. The quaint town of Sharon has one restaurant and two general stores for food and supplies.

NEW HAMPSHIRE

Road cuts, like this one in Windham, are abundant in New Hampshire and reveal the state's fascinating bedrock geology.

41. Beryl Mountain Mine

The dumps on Beryl Mountain have been worked hard, but beryl can still be collected.

Status: Restricted; no access, unless on an authorized field trip
Land manager: Private
Land type: Abandoned mine on a wooded hillside
Type of deposit: Igneous (granitic pegmatite)
Location: South Acworth, Sullivan County
GPS: Parking, N43.1792 / W72.2957; site, N43.1809 / W72.2944
Elevation: Parking, 915 feet; collecting area, 1,030 to 1,130 feet
Vehicle: Any
Best season: May through Oct
Tools: Crack hammer, chisels, safety goggles, digging tools, screen
Minerals: Albite, almandine, autunite, bertrandite, beryl, microcline, muscovite, pyrite, quartz (rose, smoky), rutherfordine, schoepite, schorl, uraninite, uranophane, zircon
Special attraction: The Fort at No. 4 Museum, Charlestown
Accommodations: Camping at Pillsbury State Park, Washington. Lodging available in Walpole and in Bellows Falls, VT.

Sites 41-49

Finding the site: From the junction of NH 10 and NH 123A in Marlow, follow NH 123A for 4.8 miles; turn left onto Beryl Mountain Road and proceed 1.1 miles. Park on right near sand pit. Cross highway and hike uphill along woods trail for about 700 feet.
Rules and regulations: Do not leave any trash.

Rockhounding

The large beryl deposit on Beryl Mountain was known at least as early as the 1820s, when specimens began to be acquired by museums in America and Europe. During the nineteenth century, crystals as long as 4 feet and weighing hundreds of pounds were unearthed. One visitor to the underground portion of the workings in the 1890s was astonished to find that at least half the tunnel walls were made of beryl. Colorful stone from the site was also used for cemetery monuments. Following the death of Ralph Waldo Emerson in 1882, Emerson's son hired mine workers to extract an enormous beryl crystal for use as a tombstone. Unfortunately the crystal couldn't be removed intact, so the decision was made to use a boulder of rose quartz instead. Emerson's rose quartz memorial can be seen in Sleepy Hollow Cemetery, Concord, Massachusetts.

Feldspar, quartz, and mica have all been mined during Beryl Mountain mine's long history. Beryl was mined during World War II as an ore of beryllium. Today the entrance to the underground mine is blocked and the open pits and extensive dumps are under thick forest cover. Beryl is still abundant—pieces of it can often be found just by scanning the top of the ground, especially on slopes where there is frequent erosion. The beryl occurs in various shades of green, blue, or yellow and is opaque or slightly translucent, not really gem quality. Screening is an effective way to search through the tailings. Most specimens are fragments, but occasionally complete crystals can be found. Rose quartz is fairly common, typically light pink. It fades in sunlight, however, so dig to find the best-quality pieces.

Beryl and rose quartz can still be found in the dumps.

42. Mine Ledge

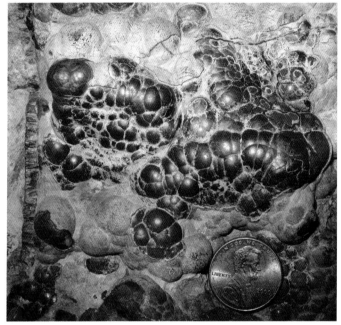

This botryoidal variety of hematite is sometimes called "kidney ore."

See map page 135.

Status: Believed to be open unless otherwise posted

Land manager: Private

Land type: Steep wooded hillside

Type of deposit: Hydrothermal deposit (silicified rock in a fault zone)

Location: Surry, Cheshire County

GPS: N43.0046 / W72.3447

Elevation: 968 feet

Vehicle: Any

Best season: May through Oct

Tools: Crack hammer, chisels, safety glasses

Minerals: Goethite, hematite (kidney ore, specularite), quartz (chalcedony, jasper, milky), romanèchite, turgite

Special attraction: Surry Mountain Dam and Lake, Surry

Accommodations: Camping at Surry Mountain Camp Ground, Surry. Lodging available in Keene.

Finding the site: From the junction of NH 12 and NH12A in Keene, proceed northeast on NH 12A (Maple Avenue) for 0.7 mile. Take third exit off of traffic circle onto Old Walpole Road; continue for 3.7 miles. Park on right, before the bridge railing.

Rules and regulations: Do not leave any trash.

Rockhounding

There is a ledge at Mine Ledge—rocky and steep and almost right beside the road—but there's no mine. If there had been a mine, we can be sure it would've been an iron mine because the ledge is loaded with iron minerals. But the deposit wasn't rich enough to work, according to nineteenth-century geologist Charles Hitchcock in his *Geology of New Hampshire* (1877). The ledge has long been a favorite site for rockhounds, however, who visit it in search of attractive specimens of botryoidal hematite and goethite. Collectors usually explore the ledge above the southwest side of the road; you can start to collect specimens just a few feet into the woods. The downward, northeast side also has specimens, but the slope is steep and hazardous. Be careful crossing the road; drivers are unaccustomed to seeing pedestrians on this country road.

The two main iron minerals at Mine Ledge are hematite and goethite. These minerals usually occur as rounded, botryoidal aggregates on quartz. Hematite is usually black, reddish black, or red. Kidney ore is another name for botryoidal hematite, especially when it's red. Crystals of metallic-gray hematite (specularite) are occasionally found associated with quartz crystals. Goethite is yellow-brown, brown, or black and generally botryoidal. Interiors of botryoids are sometimes banded. Brown or black "balls" of goethite are often attached to the sides of quartz crystals in cavities. An iridescent, multicolored mixture of hematite and goethite called turgite has also been found. The best way to distinguish hematite and goethite is by doing a streak test: Drag the mineral across the surface of a piece of unglazed porcelain, like the back of a ceramic tile. Goethite will leave a yellow-brown or brown streak; hematite will leave a rust-red streak. (Even if the color of the hematite is gray or black, it will always have a red streak.)

Romanèchite, a mineral containing barium and manganese, is another species occurring at Mine Ledge as botryoids. It is gray in color and can be distinguished from hematite and goethite by its gray streak and higher specific gravity. Cavities filled with quartz crystals occur in massive quartz, often with a thin yellowish to red iron oxide coating. Rarely quartz crystals have been found coated with periwinkle-blue chalcedony. Some of the massive red quartz appears to be the variety jasper.

43. Turner Mine

The mine pit is now flooded.

See map page 135.

Status: Restricted; no access, unless on an authorized field trip
Land manager: Private
Land type: Abandoned open-pit feldspar mine in a wooded area
Type of deposit: Igneous (complex granitic pegmatite)
Location: Marlow, Cheshire County
GPS: Parking, N43.1252 / W72.2404; site, N43.1317 / W72.2411
Elevation: Parking, 1,294 feet; site, 1,390 to 1,460 feet
Vehicle: Any
Best season: May through Oct
Tools: Crack hammer, chisels, safety goggles, digging tools, 10-power loupe
Minerals: Albite, almandine, autunite, becquerelite, bertrandite, beryl, cassiterite, columbite, curite, dickinsonite, elbaite, fairfieldite, fluorapatite, gummite, lepidolite, lithiophilite, microcline, mitridatite, montmorillonite, opal (hyalite), purpurite, pyrite, quartz (rose), schorl, sicklerite, spodumene, uraninite, uranophane, zircon
Special attraction: The Fort at No. 4 Museum, Charlestown

Accommodations: Camping at Greenfield State Park, Greenfield. Lodging available in Keene and Newbury.

Finding the site: From the junction of NH 10 and NH 123 in Marlow, follow NH 123 west for 2.6 miles. Park on the left, cross road, and hike north along woods road 0.5 mile.

Rules and regulations: Do not leave any trash.

The Turner mine is one of the few sites in New Hampshire where elbaite can be found.

Rockhounding

The Turner mine was operated by the Whitehall Company in the 1950s for feldspar, which was shipped to a processing plant in Manchester, Connecticut. The pit is now flooded, but the surrounding dumps are easily accessed. The trail to the site is used in the winter as a snowmobile trail, as indicated by signs along the way. Collectors should stay away from the dangerous high walls of the pit. Use insect repellent—the flooded pit is a breeding spot for mosquitoes.

The most productive dumps seem to be those above the quarry on the hillside. This area contains abundant white and pale blue cleavelandite—a variety of albite that has a curved lamellar or thin platy habit. Associated with the cleavelandite are tourmaline crystals (green, blue, or pink elbaite and black schorl), brown cassiterite, and abundant plates of muscovite mica. The tourmaline, though attractively colored, is rather opaque and usually not of gem quality. Green and blue crystals are far more common than pink. As far as is known, no pockets have been found in the pegmatite, with the exception of tiny cavities in albite that sometimes contain microcrystals of elbaite or fluorapatite.

Spodumene is relatively common in large masses up to several inches long, mostly in the upper dumps; rarely small white to tan crystals may be found. The spodumene at Turner has largely been altered to "pinite," a material consisting primarily of fine-grained muscovite. Radioactive minerals including uraninite, becquerelite, and uranophane have been collected at the site. Massive tan lithiophilite has been found, sometimes associated with secondary phosphate minerals such as purpurite, sicklerite, and fairfieldite, and there are likely others waiting to be discovered.

44. Tripp Mine

The Tripp mine is one of the best sites in New England to collect rose quartz. (Melissa Jeswald collection)

See map page 135.

Status: Restricted; no access, unless on an authorized field trip

Land manager: Private

Land type: Open-cut gem beryl mine

Type of deposit: Igneous (granitic pegmatite)

Location: Alstead, Cheshire County

GPS: Gilsum Village Store, N43.0481 / W72.2636; site, N43.0822 / W72.2790

Elevation: Site, 1,300 to 1,325 feet

Vehicle: 4WD

Best season: July through Sept

Tools: Crack hammer, chisels, digging tools

Minerals: Albite, almandine, beryl (aquamarine, golden), fluorapatite, microcline, montmorillonite, muscovite, quartz (rose, smoky), schorl

Special attraction: The Fort at No. 4 Museum, Charlestown

Accommodations: Camping at Surry Mountain Camp Ground, Surry. Lodging available in Keene.

Finding the site: From the junction of NH 9 and NH 10 in Keene, follow NH 10 (Gilsum Road) north for 5.8 miles. Turn left onto Main Street; proceed 0.2 mile to Gilsum Village Store. Field trip attendees will be guided to the mine from here.

Rules and regulations: Safety gear is required: hard hat, reflective safety vest, steel-toed boots, safety glasses, and gloves. Mandatory 1-hour lunch break.

Rockhounding

The Tripp mine, like so many New Hampshire pegmatite deposits, was formerly operated for feldspar and mica. Abandoned for decades, the site has recently found new life as a commercial gem and mineral specimen mine. Aquamarine is the primary focus of the miners, but gem-quality golden beryl is found as well. Most of the beryl, of course, is not gemmy; it ranges in color from yellow to yellow-green and blue-green to sky blue. When cut the aquamarine and golden beryls become valuable gems; deep red almandine and smoky quartz have been faceted as well. Rose quartz is also mined and is used for decorative purposes or made into cabochons.

The Tripp pegmatite is not enriched in lithium, so you won't find colored tourmaline, spodumene, or other minerals typical of complex pegmatites. However, good-quality black schorl crystals can be collected, and these make excellent specimens. Large, sharp crystals of muscovite, some of them color-zoned, have also been found. There are no rare or exotic minerals at the mine (as far as is known), but the quality of the species that do occur make this site a great place to collect. In fact, beryl is common enough that it's hard to imagine someone going home without having found any. Field trips to the Tripp mine are held infrequently, but if you attend one, you'll find that the mine staff is very accommodating, usually allowing you to collect in recently excavated material as well as in older dumps.

This lovely piece of beryl was found on a mineral club field trip. (Melissa Jeswald collection)

45. Beauregard Mine

Beryl is abundant at the Beauregard mine. (Dana M. Jewell collection)

See map page 135.
Status: Restricted; no access, unless on an authorized field trip
Land manager: Private
Land type: Open-cut mine and dumps
Type of deposit: Igneous (granitic pegmatite)
Location: Alstead, Cheshire County
GPS: Gilsum Village Store, N43.0481 / W72.2636; site, N43.0693 / W72.2801
Elevation: 1,200 to 1,250 feet
Vehicle: High-clearance 4WD
Best season: May through Oct
Tools: Crack hammer, sledgehammer, chisels, digging tools
Minerals: Albite, almandine, bertrandite, beryl, biotite, fluorapatite, microcline, muscovite, quartz, schorl
Special attraction: Prehistoric Native American petroglyphs, Bellows Falls, VT
Accommodations: Camping at Surry Mountain Camp Ground, Surry. Lodging available in Keene.

Finding the site: From the junction of NH 9 and NH 10 in Keene, follow NH 10 (Gilsum Road) north for 5.8 miles. Turn left onto Main Street; proceed 0.2 mile to Gilsum Village Store. Field trip attendees will be guided to the mine from here.
Rules and regulations: Required safety gear: steel-toed boots, safety glasses, and gloves.

Rockhounding

The Beauregard mine was originally a mica mine, worked for muscovite that occurred in "plates" up to 8 inches across. During those early mining operations, beryl was considered a worthless by-product and discarded onto the dumps, much to the delight of present-day mineral collectors. The site is now worked occasionally for beryl specimens, and mineral clubs are sometimes granted permission to conduct field trips. On a recent club trip, collectors found a rain-carved gully containing newly exposed beryl crystals just waiting to be picked up. Of course, collecting at the Beauregard mine is not always *that* easy, so you'll probably have to do some digging, but beryl is common enough that it would be hard for someone to go home without having found at least one piece.

For those who prefer hard-rock mining to dump digging, there is some pegmatite exposed in the cut that can be worked as well. Most of the crystals you'll find won't be gem quality, but chances are good for finding a great display specimen; beryl crystals several inches long are not uncommon. In fact, crystals as long as 3 feet are known from the mine! The color of the beryl varies: Pale-green, blue-green, blue, yellow-green, yellow, and white crystals have been found. Some crystals have a feldspar core. Other minerals reported include red almandine, black schorl, and green fluorapatite (fluorescent). Bertrandite, a rare alteration product of beryl, occurs as colorless platy microcrystals associated with beryl.

The road to the mine is pretty rough in places, but once you reach the parking area, you'll practically be at the collecting site, which makes going back to your vehicle for additional tools (or lunch) easy.

A few miles away, in the village of Gilsum, a very popular rockhound event is held every year for an entire weekend in June, and has been since the mid-1960s. The Gilsum Rock Swap features more than sixty gem, mineral, fossil, and jewelry dealers and swappers who set up under tents in a large field. There are presentations by rock and mineral experts, and fun activities for the kids, too. It's truly one of the highlights of New England rockhounding. For the latest information, visit www.gilsum.org/rockswap. If you go, be sure to stay for the famous Gilsum Rock Swap ham and bean supper, with all-you-can-eat homemade pies for dessert.

46. Chickering Mine

Heterosite is an alteration product of triphylite with a distinctive purple color.

See map page 135.
Status: Restricted; no access, unless on an authorized field trip
Land manager: Private—Daniel Webster Council, Boy Scouts of America
Land type: Abandoned open-pit mine in woods
Type of deposit: Igneous (complex granitic pegmatite)
Location: Pierre Hoge Scout Camp, Walpole, Cheshire County
GPS: Parking, N43.0836 / W72.3781; site, N43.0831 / W72.3803
Elevation: Parking, 1,100 feet; site, 1,135 to 1,162 feet
Vehicle: High-clearance 4WD
Best season: May through Oct
Tools: Crack hammer, chisels, safety goggles, 10-power loupe
Minerals: Albite, arsenopyrite, autunite, beraunite, beryl, beryllonite, brazilianite, cassiterite, childrenite, columbite, elbaite, fairfieldite-messelite, fluorapatite, goethite, gormanite-souzalite, goyazite, graphite, greifensteinite, gypsum, heterosite, hureaulite, laueite, lepidolite, löllingite, ludlamite, metavivianite, microcline, mitridatite, montebrasite, moraesite, muscovite, opal (hyalite), paravauxite, pyrite, pyrrhotite, quartz, rhodochrosite, rockbridgeite-frondelite,

schorl, scorodite, siderite, sphalerite, spodumene, strunzite, triphylite, uraninite, vivianite, wardite, whitmoreite, zircon

Special attraction: Prehistoric Native American petroglyphs, Bellows Falls, VT

Accommodations: Camping at Surry Mountain Camp Ground, Surry. Lodging available in Keene.

Finding the site: From the junction of NH 12 and NH 123 in Walpole, follow NH 123 south for 0.8 mile. Turn right onto Walpole Valley Road; proceed 3.4 miles. Turn right onto Eaton Road; proceed 0.7 mile to a woods road on the right. Park in the field. Follow woods road uphill a few hundred feet, keeping left at the fork.

Rules and regulations: Hobby collecting only.

Rockhounding

The open pit at the old Chickering feldspar and mica mine was backfilled some time ago, but collectors are still finding interesting minerals in the surrounding dumps and in exposed ledges. The most popular mineral is tourmaline (elbaite), which can be found in opaque blue or green crystals up to several inches long, in the dumps and on exposed ledges above the pit. The best-quality crystals occur embedded in quartz.

Several interesting minerals can be found in the remaining walls of the pit, including massive white to pale blue apatite and sprays of the rare phosphate mineral childrenite. Crystals of childrenite are tan to colorless, transparent to translucent, and usually well terminated. Cassiterite is relatively common at Chickering in brown crystals associated with bladed white albite (cleavelandite). The larger crystals are often crudely formed, but pseudo-octahedral microcrystals in albite can be quite good. Small pockets in massive white quartz occasionally contain crystals of fluorapatite, which may be colorless, white, pale blue, pink, or purple; some crystals are zoned blue and purple. Fluorapatite also

Elbaite at this site can be green or blue and is commonly embedded in quartz.

Collector favorites at the Chickering mine include (clockwise from top left): fluorapatite, wardite, elbaite, and childrenite.

occurs as white to yellow micro-spheres. Siderite is commonly altered, but good unaltered crystals can be found associated with quartz crystals having a quartzoid habit (crystals with truncated prisms).

Still more minerals can be collected at Chickering, including silvery löllingite with a bright metallic luster, white or pale green beryl, black columbite, gray to pale purple lepidolite, and red-brown zircon crystals (sometimes associated with uraninite). Massive spodumene is common, but most of it has been altered to white or pinkish-red "pinite." The alteration of triphylite and other phosphates has produced a large number of secondary phosphate minerals, mostly as microcrystals. Purple heterosite is common; less frequently found are white sprays of strunzite, pale green or golden radial sprays of beraunite, colorless prismatic crystals of brazilianite, yellow to orange bladed crystals of laueite, white micro-sprays of moraesite, colorless tetragonal crystals of wardite, and whitmoreite crystals exhibiting a "naval-mine" habit.

47. William Wise Fluorite Mine

Rich green fluorite from the Wise mine is world famous.

See map page 135.
Status: Restricted; no access, unless on an authorized field trip
Land manager: Private
Land type: Open-cut mine in a wooded area
Type of deposit: Hydrothermal vein deposit
Location: Westmoreland, Cheshire County
GPS: Entrance, N42.9545 / W72.4913; site, N42.9502 / W72.4861
Elevation: Entrance, 700 feet; site, 737 to 812 feet
Vehicle: High-clearance 4WD
Best season: May through Oct
Tools: Crack hammer, chisels, safety goggles, digging tools, sifting screen, bucket
Minerals: Barite, calcite, cerussite, chalcopyrite, dolomite, ferrimolybdite, fluorite, galena, malachite, molybdenite, quartz (amethyst, smoky), rutile, siderite, smithsonite, sphalerite, wulfenite
Special attraction: Chesterfield Gorge Natural Area, Chesterfield

Accommodations: Camping at private campgrounds in Swanzey and Surry. Lodging available in Keene and in Brattleboro, VT.

Finding the site: From the junction of NH 12 and NH 63 in Westmoreland, follow NH 63 south for 2.3 miles. Turn right onto River Road; proceed 2.2 miles. Turn left onto Poocham Road, then immediately right onto Reynolds Road; proceed 1.6 miles. Before the curve, turn right and continue 0.5 mile.

Rules and regulations: Rules to be provided by mine personnel.

Rockhounding

Fluorite was mined here for industrial use from the 1890s until about 1919, but the mine achieved worldwide fame for outstanding specimens of gemmy green fluorite, examples of which are on display at the Smithsonian and at many other museums around the world. The Wise mine is currently operated for mineral specimens and gem rough. The color of the fluorite ranges from soft, light green to vivid "gumdrop" green to deep, vibrant emerald green. (Less commonly, it can be colorless or purple.) Crystals of fluorite are found in large clusters of intergrown octahedrons. Transparent emerald-green fluorite makes an exquisite gemstone, but because it is far softer than most gems, the cut stones are usually used in pendants, earrings, and other settings where they are less likely to be scratched or chipped.

Fluorite from the Wise mine is prized by fluorescent mineral collectors for its distinctive bright blue fluorescence under long-wave ultraviolet light. In fact, the word *fluorescence* is derived from *fluorspar,* another name for fluorite; it was coined in 1852 by the British physicist Sir George Stokes. The peculiar blue fluorescence of Wise mine fluorite is believed to be caused by the presence of trace amounts of the rare-earth element europium.

Sift through the dumps, perhaps using a screen, to find loose pieces of fluorite, which are abundant. Quartz crystals can be found this way as well. If you happen to be at the site after a hard rain, you'll likely see some of the green beauties shining up at you from the top of the ground. Otherwise, you'll probably need to wash the dirt off your finds to see what you've got. (Fortunately the dumps are adjacent to the normally water-filled mine pit.) Larger rocks in the dumps occasionally contain groups of quartz crystals, and these can be extracted with a hammer and chisel. Metallic sulfide minerals are not common, but you may come across chalcopyrite, galena, or molybdenite. If you do find molybdenite (metallic gray and micaceous), examine the surrounding rock closely for its alteration product, ferrimolybdite; this earthy yellow species is very uncommon in New England.

40. Richmond Soapstone Quarry

This brown crystal is a pseudomorph of pinite after cordierite. (Paul Young collection)

See map page 135.
Status: Open
Land manager: Town of Richmond
Land type: Dumps of an abandoned quarry in a forest
Type of deposit: Metamorphic (amphibolite, gneiss, schist, soapstone)
Location: Richmond, Cheshire County
GPS: N42.7372 / W72.2926
Elevation: 965 to 975 feet
Vehicle: High-clearance 4WD
Best season: May through Oct

Tools: Crack hammer, chisel, safety goggles

Minerals: Anthophyllite, clinochlore, cordierite (iolite), dravite, fluorapatite, gedrite, kyanite, magnesiohornblende, microcline, muscovite, phlogopite, pinite, pyrite, quartz, rutile, talc

Special attraction: Mount Monadnock, Jaffrey

Accommodations: Camping at Monadnock State Park, Jaffrey. Lodging available in Keene.

Finding the site: From the junction of NH 32 and NH 119 in Richmond, follow NH 119 west for 0.6 mile. Turn left onto Sprague Road; proceed 0.9 mile to a brook. If brook is crossable, continue 0.5 mile to a fork. Bear left onto Parker Road (not marked), and continue 0.4 mile to an overgrown woods road between two stone walls on the left. The site is about 650 feet ENE of this point; the road does not lead to it. Use GPS and/or compass.

Rules and regulations: No commercial collecting. Hand tools only.

Rockhounding

During the nineteenth century, the Lorenzo Harris farm was the site of a soapstone quarry that was well-known to mineralogists of the time. The long-abandoned workings are located in what is now a heavily wooded area, just a mile north of the Massachusetts state line. The ground is covered with forest debris, and many of the stones are coated with moss.

The Richmond soapstone quarry is a famous locality for the mineral cordierite, which occurs here in olive-green to blue-gray barrel-shaped crystals up to several inches in length. Fine specimens of Richmond cordierite are found in mineral museums and private collections throughout the world. Many crystals are actually pseudomorphs; the original cordierite has been altered to a brownish substance called "pinite," a compact mixture of mica and clay minerals. Cordierite occurs at the site along the contact between soapstone and veins of quartz. The blue gem variety of cordierite called "iolite" was reportedly found in the nineteenth century while the quarry was still active. Cut gems of iolite exhibit an interesting property known as dichroism, which causes the stones to appear pale sky blue when viewed from one direction and violet when viewed from the other. In fact, another name for iolite is dichroite, after this property. Today massive blue to violet unaltered cordierite can be collected, but most is probably too flawed for gem use.

Rutile occurs at the site in fine dark red to black crystals up to ¾ inch long. The best area to look for it is in a small outcrop 1,000 feet due south of

Rutile occurs as reddish-black crystals in ledges south of the quarry. (Don Swenson collection)

the quarry, where bladed pale brown anthophyllite and green pseudohexagonal crystals of clinochlore can also be found.

Northeast of Richmond in the town of Jaffrey is 3,165-foot Mount Monadnock, the highest peak in southern New Hampshire. The mountain's once-forested summit was left bare after a series of fires in the nineteenth century exposed the bedrock, which consists of schist and quartzite of the Devonian Littleton Formation. Monadnock was a popular destination for the writers Ralph Waldo Emerson and Henry David Thoreau and today is one of the most climbed mountains in the world.

49. Wilton Crushed Stone Quarry

Large pieces of dark green diorite with purple fluorite have been collected at the Wilton quarry.

See map page 135.

Status: Restricted; no access, unless on an authorized field trip

Land manager: Private—Pike Industries

Land type: Active crushed stone quarry

Type of deposit: Igneous (diorite, granitic pegmatite) and metamorphic (schist, etc.)

Location: Wilton and Lyndeborough, Hillsborough County

GPS: Entrance, N42.8646 / W71.7685

Elevation: Entrance, 491 feet; quarry 650 to 800 feet

Vehicle: Any

Best season: May through Oct

Tools: Crack hammer, sledgehammer, chisels, pry bar

Minerals: Allanite-(Ce), almandine, anatase, beryl, biotite, calcite, chlorite, epidote, fluorite, goethite, hematite, microcline, muscovite, opal (hyalite), pyrite, quartz, titanite, tourmaline, zircon; also secondary sulfate minerals

Special attraction: Pack Monadnock Mountain, Miller State Park, Temple

Accommodations: Camping at Greenfield State Park, Greenfield. Lodging available in Wilton and Milford.

Finding the site: From the junction of NH 101 and NH 31 in Wilton, follow NH 31 north for 2.5 miles. Turn right onto Isaac Frye Highway; proceed 0.1 mile to gate on left.

Rules and regulations: Safety gear is required: hard hat, reflective safety vest, steel-toed boots, safety glasses, and gloves.

Rockhounding

This scenic hillside quarry with its interesting geology is a fine destination for a day of mineralogical exploration. The rocks here are certainly not the "same old, same old." You'll notice slabs consisting of dark green diorite coated with purple fluorite scattered about the rock piles on the quarry floor. The fluorite occurs with calcite in seams in the diorite. The diorite tends to split along these seams during quarry operations, exposing the purple fluorite. Very little of the fluorite occurs as crystals, but if you look closely with a loupe, you might find some microcrystals. Rarely bipyramidal, butterscotch-colored crystals of anatase are associated. The titanium in the anatase appears to have been derived from the mineral titanite, which is abundant in the diorite.

On the upper bench of the quarry, pegmatite veins occur in which collectors have found pale yellow beryl, red almandine garnet, and pale greenish feldspar. Cavities filled with milky quartz crystals have been collected, too; slabs up to several inches across covered with quartz crystals make attractive specimens. The metamorphic rocks in the quarry contain abundant pyrite—its decomposition upon exposure to the atmosphere gives rise to a suite of secondary sulfate minerals, including what appear to be copiapite (yellow) and halotrichite (white hairlike crystals). These minerals can only be collected during dry weather; put them in a protective container, as they are fragile and soluble in water.

The summit of Pack Monadnock Mountain (elevation 2,290 feet) in the nearby town of Temple offers spectacular views of the surrounding countryside. The mountain, in Miller State Park, is the highest in the county. The park entrance is 7.5 miles from the Wilton Quarry; you can either drive or hike up to the summit. In addition, two rock shops in the neighboring town of Milford (see Appendix C) are worth a visit.

50. Hooksett Crushed Stone Quarry

Sphalerite, the chief ore of zinc, has been found at this site as yellowish-brown masses.

Status: Restricted; no access, unless on an authorized field trip
Land manager: Private—Pike Industries
Land type: Active crushed stone quarry
Type of deposit: Igneous (granite, granitic pegmatite, mafic dikes), metamorphic (metasedimentary rocks), hydrothermal quartz veins
Location: Hooksett, Merrimack County
GPS: N43.0861 / W71.4778
Elevation: 370 to 456 feet
Vehicle: Any
Best season: May through Oct
Tools: Crack hammer, chisels, digging tools
Minerals: Almandine, arsenopyrite, calcite, chalcopyrite, chlorite, dravite, epidote, fluorapatite, fluorite, galena, hematite, malachite, microcline, muscovite, olivine, opal (hyalite), pyrite, quartz (colorless, chalcedony), schorl, sphalerite

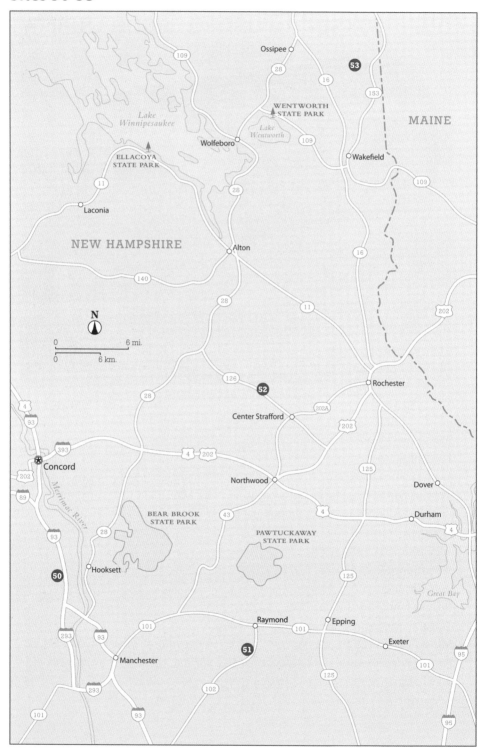

Special attraction: The Little Nature Museum, Warner

Accommodations: Camping at Bear Brook State Park, Allenstown. Lodging available along US 3 in Hooksett.

Finding the site: From I-93, exit 11, turn right onto Hackett Hill Road; proceed 0.4 mile. Turn right onto Cate Road; proceed 0.3 mile to site.

Rules and regulations: Safety gear is required: hard hat, reflective safety vest, steel-toed boots, safety goggles, and gloves.

This colorless quartz (or "rock crystal") was found by dissolving the calcite that had enclosed it.

Rockhounding

This huge crushed stone quarry contains a variety of rock types and to date has not been thoroughly explored by mineral collectors. The most interesting minerals found so far are metallic sulfides—pyrite, sphalerite, galena, chalcopyrite, and arsenopyrite—often in small but well-formed crystals. Most of the sulfide minerals, including hand-size chunks of sphalerite, seem to occur in the southeast part of the quarry near the entrance and also along the quarry access road, where this material was dumped. In places, bronzy chalcopyrite has been partially altered to green malachite. Quartz and calcite crystals, massive purple fluorite, and brown crystals of the tourmaline mineral dravite are also noteworthy. Fluorescent mineral collectors should look for coatings of hyalite (bright green fluorescence) and crystals of green fluorapatite (yellow fluorescence). The best approach here is to keep an open mind while exploring the site; your luck will depend in part on what part of the quarry is being worked. No doubt, the list of minerals will grow much longer in the future.

Pegmatite is the host of many rare and beautiful minerals in New England—but at this site the pegmatites appear to be simple and lacking in unusual minerals. Schorl and almandine occur in the pegmatite veins, but beryl apparently hasn't been found. However, high-quality beryl has been collected elsewhere in Hooksett, so it would be wise to carefully examine all pegmatite exposures in the quarry.

If time permits, take a trip to the Little Nature Museum in Warner. You'll find displays of rocks and minerals, including fluorescent ones, as well as fossils and all sorts of natural wonders and ancient artifacts. There's a gift shop that sells rocks and minerals, and kids will enjoy making their own rubbings of fossils and animal tracks to take home.

51. Raymond Quarry

Collectors search these quarry rocks for crystal-lined cavities.

See map page 156.

Status: Restricted; no access, unless on an authorized field trip

Land manager: Private—Aggregate Industries Northeast Region

Land type: Active crushed stone quarry

Type of deposit: Igneous (plutonic and volcanic rocks; granitic pegmatite) and metamorphic (metasedimentary rocks)

Location: Raymond, Rockingham County

GPS: N42.9974 / W71.1853

Elevation: Entrance, 208 feet; quarry, 131 to 296 feet

Vehicle: 4WD

Best season: May through Oct

Tools: Crack hammer, chisels, 10-power loupe

Minerals: Albite, almandine, anatase, bertrandite, beryl, biotite, calcite, fluorite, goethite, gypsum, microcline, molybdenite, muscovite, pyrite, quartz (smoky), schorl, siderite, sphalerite, zircon

Special attraction: Seacoast Science Center, Odiorne Point State Park, Rye

Accommodations: Camping at Pawtuckaway State Park, Nottingham. Lodging available in Exeter and Manchester.

Finding the site: From NH 101, exit 5, in Raymond, follow NH 102 west for 2.6 miles.

Rules and regulations: Safety gear is required: hard hat, reflective safety vest, steel-toed boots, safety glasses, and gloves.

Rockhounding

The Raymond quarry is located at Little Rattlesnake Hill, the site of one of three small volcanoes that were active about 114 million years ago in Early Cretaceous time. According to a 1950 report by geologist Jacob Freedman, the other volcanoes were located at Hook Hill, 0.5 mile northeast, and another hill 0.5 mile to the southeast. Little Rattlesnake Hill itself has largely been removed by quarrying operations, leaving its fascinating geology open to view in the quarry walls. Originally coarse-grained igneous rocks such as gabbro, monzonite, and syenite were injected forcefully into metamorphic rocks of the Berwick Formation, possibly at different times. Hook Hill erupted explosively with felsic magma, possibly followed by the other two volcanoes. The volcanoes themselves have long since eroded away; what remains are the rocks that filled the volcanic vents, including rhyolite, andesite, and keratophyre.

Smoky quartz crystals are common at this site.

Light-colored, coarse-grained igneous rock at the site superficially resembles the Conway granite of Moat Mountain and elsewhere in the White Mountains. It contains abundant cavities, most of them small but occasionally up to an inch or so across. The cavities commonly contain crystals of colorless or smoky quartz, fluorite, siderite, pyrite, and feldspar. Fluorite occurs as well-formed crystals, usually colorless but sometimes a pale shade of purple, blue, green, or yellow, often perched on quartz crystals. Siderite is found in groups of curved crystals—red, orange, or tan—on quartz and feldspar; often the crystals are surficially altered with an iridescent red or brown iron oxide coating. Less common species include calcite as yellow-white rhomb-shaped crystals; zircon as micro brown octahedrons on feldspar; goethite as tiny black balls; molybdenite as thin, bright metallic crystals looking sort of like bits of tin foil; and sphalerite as red-brown to black crystals.

Rocks unrelated to the plutonic/volcanic complex can also be found in the quarry, including schist, gneiss, and granitic pegmatite. The pegmatite contains light blue and light green beryl, muscovite (some as "ball" mica), schorl, and almandine.

52. Parker Mountain Mine

The Parker Mountain mine has long been a popular collecting site.

See map page 156.

Status: Restricted; no access, unless on an authorized field trip
Land manager: Private
Land type: Abandoned mine in woods
Type of deposit: Igneous (complex granitic pegmatite)
Location: Strafford, Strafford County
GPS: Parking, N43.2929 / W71.1603; site, N43.2935 / W71.1575
Elevation: Parking, 921 feet; site, 760 to 815 feet
Vehicle: Any
Best season: May through Oct
Tools: Crack hammer, chisels, safety goggles, digging tools, rake
Minerals: Albite, almandine, arsenolite, arsenopyrite, autunite, bertrandite, beryl, biotite, cassiterite, columbite, cookeite, corkite, cymatolite, diadochite, eucryptite, ferrisicklerite, fluorapatite, goethite, graftonite, graphite, hematite,

heterosite, hydroxylherderite, jahnsite, laueite, löllingite, ludlamite, magnetite, microcline, montmorillonite, muscovite, opal (hyalite), pharmacosiderite, pyrite, quartz, rhodochrosite, rockbridgeite, schorl, scorodite, siderite, spodumene, stewartite, strengite, strunzite, sulphur, triphylite, uraninite, uranophane, vivianite, whitlockite, zircon

Special attraction: Woodman Institute Museum, Dover

Accommodations: Camping at Pawtuckaway State Park, Nottingham. Lodging available in Rochester and Dover.

Finding the site: From the junction of NH 202A and NH 126 in Center Strafford, follow NH 126 north for 2.5 miles to Spencer Smith Trail parking area. Carefully walk across highway and downhill about 30 feet; follow path into the woods, down a steep embankment, and 200 feet to a trail on the left. Follow that trail a few hundred feet.

Rules and regulations: Hand tools only.

Rockhounding

The Parker Mountain mine, formerly known as the Foss or Buzzo mine, was operated for mica and feldspar periodically from the 1880s to 1959. Now surrounded by dense woods, yet still fairly accessible, the site has been a popular destination for collectors for many decades. The easy pickings are gone; considerable searching is required to find good specimens.

Massive dark green fluorapatite (manganapatite) is one of the most conspicuous minerals you'll see at Parker Mountain. It's fairly distinctive, but if you have any doubt, shine a shortwave UV light on it when you get home—it will fluoresce bright yellow. Black schorl and orange-red almandine crystals are frequently associated with the fluorapatite. Beryl is not uncommon; it's usually light green or blue-green but rarely, if ever, gem quality. Spodumene is abundant, but most of it has been altered to cymatolite, a pseudomorph consisting of mica

Cymatolite is a mica and feldspar pseudomorph after spodumene.

Minerals from the Parker Mountain mine include (clockwise from top left): fluorapatite (variety "manganapatite"), heterosite, eucryptite (daylight), and eucryptite (shortwave UV).

and feldspar. Cavities are rare, but occasionally small ones are found filled with crystals of quartz, albite, or other minerals.

Parker Mountain is perhaps most famous for eucryptite, a rare lithium species that is highly prized by collectors of fluorescent minerals. Dull gray in daylight, eucryptite comes alive with a beautiful rose-red glow under shortwave ultraviolet light. This mineral is always found in massive form, never in crystals. It was formerly pretty common on the dumps, even on the surface, but collectors have scooped so much of it up that you'll probably have to dig to find it.

Löllingite, a silvery-gray arsenic mineral, is not uncommon, but good crystals are rare. Triphylite occurs in the pegmatite, and you'll see scattered pieces on the dumps. But unlike at the Palermo mines (Sites 56, 57), collectible secondary phosphates resulting from the alteration of triphylite are scarce. Nonetheless, micromineral collectors have found some rare and interesting species, and the possibility that the list will be extended is good.

53. Ham and Weeks Mine

Blue is the typical color for beryl at this site. (Don Swenson collection)

See map page 156.

Status: Restricted; no access except by members of the Maine Mineralogical and Geological Society (MMGS) and authorized guests

Land manager: MMGS

Land type: Abandoned open-pit mine

Type of deposit: Igneous (granitic pegmatite)

Location: Wakefield, Carroll County

GPS: Entrance, N43.6704 / W71.0079

Elevation: Entrance, 767 feet; site, 720 to 725 feet

Vehicle: Any

Best season: May through Oct

Tools: Crack hammer, sledgehammer, chisels, safety goggles, digging tools; Geiger counter (optional)

Minerals: Albite, almandine, autunite, beryl, chalcopyrite, chrysoberyl, columbite-(Fe), fluorapatite, fluorite, gummite, magnetite, malachite, microcline, molybdenite, muscovite, phenakite, pyrite, quartz, samarskite-(Y), spessartine, synchysite-(Ce), uraninite, zircon (cyrtolite)

Special attraction: Wentworth State Park, Wolfeboro
Accommodations: Private campgrounds located in East Wakefield and Effingham. Lodging available along NH 16, Wakefield.
Finding the site: From the junction of NH 109 and NH 153 in Wakefield, follow NH 153 north for 9.4 miles. Turn left onto Pick Pocket Road and proceed 1 mile.
Rules and regulations: MMGS membership card and vehicle decal required. Hand tools only. No commercial collecting. MMGS safety rules and per-day collecting limits apply.

Rockhounding

The Ham and Weeks mine was worked at various times beginning in 1877 for mica, feldspar, and beryl. The mica was originally sold for use in stove windows and lamp chimneys, and much later for use in gas masks worn by soldiers during World War I and for insulation in crystal radio sets. Today the site is best known for its distinctive powder-blue beryl crystals.

Yellow-green chrysoberyl on blue beryl is an attractive combination. (Don Swenson collection)

The beryl is rarely gemmy enough to be faceted, but the material does make attractive cabochons. In 2012 the MMGS conducted a blast at the site to uncover new material. Afterwards, the first collectors to scramble onto the scene procured some choice beryl crystals, some several inches long. Seekers of rare but less showy species also came away with interesting finds.

Ham and Weeks is one of the few sites in New England where collectors have a reasonable chance of finding chrysoberyl, a beautiful but uncommon beryllium mineral. Here it is usually found emplaced on the sides of blue beryl crystals. Citrusy, yellow-green chrysoberyl on powder-blue beryl is a visually striking combination. Radioactive species such as uraninite, samarskite-(Y), and cyrtolite are popular with some collectors. Garnet—almandine or spessartine—is not common, but can be found in attractive red to orange crystals. Fluorapatite occurs both in massive form and as crude hexagonal crystals up to several inches long, usually with a pale gray color that makes it difficult to identify in the field. However, under shortwave ultraviolet light the mineral

Recent blasting exposed light blue beryl in one of the pit walls.

comes alive with very bright, yellow fluorescence. This is one of the best localities in New England for this variety of fluorapatite, called "manganapatite" for manganese, the activator of its fluorescence.

Branchlike dendrites on feldspar look so much like plant fossils that they are frequently mistaken for them. These "pseudofossils" are formed by manganese oxides that crystallize on cleavage and fracture surfaces in the rock. Dendrites are common at many pegmatite localities in New England, but at Ham and Weeks they make especially attractive specimens when found on peach-colored microcline feldspar.

Other minerals at the site include microcrystals of phenakite, fluorite, and secondary beryl from cavities within larger corroded beryl crystals. The fluorite is deep purple and at first glance looks like purple fluorapatite, which is well-known from some of the Maine pegmatites but has not been found here. Other rare species have been reported from Ham and Weeks but are not listed above because they are still unverified. However, there is little doubt that diligent searching by collectors will turn up new and unusual species for the site.

Dendrites of manganese oxides often resemble plant fossils.

54. Ruggles Mine

"Gummite" is not a valid mineral, but a mixture of uraninite and secondary uranium minerals. Ruggles mine is a world-famous gummite locality. (Dana M. Jewell collection)

Status: Open on a fee basis, weekends from mid-May to mid-June, daily from mid-June to mid-Oct, 9 a.m. to 5 p.m. For more information, visit www.rugglesmine.com.
Land manager: Private—Ruggles Mine, Inc.
Land type: Former mica mine—large open pit and tunnels
Type of deposit: Igneous (complex granitic pegmatite)
Location: Grafton, Grafton County
GPS: N43.5908 / W71.9913
Elevation: Parking, 1,625 feet; mine, 1,470 to 1,645 feet
Vehicle: Any
Best season: Mid-May to mid-Oct
Tools: Crack hammer, chisels, safety goggles, digging tools, 10-power loupe, flashlight. Collecting gear can be rented on-site.
Minerals: Albite, almandine, anglesite, autunite, bertrandite, beryl (aquamarine, golden), beryllonite, beta-uranophane, biotite, bismuth, chrysoberyl, columbite,

fluorapatite, galena, goethite, gummite, kasolite, löllingite, microcline, montmorillonite, muscovite, parsonsite, paulscherrerite, phosphuranylite, pyrite, pyrrhotite, quartz, schoepite, schorl, sillimanite, sklodowskite, soddyite, staurolite, torbernite, triphylite, uraninite, uranophane, vandendriesscheite, vivianite, zircon (cyrtolite)

Special attraction: Cardigan Mountain State Park, Orange

Accommodations: Camping at AMC's Cardigan Lodge & Campsites, Alexandria. Lodging available in New London, Sunapee, and Lebanon.

Finding the site: From US 4 in Grafton, take Riddle Hill Road west for 1.2 miles. Turn right onto Ruggles Mine Road; continue for 1 mile.

Rules and regulations: Keep out of restricted areas.

Rockhounding

Ruggles mine, located high atop Isinglass Mountain, has been nicknamed "The Mine in the Sky." Opened about 1803 by Sam Ruggles, it was the first commercial mica mine in the United States (*isinglass* is an old name for mica). A giant plate of muscovite mica, 5 feet long by 3 feet wide, was reportedly extracted in the nineteenth century and delivered to Windsor Castle in England. Beginning in 1912, feldspar was also mined; later beryl as well, as an ore of beryllium. The mine began operating as a tourist attraction in 1963. A museum on the site displays minerals, mining artifacts, and local history items. The gift shop sells minerals, fossils, and jewelry from around the world, and there's a snack bar and picnic area with scenic views of the mountainous countryside.

The open pit, tunnels, and underground chambers of Ruggles mine are fun to explore, even for non-rockhounds. Kids love this place. Many visitors are first-time collectors, so for them picking up a few pretty rocks in the mine is an enjoyable enough experience. Many seasoned rockhounds, on the other hand, have been skeptical about whether anything worthwhile remains to be collected, especially after decades of over-collecting and without any new excavating activity. Old-timers remember the days when intensely colored secondary uranium minerals like the bright orange-and-yellow specimens of "gummite" and other minerals seen in museums around the world were collected. However, in the past few years the situation has improved. Occasional blasting is now being done at the far end of the quarry, where miners are searching for gem-quality beryl and other valuable minerals, and this has opened up new opportunities for visiting collectors as well. The employees

Sites 54-57

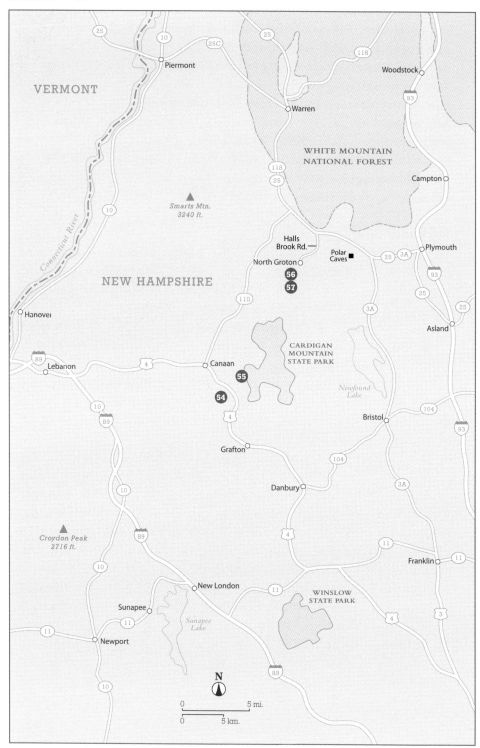

Access to the main pit of Ruggles mine is through a tunnel.

who patrol the collecting area are quite knowledgeable about the mineralogy of the mine and are eager to assist visitors.

A smart strategy for maximizing your collecting experience at Ruggles would be to contact the mine office and ask when the next blast is scheduled, and plan to visit after that. Dig deep into the dumps to find the good stuff that others have missed—keep in mind that most visitors simply scan the surface. Micromineral collectors should search for pockets in albite; these sometimes contain tiny hexagonal fluorapatite crystals. Massive greenish-gray triphylite is associated with orange-red almandine and pyrite. Black schorl and scattered pieces of blue-green beryl are fairly common.

The open pit can get very hot in the summer, so dress accordingly and bring plenty of water. Gloves are advisable if you plan to do any digging because the quartz and mica fragments can be sharp. Spectacular views of colorful fall foliage are a bonus if you visit in early October.

55. Hoyt Hill Mica Mine

The flooded Hoyt Hill mine is located deep in the forest.

See map page 168.

Status: Restricted; open only to members of the Capital Mineral Club (CMC) and designated guests

Land manager: State of New Hampshire; mineral rights belong to CMC

Land type: Abandoned mica mine on a forested hilltop

Type of deposit: Igneous (granitic pegmatite)

Location: Frank H. Jackson Forest, Orange, Grafton County

GPS: Mine road entrance, N43.6458 / W71.9466; site, N43.6348 / W71.9487

Elevation: Mine road entrance, 1,667 feet; site, 1,980 feet

Vehicle: High-clearance 4WD

Best season: Mid-May through Oct

Tools: Crack hammer, chisels, safety goggles, digging tools

Minerals: Albite, almandine, beryl, fluorapatite, microcline, muscovite, quartz, schorl, zircon

Special attraction: Cardigan Mountain State Park, Orange

Accommodations: Camping at AMC Cardigan Lodge, Alexandria. Lodging available in New London, Sunapee, and Lebanon.
Finding the site: From the junction of US 4 and NH 118 in Canaan, follow NH 118 north for 0.5 mile. Turn right onto Cardigan Mountain Road; continue for 3.2 miles. Park by woods road on right; hike along woods road about 1.1 miles to the site.
Rules and regulations: Noncommercial, hobby collecting only.

Muscovite mica was mined on Hoyt Hill beginning in the 1870s.

Rockhounding

Mica plates as large as 8 inches square came out of the old Hoyt Hill mica mine, which was operated intermittently from the 1870s to the 1940s and consisted of an open cut as well as underground workings. Today the site is typical of hundreds of nearly forgotten (and forgotten) abandoned mica and feldspar mines that dot the hills of New Hampshire. The pit is flooded, the dumps are mostly overgrown, and much of the mine road is inaccessible to vehicles of any kind. Aside from the occasional hunter stumbling across the old pit, few have ever seen the site since mining ceased. But mineral collectors are an adventurous lot, and members of the Capital Mineral Club are no exception as they seek to uncover whatever treasures might await them.

Although beryl was not mentioned in early government mining reports, it has in fact been found by collectors searching in the dumps. Whether any gem material will be found remains to be seen. Large plates of muscovite mica can be collected at this site, as well as other typical pegmatite minerals such as black schorl, orange-red to red almandine, and masses of green manganoan fluorapatite, which exhibits a bright mustard-yellow fluorescence under shortwave UV light. Cavities appear to be rare in the pegmatite; however, tiny vugs containing well-formed albite and muscovite crystals have been found.

Hoyt Hill is in a remote forested area frequented by hunters, so it's a good idea to wear bright-colored clothing, especially during the fall hunting season. Moose droppings are common along the trail, so seeing a moose is not out of the question. Bring your camera! Bug spray is essential, as ticks, mosquitoes, and deerflies are unfortunately both abundant and persistent.

56. Palermo No. 1 Mine

The Palermo No. 1 mine is one of the most famous mineral localities in the world.

See map page 168.
Status: Restricted; no access, unless on an authorized field trip
Land manager: Private
Land type: Mine and dumps on a wooded hillside
Type of deposit: Igneous (complex granitic pegmatite)
Location: North Groton, Grafton County
GPS: N43.7509 / W71.8902
Elevation: 1,580 to 1,660 feet
Vehicle: High-clearance 4WD
Best season: Mid-May through Oct
Tools: Crack hammer, chisels, digging tools, 10-power loupe
Minerals: Albite, allaudite/ferroallaudite, almandine, anapaite, anatase, arrojadite-(KFe), arsenopyrite, augelite, autunite, azurite, barbosalite, beraunite, bermanite, bertrandite, beryl (golden, aquamarine), beryllonite, beta-uranophane, biotite,

birnessite, bismuth, bismuthinite, bjarebyite, bornite, brazilianite, brushite, cacoxenite, cerussite, chalcopyrite, childrenite, chlorapatite, chlorite, collinsite, columbite, covellite, crandallite, cuprite, diadochite, dickinsonite, djurleite, dufrénite, eosphorite, fairfieldite, falsterite, ferrisicklerite, ferrostrunzite, fluorapatite, galena, goedkinite, goethite, gordonite, gormanite, goyazite, graftonite, greifensteinite, gummite, gypsum, hagendorfite, hematite, heterosite, hinsdalite, hisingerite, hollandite, hopeite, hureaulite, hydroxylapatite, hydroxylherderite, jahnsite, keckite, kryzhanovskite, kulanite, laueite, lazulite, leucophosphite, löllingite, ludlamite, magnetite, malachite, marcasite, melanterite, messelite, metavivianite, microcline, mitridatite, montebrasite, montmorillonite, moraesite, muscovite, nizamoffite, nontronite, opal (hyalite), palermoite, parascholzite, paravauxite, paulscherrerite, phosphoferrite, phosphophyllite, phosphosiderite, phosphuranylite, pseudolaueite, pseudomalachite, pyrite, pyromorphite, pyrrhotite, quartz, rhodochrosite, rockbridgeite, rutherfordine, samuelsonite, sarcopside, schoepite, schoonerite, schorl, scorzalite, siderite, sillimanite, sinkankasite, smithsonite, souzalite, sphalerite, stewartite, strengite, strunzite, tavorite, todorokite, torbernite, triphylite, triploidite, uraninite, uranophane, ushkovite, vandendriesscheite, vivianite, wardite, whiteite, whitlockite, whitmoreite, wolfeite, xanthoxenite, zanazziite, zircon

Special attraction: Sculptured Rocks, Groton

Accommodations: Campgrounds located in Plymouth and Wentworth. Lodging available along I-93, Ashland to Franconia.

Finding the site: From I-93, exit 26, follow NH 25 west for 8.5 miles. Turn left onto Halls Brook Road; proceed 3.7 miles. Turn left onto North Groton Road; proceed 0.2 mile. Turn right and follow Edgar Albert Road 0.9 mile to gate; proceed 0.4 mile to site.

Rules and regulations: Hard hat, safety goggles, long pants, and sturdy footwear are required. Climbing walls or large rocks is prohibited.

Rockhounding

The Palermo No. 1 mine is one of the most famous pegmatite mineral localities in the world. Twelve new mineral species have been discovered here, most recently falsterite (2011) and nizamoffite (2012). While best known for its unusual phosphate mineralogy, there are treasures at Palermo for everyone. Whether you're looking for cabinet specimens or micromounts, rare species or gem rough, fluorescent minerals or just pretty yard rock, a visit to the mine will rarely leave you disappointed.

Opened in 1863, the Palermo No. 1 mine has been operated commercially for mica, feldspar, quartz, and beryl. Since the 1970s gem beryl (aquamarine

This fabulous beryl crystal was discovered on a mineral club field trip.

and golden) and mineral specimens have been the primary focus. Beryl crystals are sometimes seen embedded in massive quartz in mine walls; these tantalizing beauties are very difficult to extract intact. It's better to search the dumps for beryl that has been blasted out, discarded, or missed. Lucky collectors have even found colorful crystals lying on mine roads, exposed by the rain.

Quartz crystals are common, usually colorless or smoky. Sometimes a thin coating of iron oxide gives the quartz a yellowish hue. Quartz in massive form can be milky, pale rose, or even tinted green or blue when associated with phosphate minerals. Albite commonly contains small cavities, many containing green or blue crystals of fluorapatite.

Triphylite, one of the primary phosphate minerals at the mine, is grayish green or blue with a greasy luster and is often seen embedded in walls or in loose pieces scattered about the dumps. Sulfide minerals such as pyrite, pyrrhotite, chalcopyrite, and arsenopyrite are commonly associated. Triphylite is the source of many of the interesting secondary phosphate species that the mine is famous for. Use a 10-power loupe to closely examine loose pieces of triphylite or tan to brownish siderite. Some of the more abundant phosphate minerals include blue vivianite in bladed crystals, orange laueite, apple-green ludlamite, and straw-colored fibrous strunzite. Wrap up some promising pieces to take home with you to examine later with your loupe or a microscope. Don't be discouraged if you can't identify everything you find. Even experts can get stumped, and there are probably several new mineral species here yet to be discovered.

On hot summer days, you can sit at the entrance of the underground workings and cool off as air exits the tunnel like natural air-conditioning, chilled by ice that sometimes persists in the mine as late as July.

57. Palermo No. 2 Mine

The flooded pit of the Palermo No. 2 mine is behind this ridge.

See map page 168.
Status: Restricted; no access, unless on an authorized field trip
Land manager: Private
Land type: Open-pit mine
Type of deposit: Igneous (complex granitic pegmatite)
Location: North Groton, Grafton County
GPS: N43.7518 / W71.8928
Elevation: 1,760 to 1,788 feet
Vehicle: High-clearance 4WD
Best season: Mid-May through Oct
Tools: Crack hammer, chisels, digging tools, 10-power loupe

This black schorl crystal is partially coated with green mitridatite.

Minerals: Albite, almandine, arsenopyrite, augelite, autunite, beraunite, bertrandite, beryl (aquamarine, golden), biotite, bismuth, bornite, chalcopyrite, childrenite, chlorapatite, chlorite, collinsite, columbite-(Fe), crandallite, diadochite, eosphorite, fairfieldite, ferrisicklerite, ferrohagendorfite, fluorapatite, frondelite, galena, gordonite, gormanite, goyazite, graftonite, gypsum, hematite, heterosite, hydroxylapatite, jahnsite, kryzhanovskite, laueite, lazulite-scorzalite, leucophosphite, löllingite, ludlamite, magnetite, messelite, metavivianite, microcline, mitridatite, monazite-(Ce), montebrasite, muscovite, paravauxite, phosphoferrite, phosphosiderite, pseudolaueite, pyrite, quartz, rockbridgeite, rutile, sarcopside, schorl, siderite, souzalite, sphalerite, stewartite, strengite, strunzite, tapiolite-(Fe), torbernite, triphylite, uraninite, ushkovite, vivianite, whiteite, whitmoreite, wolfeite, xenotime-(Y), zircon

Special attraction: Polar Caves Park, Rumney

Accommodations: Campgrounds located in Plymouth and Wentworth. Lodging available along I-93, Ashland to Franconia.

Finding the site: From North Groton Road, follow Edgar Allen Road 1.3 miles to the Palermo No. 1 mine parking area; take the trail on the left 0.25 mile to the mine.

Rules and regulations: Safety goggles, long pants, and sturdy footwear are required.

Rockhounding

The Palermo No. 2 mine is a bit higher up the mountain and a lot smaller than its sister mine, but is an outstanding mineral locality in its own right. It began as an open-cut mica mine in the nineteenth century and is now a source of gem aquamarine and golden beryl, as well as a variety of other minerals including rare phosphate species. The mineral list is similar to but less extensive than the list for Palermo No. 1. Though close in proximity, there are some obvious differences between the two sites. For example, schorl is far more common at No. 2 than No. 1. As you search through the dumps, you'll notice other differences as well. Some minerals reported at the No. 2 mine have not yet been reported from Palermo No. 1, including ferrohagendorfite, frondelite, monazite, rutile, tapiolite-(Fe), and xenotime-(Y). Look through the dumps for brown altered triphylite and check for cavities that might contain unusual microminerals.

Wildlife abounds in the vicinity of the Palermo mines. Moose, deer, and black bear all frequent the area. One of these visitors—the eastern moose, *Alces alces americana*—is a huge animal; males can be up to 7 feet tall at the shoulders and on average weigh 1,400 pounds. If you're lucky, you might see one munching on the leaves and twigs of hardwood trees near the mines. The forest clearings in the mine area provide perfect habitat for wildflowers and butterflies. On a recent field trip, a rare daytime sighting of a green luna moth, several inches long, caused considerable excitement; several rockhounds took a break from collecting to snap photos. Snakes are sometimes encountered in the dumps; however, the area is far north of the ranges of any poisonous species.

58. Wild Ammonoosuc River— Gold Panning

The Wild Ammonoosuc River is the most popular stream in New Hampshire to pan for gold.

Status: Open; permit required from Twin Rivers Campground
Land manager: Private—Twin River Campground and Cottages
Land type: Rocky river
Type of deposit: Alluvial placer deposit
Location: Bath, Grafton County
GPS: N44.1518 / W71.9755
Elevation: Campground entrance, 492 feet
Vehicle: Any
Best season: Summer, when water level is low. Campground season: May 15 to Oct 15.
Tools: Lightweight plastic gold pan, plastic pail or bucket, small shovel or garden trowel, tweezers, small plastic bottle for gold. Equipment can be purchased at the campground store. Sluices are available for rent (state permit required).
Minerals: Almandine, chalcopyrite, gold, magnetite, molybdenite, pyrite
Special attraction: The Brick Store (general store established ca. 1790), Bath

Sites 58-65

Accommodations: Camping at Twin River Campground and Cottages. Lodging available in Lincoln and Franconia.
Finding the site: Campground is on NH 112 at the junction of US 302.
Rules and regulations: State permit required to use a sluice or dredge.

Rockhounding

The discovery of gold at the Orchard mine in Lyman by Professor Henry Durtz in 1864 set off a minor gold rush in New Hampshire. Several small mines with shafts were opened, as well as

This 0.115-gram gold nugget is from the Wild Ammonoosuc River.

two milling operations. The region became known as the Ammonoosuc Gold District and included Lyman, Monroe, Bath, and parts of Littleton, Landaff, and Lisbon. Gold was found in veins with sulfide minerals and as free gold in quartz. Though streams in the area were not worked commercially for placer gold, many have long been known to contain deposits of gold.

The Wild Ammonoosuc River, a 15-mile-long tributary of the Ammonoosuc River, is one of the most popular places to pan in New England. The gravel at the bottom of the river contains gold, and because gold is not subject to weathering when you find it, it will look just like you'd expect. (But be careful—at first glance, mica and pyrite can look like gold, too.) The goal of hunting for gold in streams is to separate any gold flakes and nuggets from gravel, and panning is an easy, time-honored way to do this. Nuggets weighing up to 0.75 ounce are said to have been recovered from the "Wild A," but most of the gold you'll find will be dust or flakes. The largest gold is reportedly found near the middle of the river.

Before you begin, dress so that you can wade into the river. Put on some sunscreen and insect repellant. Find a good spot along the river, up to about a mile from the campground. Look for stream gravel that has settled in between boulders and scoop some up into your pan, filling it about three-quarters of the way while discarding any large stones. Shake the pan back and forth just under the surface of the water, so that heavier minerals will settle to the bottom and lighter ones will be washed away by the current. Eventually, as you repeat this, only dark sand containing heavier minerals such as magnetite, almandine, and, if you're lucky, gold will remain in the pan. Use tweezers to remove any gold you see, and place it into your small plastic container. Be aware that once you find your first gold, there's a good chance you'll be hooked!

59. Tunnel Brook—Gold Panning

Metamorphic rock crops out at Tunnel Brook near the parking area.

See map page 178.

Status: Open

Land manager: White Mountain National Forest (WMNF), Pemigewasset Ranger District

Land type: Brook in forest

Type of deposit: Alluvial placer deposit

Location: Benton, Grafton County

GPS: Parking, N44.0743 / W71.8366

Elevation: Parking, 1,410 feet

Vehicle: Any

Best season: Mid-May through Oct

Tools: Gold pan, shovel, trowel, plastic vial, tweezers; handheld sluice box (optional)

Type of deposit: Placer

Minerals: Almandine, gold, magnetite

Special attraction: Lost River Reservation, North Woodstock

Accommodations: Camping at WMNF Wildwood Campground, Easton, and Lost River Valley Campground, North Woodstock. Lodging available in North Woodstock and Lincoln.

Finding the site: From I-93, exit 32, in North Woodstock, follow NH 112 west for 11 miles. Turn left onto Tunnel Brook Road; proceed 1.4 miles to bridge.

Rules and regulations: Hobby gold hunting for personal, noncommercial use is allowed. Hand tools only—no power or mechanized equipment or explosives. Sluice boxes more than 3 feet long, rocker boxes, and dredges are prohibited. Care must be taken to protect water quality and aquatic habitat. Disturbance of stream banks is prohibited.

Rockhounding

Tunnel Brook, at the northern foot of 4,802-foot Mount Moosilauke, has plenty of quiet spots to do some good old-fashioned gold panning. Metamorphic rocks of the Devonian Littleton Formation crop out in the brook just south of the bridge on Tunnel Brook Road. You could settle in there to do some panning, or if you prefer, set up a sluice box. There are other good spots downstream along Tunnel Brook Road to pan as well. If you'd rather try your luck upstream, you'll have to walk; a gate currently blocks the road leading south from the parking area because of extensive damage caused by Hurricane Irene in 2011. Large sections of the road were completely washed away. The roaring floodwaters no doubt moved a lot of gold around as well, so prospecting in that area could be worthwhile.

Tunnel Brook has been a favorite stream for gold hunters for many years—coarse gold and occasionally even a gold nugget have turned up in many a pan. It's not uncommon to see well-formed crystals of almandine and magnetite in a gold pan, a sign that their bedrock source is not far upstream, likely in mica schist of the Littleton Formation.

Lost River Reservation (also called Lost River Gorge and Boulder Caves) is 6.4 miles away on NH 112. It's owned by the nonprofit Society for the Protection of New Hampshire Forests. The reservation features a babbling river that plays hide-and-seek as it winds through a rocky gorge, over waterfalls, and through caves formed by a jumble of giant boulders. The society has owned the land since 1912, when they purchased it to protect it from logging operations. Visitors can experience the site via a wooden boardwalk that weaves its way through the gorge and caves.

60. North Sugarloaf Mountain

Bertrandite is one of the many uncommon minerals that occur as good microcrystals at this site.

See map page 178.

Status: Open; nominal day-use fee required

Land manager: White Mountain National Forest (WMNF), Pemigewasset Ranger District

Land type: Forested mountainside

Type of deposit: Igneous (granite with miarolitic cavities)

Location: Bethlehem, Grafton County

GPS: Trailhead, N44.2538 / W71.5042; summit, N44.2578 / W71.5178

Elevation: Trailhead, 1,643 feet; summit 2,310 feet

Vehicle: Any

Best season: Mid-May through Oct

Tools: Crack hammer, chisels, safety goggles, pry bar, 10-power loupe, hand trowel or small shovel

Minerals: Albite, anatase, bastnäsite-(Ce), bazzite, bertrandite, beryl, biotite, cassiterite, cerianite-(Ce), columbite/tantalite, danalite, fergusonite, fluocerite-(Ce), fluorite, gadolinite, genthelvite, goethite, hematite, hingganite-(Y), ilmenite, microcline, microlite, molybdenite, muscovite, opal (hyalite), phenakite, pyrite, pyrochlore, quartz (amethyst, smoky), siderite, uvite, xenotime-(Y), zinnwaldite, zircon

Special attraction: Mount Washington Cog Railway, Bretton Woods

Accommodations: WMNF campgrounds Zealand, Sugarloaf I, and Sugarloaf II are nearby. Lodging available in Twin Mountain and Bethlehem.

Finding the site: From the junction of US 3 and US 302 in Twin Mountain, follow US 302 east for 3.1 miles. Turn right onto Zealand Road; proceed 0.9 mile. Park and pay day-use fee at self-service station. Cross bridge and hike along the Sugarloaf Trail about 1.1 miles to the collecting area.

Rules and regulations: Hobby mineral collecting is allowed using hand tools only and resulting in no more than minor surface disturbance. Before leaving, fill in holes, restore natural contours, and spread the original soil cover of natural organic debris. Cutting trees or other vegetation is forbidden.

Rockhounding

The Sugarloaf Trail is a popular hiking trail that rises through dense woods past large, frequently moss-covered boulders. The rocky summit of North Sugarloaf provides fabulous views of the surrounding White Mountains. The hike is not difficult for about the first 0.7 mile, but the last half mile is a bit rougher. Talus boulders along the trail to the summit occasionally contain crystal-filled cavities. The main collecting area is alongside the trail, just below the summit. Smoky quartz crystals are often very dark, even black, and these are the most popular, but lighter brown and colorless quartz occurs as well.

Several unusual minerals have been collected on North Sugarloaf, some of them very uncommon in New England. Most of these species occur as microcrystals. Pockets in crumbly, decaying Conway granite contain crystals of rare-earth minerals such as red bastnäsite-(Ce), yellow-brown xenotime-(Y), and gadolinite in wheat-sheaf-like groups of brown crystals. Collectors have also found pale blue microcrystals of bazzite, salmon-pink danalite, yellow or blue genthelvite, and yellow to orange octahedrons of pyrochlore. Fluorite is relatively common as colorless, pale blue, and purple cubic crystals; some colorless crystals have purple corners, and some have yellow-green muscovite inclusions. Siderite crystals are also common, frequently showing alteration to goethite. Beryl can be found as crudely formed pale green crystals as long as 8 inches, but is often overlooked because of its poor quality.

North Sugarloaf is one of the best New England localities for the beryllium mineral bertrandite. Crystals have been found as classic heart-shaped "V" twins. Phenakite occurs in colorless crystals, usually less than 3 millimeters long. One amazing gem crystal, 1¾ inches long, was found by collectors who believed it to be topaz; much later it was proven to be the much rarer phenakite and is now at the Smithsonian Institution.

Ramsbeckite (blue-green), a rare copper-zinc sulfate mineral, has been found on the shore of Mascot Pond.

See map page 178.

Status: Believed to be open, subject to restrictions

Land manager: New Hampshire Department of Resources and Economic Development (DRED), Division of Forests and Lands

Land type: Dumps of an abandoned lead mine on a mountainside

Type of deposit: Hydrothermal breccia vein deposit

Location: Gorham, Coos County

GPS: Parking, N44.4024 / W71.1993; site, N44.4006 / W71.1790

Elevation: Parking, 780 feet; site, 1,053 to 1,280 feet

Vehicle: Any

Best season: May through Oct

Tools: Knapsack, 10-power loupe, wrapping material

Minerals: Acanthite, anglesite, aragonite, arsenopyrite, aurichalcite, biotite, brochantite, calcite, cerussite, chalcopyrite, chamosite, cuprite, galena, gypsum, hemimorphite, hydrozincite, linarite, malachite, metazeunerite, muscovite, posnjakite, pyrite, pyrrhotite, quartz, ramsbeckite, schulenbergite, serpierite, siderite, silver, smithsonite, sphalerite

Special attractions: Mount Washington Auto Road, Pinkham Notch

Accommodations: Camping at Moose Brook State Park and elsewhere in Gorham. Lodging also available in Gorham.

Finding the site: From the junction of US 2 (Lancaster Road) and NH 16 (Main Street) in Gorham, follow NH 16 north for 0.4 mile to the parking area by the steel railroad bridge. Use footbridge to cross Androscoggin River. Follow dirt road on left 0.25 mile to junction of old rail bed; continue 1,000 feet to bridge. Cross bridge and immediately turn right onto trail. Turn right again in 400 feet; proceed 0.4 mile to sign for AMC Mahoosuc Trail (before the dam). Follow AMC trail 2,000 feet; turn at trail sign marked Mascot Pond and continue 0.25 mile.

Rules and regulations: Mechanized equipment and hand tools are prohibited. Keep out of tunnels.

Rockhounding

Located on the steep southwestern side of Mount Hayes, the Mascot mine produced lead and silver from 1881 to 1885 and again for a short time in the early twentieth century. The deposit is basically a breccia vein consisting of fragments of altered granitic rock and the minerals siderite, quartz, galena, sphalerite, and chalcopyrite. The dumps are on a very steep slope, so use abundant caution while collecting.

Siderite is very common on the mine dumps, both massive and as tan-colored crystals up to 2 centimeters long. The metallic minerals galena, chalcopyrite, and pyrite are also common but are often obscured by a dark brown surface coating. Check weathered brown stones on the dump for a greater than average "heft"; heavier stones will likely contain one or more of the metallic minerals. In tailings along the shore of Mascot Pond, brightly colored secondary lead, zinc, and copper minerals resulting from the alteration of galena, sphalerite, and chalcopyrite can be

Native silver often occurs as tiny "wires." (Tom Mortimer collection) Photo by Tom Mortimer

Linarite (azure-blue), a lead-copper sulfate mineral, is popular with micromount collectors.

found. These secondary minerals are commonly a shade of blue or green and include linarite, brochantite, malachite, aurichalcite, posnjakite, ramsbeckite, and schulenbergite. Most occur as microcrystals, but a few larger specimens have been found as well.

Entrances to underground portions of the mine are blocked with steel gates to protect a population of about 1,500 bats. Five different species spend winters hibernating in the mine, including the endangered eastern small-footed bat, *Myotis leibii*. You can climb the slope up to the mine entrances and look inside. The fabulous view of Mascot Pond and the White Mountains alone is worth the effort.

The Mount Washington Auto Road in Pinkham Notch, 7.5 miles south of Gorham, is a privately operated toll road that climbs to the summit of the 6,288-foot peak, the highest in the Northeast. The windswept summit area has an arctic/alpine climate—you can see rare plant species along the Alpine Garden Trail. There's a summit weather observatory and museum, too. Mount Washington is notorious for severe weather; high winds and snowstorms can happen any time of the year. The steep 7.6-mile auto road is open mid-May to October, weather permitting, of course.

62. Iron Mountain Mines

Danalite, first reported from Iron Mountain in 1880, occurs as reddish octahedral crystals. (Tom Mortimer collection) Photo by Tom Mortimer

See map page 178.

Status: Open

Land manager: White Mountain National Forest (WMNF), Saco Ranger District

Land type: Abandoned mines on forested mountainside

Type of deposit: Hydrothermal (metasomatically replaced granite)

Location: Bartlett, Carroll County (trailhead is in Jackson)

GPS: Trailhead, N44.1432 / W71.2312; higher pit, N44.1249 / W71.2370; lower adit pit, N44.1232 / W71.2376

Elevation: Trailhead, 1,912 feet; summit, 2,726 feet; higher pit, 2,060 feet; lower adit pit, 1,800 feet

Vehicle: High-clearance 4WD

Best season: Mid-May through Oct

Tools: Crack hammer, chisels, safety goggles, pry bar, digging tools, 10-power loupe

Minerals: Adularia, albite, bazzite, bertrandite, beryl, biotite, chalcopyrite, chrysoberyl, danalite, diopside, ferrosilite, fluorite, galena, genthelvite, hedenbergite, helvite, hematite, magnetite, microcline, phenakite, pyrite, pyrochlore, quartz, scheelite, sphalerite, vesuvianite, xenotime-(Y), zircon

Special attraction: Glen Ellis Falls, Jackson

Accommodations: Camping at Crawford Notch State Park. Lodging available in Jackson, Bartlett, and North Conway.

Finding the site: From the junction of US 302 and NH 16 in Glen, follow NH 16 north for 2.5 miles. Turn left onto Green Hill Road; proceed 1.2 miles. Turn left onto Iron Mountain Road/FR 119 and proceed 1.4 miles to the Trail sign on left. Hike 0.9 mile to the summit of Iron Mountain; continue south for 0.6 mile. Follow side trail to the left 0.2 mile to the mines. Total round-trip hiking time is about 3 hours.

Rules and regulations: Hobby mineral collecting is allowed using hand tools only and resulting in no more than minor surface disturbance. Before leaving, fill in holes, restore natural contours, and spread the original soil cover of natural organic debris. Cutting trees or other vegetation is forbidden.

Rockhounding

Originally called Baldface, Iron Mountain was named for the nineteenth-century iron-mining operations that took place on its south face. The deposit of iron ore is thought to have been formed by replacement of Jurassic-age Conway granite near its contact with gneiss of the Devonian-age Littleton Formation. There were at least four mines on the mountain, both underground workings and open cuts, and there are extensive dumps. Much of the area has yet to be investigated by collectors. Look for rocks with cavities or vugs that might contain crystals, and break open weathered rocks that feel especially heavy to search for sulfide minerals like galena.

The most common minerals on the dumps are quartz and the iron ores hematite and magnetite. Others you're likely to encounter include galena (sometimes altered to cerussite), sphalerite (yellow, brown, or black), chalcopyrite, and fluorite (purple or white). Crystals of these minerals are uncommon, however.

The real treasures on Iron Mountain are microcrystals of various rare minerals. These include phenakite (colorless crystals up to 3 millimeters long), bertrandite (colorless), and ferrosilite (brown). Pale blue hexagonal crystals of bazzite, a mineral related to beryl that contains scandium, were found in the 1990s. Two other beryllium minerals—danalite (red) and helvite (yellow)—were first reported from Iron Mountain in 1880; both have been found again in recent years as well-formed crystals.

Glen Ellis Falls, a 65-foot waterfall on the Ellis River, is a short distance from Iron Mountain. The falls plunge over metamorphic bedrock of the Silurian-age Rangeley Formation that forms the headwall of an ice age valley. They can be reached via a 0.2-mile trail from a WMNF parking area on NH 16.

63. Moat Mountain

Moat Mountain is famous for smoky quartz, the state gem of New Hampshire; this faceted stone is 11.7 carats. (Cliff Trebilcock collection)

See map page 178.

Status: Open

Land manager: White Mountain National Forest (WMNF), Saco Ranger District

Land type: Forested mountainside

Type of deposit: Igneous (granite with miarolitic cavities)

Location: Hale's Location, Carroll County

GPS: Trailhead, N44.0217 / W71.1695; site, N44.0315 / W71.1831

Elevation: Trailhead, 891 feet; site, 1,175 to 1,300 feet

Vehicle: Any

Best season: Mid-May through Oct

Tools: Crack hammer, chisels, safety goggles, hand trowel, 10-power loupe

Minerals: Albite, allanite-(Ce), anatase, annite, arsenopyrite, bastnäsite-(Ce), bavenite, bertrandite, calcite, cassiterite, chamosite, danalite, epidote, fergusonite, ferrogedrite, fluorapatite, fluorite, gadolinite, helvite, hematite, magnetite, microcline, milarite, molybdenite, muscovite, opal (hyalite), pharmacosiderite, quartz (smoky), riebeckite, titanite, topaz, trögerite, uraninite, wulfenite

Special attractions: Madison Boulder, Madison; Echo Lake State Park, Conway

Accommodations: WMNF campgrounds located along the Kancamagus Highway (NH 112). Lodging and camping available in Conway and North Conway.

Finding the site: From NH 16 north in Conway, turn left onto Washington Street; proceed 0.2 mile. Bear left onto West Side Road; continue for 0.7 mile. Turn left onto Passaconaway Road; proceed 1.2 miles. Turn right onto High Street; follow signs to trailhead parking area. Hike 0.9 mile to the collecting area.

Rules and regulations: Hobby mineral collecting is allowed using hand tools only and resulting in no more than minor surface disturbance. Before leaving, fill in holes, restore natural contours, and spread the original soil cover of natural organic debris. Cutting trees or other vegetation is forbidden.

Rockhounding

Moat Mountain is famous for smoky quartz crystals. The crystals are plentiful even after decades of collecting, so even novice rockhounds should have no problem finding some. The trail to the site takes you through a tranquil, pine-scented forest to a WMNF digging area clearly marked with a sign. It is not a particularly difficult hike, though there are a couple of steep gullies along the way. When you first arrive, check out the tailings left by other collectors to familiarize yourself with the rocks. The smoky quartz crystals originate in "pockets" in the granite called miarolitic cavities; you can use a hammer and chisel to break up rocks and boulders that contain these cavities, or dig and sift through the soil formed by crumbling, weathered granite (locally called rottenstone) to search for loose crystals. The crystals can be several inches long, though most are considerably smaller.

Microcline is common at the site as large white or tan blocky crystals; more rarely it is pale green or blue (amazonite). Albite is found in cavities as sharp white crystals with dark green chamosite. Fluorite can be found as green or purple octahedral crystals. Rarer minerals include topaz, in colorless to pale blue crystals, and pinkish-red danalite—easily mistaken for garnet, which does not occur here. The rare beryllium mineral milarite occurs as elongated sprays of white crystals which glow blue under mid-wave ultraviolet light. Hyalite occurs as clear to white bubbly coatings on feldspar and quartz, and shows strong green fluorescence under shortwave ultraviolet light.

First-time visitors to Moat Mountain often try to collect too much, which is understandable given all the glimmering crystals at the site, but the nearly 1-mile walk back to your vehicle will be much easier if you're not lugging 50 pounds of rock. Sort through your finds at the end of the day, trim your specimens down to a manageable size, and pack up only the best to take home.

64. South Baldface

Phenakite is a rare beryllium mineral that is occasionally used as a gemstone. (Cliff Trebilcock collection)

See map page 178.

Status: Open

Land manager: White Mountain National Forest (WMNF), Saco Ranger District

Land type: High mountain ledges

Type of deposit: Igneous (granite with miarolitic cavities)

Location: North Chatham, Carroll County

GPS: Trailhead, N44.2387 / W71.0164

Elevation: Trailhead, 502 feet; summit, 3,569 feet

Vehicle: Any

Best season: Mid-May to mid-Oct

Tools: Backpack, crack hammer, chisels, safety goggles, hand trowel, topo map

Minerals: Albite, biotite, fluorite, microcline (amazonite), phenakite, quartz, topaz

Special attraction: Maine Mineral and Gem Museum, Bethel, ME

Accommodations: Camping at WMNF Cold River and Basin Campgrounds, Chatham. Appalachian Mountain Club's (AMC) Cold River Camp, Chatham, has cabins. Lodging available in Conway and Gorham, NH, and in Bethel, ME.

Finding the site: From the junction of US 302 and ME 113 in Fryeburg, ME, follow ME/NH 113 north for 17.2 miles to AMC Road. Continue 0.2 mile to the Baldface Circle trailhead. The trail is steep and rough; allow 3.5 to 4 hours for the 3.75-mile hike to the collecting area, and you'll need the same amount of time to hike back. Carry plenty of food and water, and extra clothing in case of bad weather. At 0.7 mile there is a trail junction; take the left-hand trail toward South Baldface. There is a shelter at about 2,100 feet. Collecting is possible within a large area near the summit; it's best to go with a guide to find specific spots.

Rules and regulations: Hobby mineral collecting is allowed using hand tools only and resulting in no more than minor surface disturbance. Before leaving, fill in holes, restore natural contours, and spread the original soil cover of natural organic debris. Cutting trees or other vegetation is forbidden.

Rockhounding

South Baldface became famous for gem-quality topaz soon after its discovery on the mountain in 1888. Many exceptional crystals of the rare mineral phenakite were found as well. Topaz and phenakite can still be found in miarolitic cavities in granite ledges and boulders near the summit, or loose in talus on the mountainside. A long, challenging hike is required to get to the locality, but the possibility of finding outstanding specimens can be worth the effort.

South Baldface topaz is often completely colorless, but some crystals have a light blue or sherry tint. Crystals as long as 3½ inches are known, though most are much smaller. Brilliant, gleaming gemstones have been faceted from the topaz—the Smithsonian Institution has a 12.4-carat colorless stone in its collection. Phenakite occurs as colorless crystals attached to smoky quartz, topaz, or microcline. Green microcline (amazonite) is occasionally associated with smoky quartz, and specimens of this pairing are often spectacular.

A collecting trip to the high elevations of South Baldface should not be attempted alone, even if you are an experienced hiker. If possible, go with someone who is familiar with the site, or better yet, see if you can participate on a field trip led by an experienced guide. You'll want to take full advantage of the short amount of time available before you'll need to head back down the mountain. Bring enough food, water, and bug spray for a long hike. Be prepared for changes in weather—a rain poncho is a smart thing to pack. In the spring and fall, there may be snow high on the mountain, even when conditions look fine at the base. The views of the surrounding White Mountains from the summit are breathtaking and rewarding in their own right, but with proper planning and a little luck, you've got an excellent chance of bringing back some mineral treasures as well.

65. Madison Mine

Gray galena and brown sphalerite were the primary ore minerals at the Madison mine.

See map page 178.

Status: Open

Land manager: Town of Madison

Land type: Dumps of an abandoned mine

Type of deposit: Hydrothermal fault breccia deposit

Location: Goodwin Town Forest, Madison, Carroll County

GPS: Parking, N43.8540 / W71.1550

Elevation: Parking, 558 feet; site, 600 feet

Vehicle: Any

Best season: May through Oct

Tools: Crack hammer, chisels, safety goggles

Minerals: Albite, anglesite, aragonite, arsenopyrite, biotite, calcite, chalcopyrite, chlorite, danalite, fluorite, galena, goethite, greenockite, helvite, hematite, hemimorphite, hisingerite, hydrozincite, microcline, muscovite, pyrite, pyromorphite, quartz, siderite, smithsonite, sphalerite, titanite, uvite, wulfenite

Special attraction: Madison Boulder Natural Area, Madison

Accommodations: Camping at WMNF White Ledge Campground, Conway, and White Lake State Park, Tamworth. Lodging available in Conway.

Finding the site: From the junction of NH 16 and NH 41 in Ossipee, follow NH 41 north for 2.2 miles. Turn right onto East Shore Drive; proceed 1.2 miles. Turn right onto Lead Mine Road (closed in winter); continue for 0.5 mile and park on left. Cross road and walk 100 feet uphill.

Rules and regulations: Hand tools only. Do not leave any trash.

Rockhounding

The Madison mine opened in 1826, when the area was part of the town of Eaton, and was worked for lead, silver, zinc, and iron. At its peak around 1870, twenty-two miners were employed—eleven above ground and eleven below. Operations ceased in 1918, and today the main shaft is filled with water, with only scattered dumps and ruins remaining. Masses of lead ore (galena) and zinc ore (sphalerite) are the most common minerals at the site. Small cavities lined with quartz crystals are sometimes found containing colorful secondary minerals like pyromorphite and wulfenite. Hydrozincite occurs as white crusts on massive sphalerite; it exhibits brilliant blue-white fluorescence under shortwave ultraviolet light. The Madison mine is perhaps the best locality in New England to collect good specimens of this mineral.

Before exploring the dumps, examine the mine road itself and the gullies alongside it, where erosion may have exposed some collectible material. Check the open, flat area in front of the water-filled mine, where good micros have been found. Finally, search the scattered dumps, many of which are partially covered with forest debris. On the opposite side of Lead Mine Road, a path descends down to Cooks Pond, which is popular with canoeists and kayakers. Mine tailings and ruins can be seen on the slope on the way down to the pond.

While in Madison, don't miss seeing one of the largest glacial erratics in the world, Madison Boulder. Located at the end of Boulder Road off of NH 113, this National Natural Landmark is 23 feet high by 83 feet long by 37 feet wide and is estimated to weigh nearly 6,000 tons! Geologists believe the boulder was plucked by an advancing glacier during the last ice age from a ledge some distance to the northwest. This is because Madison Boulder consists of Conway granite, whereas the bedrock underneath it consists of an entirely different type of granite known as Concord granite.

MAINE

Rockhounds from around the world come to Maine to search for the state's hidden mineral treasures.

66. Estes Quarry

This hillside crushed stone quarry hosts a variety of rare and unusual minerals.

Status: Restricted; no access, unless on an authorized field trip
Land manager: Private—P. Y. Estes & Son, Inc.
Land type: Active crushed stone quarry
Type of deposit: Igneous (complex granitic pegmatite)
Location: West Baldwin, Cumberland County
GPS: N43.8585 / W70.7892
Elevation: 400 to 485 feet
Vehicle: Any
Best season: May through Oct
Tools: Crack hammer, chisels, digging tools, 10-power loupe
Minerals: Albite, almandine, aragonite, arsenopyrite, autunite, beraunite, beryl, beryllonite, chalcopyrite, chlorite, columbite, diadochite, dolomite, elbaite, eosphorite, fairfieldite, falsterite, fluorapatite, gahnite, galena, graphite, greenockite, greifensteinite, heterosite, hydoxylapatite, hydoxylherderite, jahnsite, lithiophilite, löllingite, microcline, mitridatite, molybdenite, montebrasite, moraesite, muscovite, opal (hyalite), phosphosiderite, purpurite, pyrite, pyrrhotite, quartz (rose, smoky), rhodochrosite, rockbridgeite, roscherite, schoonerite, schorl, siderite, sphalerite, strunzite, switzerite, todorokite, triphylite, uralolite, uraninite, väyrynenite, vivianite, zircon

Sites 66-93

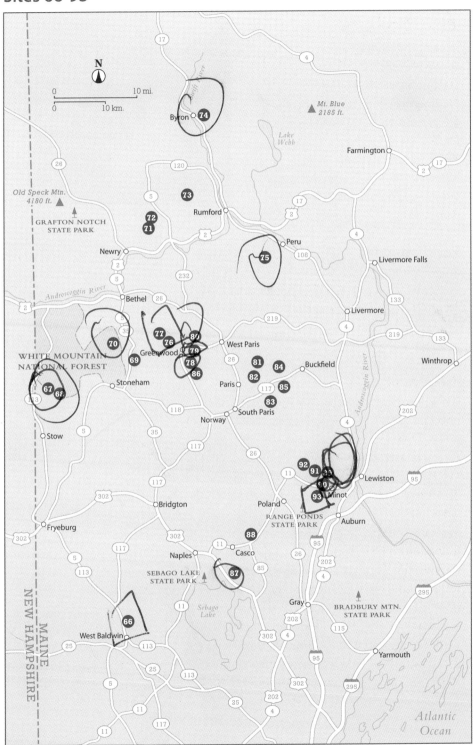

Special attraction: 19th Century Willowbrook Village, Newfield

Accommodations: Camping at Sebago Lake State Park, Naples. Lodging available in Cornish.

Finding the site: From the junction of ME 117 and ME 5/113 in Hiram, follow ME 5/113/117 south for 1.7 miles.

Rules and regulations: Safety gear is required: hard hat, reflective safety vest, steel-toed boots, safety goggles, and gloves.

Fairfieldite (white) and eosphorite (orange) are frequently found together at this site.

Rockhounding

Since opening in 1997, the Estes quarry has become well-known among collectors of rare minerals. Though a large part of the deposit consists of a complex pegmatite, the quarry is currently being operated commercially for crushed stone for construction purposes. Fortunately sharp-eyed collectors have been able to save many rare and beautiful mineral specimens from the crusher. The most interesting minerals are secondary phosphates including outstanding examples of fairfieldite, eosphorite, and greifensteinite. Vivianite is abundant as blue stains and coatings and occasionally is found as dark blue, bladed crystals. Falsterite, known elsewhere only from the Palermo No. 1 mine in New Hampshire, and väyrynenite, a rare pink mineral resembling rhodochrosite, are two further examples of the unusual mineralogy at the site.

Depending on what part of the hillside is being blasted by the quarry operators, interesting material might (or might not) be available. Examine stone piles to look for coarse pegmatite with cavities. Boulders of promising rock could have been moved some distance, so look over the entire site. Cavities in the pegmatite frequently contain colorless, striated albite crystals. Fluorapatite occurs as exquisite hexagonal crystals in various pale tints, sometimes frosted with a white or reddish coating. Muscovite, usually a rather boring mineral, is found in sharp, pale green microcrystals. Examine these pockets carefully with a loupe to look for crystals of colorful, rare phosphates. Occasionally you'll find columbite, sphalerite, pyrite, and crystals of smoky or rose quartz. For some reason, tourmaline is very rare in the pegmatite, though it does occur in the schist country rock.

67. Deer Hill

This lovely purple gem was cut from Deer Hill amethyst.
(Linda Trebilcock collection)

See map page 197.

Status: Open; fee and permit required

Land manager: White Mountain National Forest
(WMNF), Saco Ranger District

Land type: Forested mountainside

Type of deposit: Igneous (granitic pegmatite)

Location: Stow, Oxford County

GPS: Trailhead, N44.2315 / W70.9799

Elevation: Trailhead, 689 feet

Vehicle: Any

Best season: Mid-May through Oct

Tools: Crack hammer, chisels, safety goggles,
digging tools, screen

Amethyst from Deer Hill is
sometimes deep royal purple.
(Cliff Trebilcock collection)

Minerals: Albite, almandine, beryl (aquamarine), biotite, columbite-(Fe), kaolinite,
microcline, muscovite, pyrite, quartz (amethyst, smoky, milky, colorless)

Special attraction: Maine Mineral and Gem Museum, Bethel

Accommodations: Camping at WMNF Basin and Cold River Campgrounds,
Chatham, NH. Lodging available in Fryeburg.

Finding the site: From the junction of US 302 and ME 113 in Fryeburg, follow ME 113 north for 16.4 miles, crossing the border into New Hampshire. Turn right onto Deer Hill Road (Windgan Road); continue for 2.2 miles to the Deer Hill Mineral Collecting Area trailhead. Pay fee at the self-service pay station. A map at the kiosk shows trails to three collecting sites, the boundaries of which are clearly marked. (**Note:** Authorized collecting sites may change over time.) Hike about 0.5 mile to the sites.

Rules and regulations: Hobby mineral collecting is permitted in designated areas on Deer Hill. Only hand tools may be used, resulting in no more than minor surface disturbance. Before leaving, fill in holes, restore natural contours, and spread the original soil cover of natural organic debris. Cutting trees or other vegetation is forbidden.

Rockhounding

For collectors, the name Deer Hill is practically synonymous with amethyst, which was discovered at the site as far back as 1875 to 1880. The first real mining for amethyst began about 1920 and really boomed in the 1950s and '60s; single amethyst crystals up to 8 inches long were found. Deer Hill remains very popular with collectors today seeking to find their own gems. Besides true purple, many crystals appear somewhat brownish, like a cross between amethyst and smoky quartz. Other specimens have been found that consist of a purple crystal on top of a milky white stem. The best of the gem-quality material, however, is deep royal purple. When faceted, some of the gemstones exhibit flashes of red; others alternate between colorless and shades of purple. Cut stones can be seen in major museums across the United States; the largest, a 161.75-carat pear-shaped gem, is privately owned.

To find loose crystals, dig through the soil using a hand trowel and sift it with a screen. If one area isn't productive, try digging in one of the other designated areas on the hill. Wrap your finds in newspaper or place them into ziplock bags to protect them. Don't forget to bring plenty of food, water, sunscreen, and insect repellent for the hike up and back.

Besides the WMNF prospects, there is a privately owned excavation on Deer Hill known as the Intergalactic Pit that is closed to the public (but has been occasionally accessible to collectors on authorized field trips). A major find of amethyst took place there in the summer of 1993, generating much publicity. The first amethyst pocket to be discovered, the 4th of July Pocket, produced an 11-pound crystal that the owners dubbed the Grape of Maine. Overall the Intergalactic Pit produced well over a ton of amethyst, a significant amount of it gem quality, making it one of the biggest gem strikes ever in New England.

68. Lord Hill

Lord Hill is one of the best topaz localities in New England; this crystal is 1¼ inches long. (Don Swenson collection)

See map page 197.

Status: Open

Land manager: White Mountain National Forest (WMNF), Saco Ranger District

Land type: Forested mountain

Type of deposit: Igneous (complex granitic pegmatite)

Location: Stoneham, Oxford County

GPS: Parking, N44.2113 / W70.9510; site, N44.2240 / W70.9538

Elevation: Parking, 683 feet; site, 1,240 feet

Vehicle: 4WD

Best season: Mid-May through Oct

Tools: Crack hammer, chisels, safety goggles, digging tools, 10-power loupe

Minerals: Albite, almandine, autunite, beraunite, bermanite, bertrandite, beryl, beryllonite, biotite, bismuth, bismuthinite, bismutite, cassiterite, columbite-(Fe), cryptomelane, elbaite, eosphorite, fluorapatite, fluorite, gahnite, goethite, goyazite, hureaulite, hydoxylapatite, hydoxylherderite, jahnsite, kaolinite, metatorbernite, microcline, mitridatite, montmorillonite, muscovite, opal (hyalite), phenakite, phosphosiderite, pyrite, pyrrhotite, quartz (milky, smoky), rockbridgeite, siderite, sphalerite, strunzite, todorokite, topaz, torbernite, triplite, uraninite, uranophane, vivianite, zircon

Special attraction: Maine Mineral and Gem Museum, Bethel

Accommodations: Camping at WMNF Crocker Pond Campground, East Stoneham. Lodging available in Bethel.

Finding the site: From the junction of ME 5 and ME 93 in Lovell, follow ME 5 north for 2.4 miles. Turn left onto West Lovell Road; proceed 2.7 miles. Bear left onto Foxboro Road; continue for 1.5 miles. Turn right onto a gravel road; proceed north 1 mile. Park near side road on left; continue on foot on quarry road for just over 1 mile.

Rules and regulations: Hobby collecting only, using small hand tools. An excavation cannot exceed 1 cubic yard; only 1 site at a time can be dug. Holes cannot be more than 3 feet deep and must be filled in before leaving. Digging under trees is prohibited.

Rockhounding

Collectors have visited Lord Hill in search of interesting minerals since at least as early as the 1880s, when the hill was known as Harndon Hill. It wasn't until the 1940s that commercial mining began for feldspar. But for collectors, topaz is the major attraction at Lord Hill; in fact, this was the first locality in New England to produce good-quality crystals of this mineral. White, pale blue, and pale green crystals have been found, some of them gem quality and as long as 2½ inches. Even larger non-gem crystals have been recovered, in some cases weighing more than 50 pounds! Topaz crystals from Lord Hill sometimes contain interesting liquid bubble inclusions; look closely with a loupe to see them.

Gem-quality smoky quartz is another mineral highlight of Lord Hill, and many fabulous specimens have been collected. One enormous crystal collected in the 1960s weighed 573 pounds and was nearly 4 feet long. Cut gems of Lord Hill smoky quartz can be quite large—examples weighing over 100 carats are known.

Other interesting minerals from Lord Hill include fluorapatite in blue, green, and purple hexagonal crystals, and phenakite in small colorless to white crystals and in larger aggregates coating quartz crystals. Autunite is common as small yellow-green crystals that are highly fluorescent; occasionally it is found in large clusters of crystals. Pink to purple fluorite, colorless to pale green beryl, black columbite, silvery "balls" and large crystal clusters of muscovite, and several rare phosphate minerals also occur at the site. Pink montmorillonite sometimes fills cavities in cleavelandite.

Visitors to Lord Hill are rewarded with fabulous views of Horseshoe Pond, Square Dock Mountain, and other surrounding mountains, making this one of the most enjoyable sites in New England to collect.

69. Bumpus Mine

The Bumpus mine is a well-known locality for rose quartz. (Patricia Barker collection)

See map page 197.

Status: Restricted; no access, unless on an authorized field trip

Land manager: Private

Land type: Mine dumps in an open area

Type of deposit: Igneous (granitic pegmatite)

Location: Albany Township, Oxford County

GPS: N44.3128 / W70.7818

Elevation: 640 to 680 feet

Vehicle: Any

Best season: May through Oct

Tools: Crack hammer, chisels, safety goggles, sifting screen, digging tools

Minerals: Albite, almandine, autunite, bertrandite, beryl (aquamarine, golden), biotite, chalcopyrite, chamosite, columbite, cryptomelane, fluorapatite, foitite, goethite, hematite, hydroxylapatite, hydroxylherderite, kaolinite, microcline, muscovite, nontronite, pyrite, pyrrhotite, quartz (rose, smoky), rutile, schorl, scorzalite, siderite, todorokite, torbernite, uraninite, vivianite, zircon

Special attraction: Maine Mineral and Gem Museum, Bethel

Accommodations: Camping at Bethel Outdoor Adventure, Bethel. Lodging also available in Bethel.

Finding the site: From the junction of US 2 and ME 35/5 in Bethel, proceed south on ME 35/5 for 7.5 miles to the mine entrance on the left.

Rules and regulations: Rules to be provided by field trip leaders.

Rockhounding

The Bumpus mine is famous for having produced some of the largest beryl crystals ever found in the United States. The American Museum of Natural History in New York has in its collection a gigantic crystal measuring 7 by 4 feet and weighing about 4 tons. Dwarfing even that one, however, was a true monster of a crystal—27 feet long and 26 tons—that was mined for beryllium.

The Bumpus mine opened in 1927 and was worked for feldspar and mica in addition to beryl. The feldspar was shipped to a mill in West Paris to be processed before being shipped off to be used in manufacturing products such as porcelain, scouring powder, and soap. A large amount of rose quartz was also extracted from the mine for use as decorative stone. In 1949 alone, about 50 tons of rose quartz was mined; one enormous piece weighed nearly a ton.

Nowadays collectors are still finding beryl in the dumps, but in more manageable crystals measured in inches rather than feet. The combination of blue-green beryl in soft pink rose quartz is a strikingly beautiful classic of Maine mineralogy, but such specimens are now hard to come by. Beryl can also be found as pale green or yellow (golden) crystals. Glossy black schorl is abundant, and many crystals are well terminated. Green fluorapatite (fluorescent variety "manganapatite"), red almandine, and tan-colored microcline crystals are also common. Less common finds include uraninite, columbite, and deep blue scorzalite.

Visitors to the mine sometimes have an opportunity to take a guided tour of the lower tunnel—but collecting is not allowed underground. The extensive dumps at the site offer plenty of good hunting grounds. Sunscreen and a hat are recommended in the largely shadeless collecting area. Wear sturdy shoes or boots for navigating the rocky ground.

70. Pingree Ledge

These pieces of etched beryl were found in the dumps. (Dana M. Jewell collection)

See map page 197.

Status: Open

Land manager: White Mountain National Forest (WMNF), Androscoggin Ranger District

Land type: Abandoned mica prospect on a forested hillside

Type of deposit: Igneous (granitic pegmatite)

Location: Albany Township, Oxford County

GPS: Parking, N44.3237 / W70.8273; site, N44.3242 / W70.8305

Elevation: Parking, 835 feet; site, 890 to 910 feet

Vehicle: Any

Best season: Mid-May through Oct

Tools: Crack hammer, chisels, safety goggles, 10-power loupe, digging tools, screen

Minerals: Albite, almandine, autunite, bertrandite, beryl, biotite, columbite-(Fe), fluorapatite, fluorite, goethite, hematite, microcline, muscovite, phosphuranylite, quartz, schoepite, schorl, uranophane, zircon

Special attraction: Maine Mineral and Gem Museum, Bethel

Accommodations: Camping at WMNF Crocker Pond campground, Albany. Lodging available in Bethel.

Finding the site: From the junction of US 2 and ME 35 in Bethel, proceed south on ME 35 for 4.6 miles. Turn right onto Patte Brook Road; continue for 2.9 miles. Turn left onto FR 18; proceed 0.2 mile to woods road on right. Park and walk along road 600 feet to a fork; bear right and continue 400 feet to site.

Rules and regulations: Hobby mineral collecting is allowed using hand tools only and resulting in no more than minor surface disturbance. Before leaving, fill in holes, restore natural contours, and spread the original soil cover of natural organic debris. Cutting trees or other vegetation is forbidden.

Rockhounding

Gem-quality beryl was found in the extreme western part of Albany Township on the C. P. Pingree farm, at a ledge prospected for mica from 1878 to 1879 and again in 1900. The site continues to produce beryl crystals, though most of what is found is the common opaque variety. Digging and sifting through the tailings, however, has produced some nice crystals and fragments of etched blue-green and golden beryl.

Pingree Ledge is also the source of a number of other interesting minerals, including crystals of well-terminated black schorl, lavender-colored fluorapatite, and colorless, milky, and smoky quartz. Several kinds of quartz crystals can be found, including doubly terminated "floaters," scepters, and ones containing bubble inclusions. Smoky quartz in groups of parallel-growth crystals up to 6 inches across has been unearthed in recent years. Collectors have also turned up attractive crystals of white and light green fluorapatite, red almandine, and sharp, silvery, pseudohexagonal muscovite. Bertrandite occurs in clusters of good-quality colorless microcrystals.

Easy accessibility has contributed to making this a popular collecting site, so you'll need to do a lot of searching to find the good stuff. Look for promising pieces to break up below the ledge. Some of the best rocks are in a marshy area and will be wet and muddy, so be prepared to get dirty. Don't forget to bring bug spray and to wear sturdy footwear. Keep your eye out for moose, especially in the early morning or at dusk. Maine has the second-highest population of moose in the United States, estimated at about 75,000; your chances of sighting one in the national forest are best from mid-May through July and during their breeding season in the fall.

71. Newry I—Dunton Gem Mine and Crooker Quarries

The views from the Crooker quarries are magnificent.

See map page 197.

Status: Restricted; no access, unless on an authorized field trip

Land manager: Private—Plumbago Timber and Quarries LLC

Land type: Gem tourmaline mines on a mountain

Type of deposit: Igneous (complex granitic pegmatite)

Location: Plumbago Mountain, Newry, Oxford County

GPS: Base parking, N44.5113 / W70.7276; Dunton, N44.5428 / W70.7233; Crooker, N44.5446 / W70.7243

Elevation: Base parking, 1,200 feet; site, 1,350 to 1,525 feet

Vehicle: High-clearance 4WD

Best season: Mid-May through Oct

Tools: Crack hammer, chisels, digging tools, 10-power loupe, screen

Minerals: Dunton and Crooker: albite, almandine, autunite, bertrandite, beryl, cassiterite, columbite, cookeite, cryptomelane, diadochite, earlshannonite, elbaite, eosphorite, fluorapatite, foitite, goethite, hematite, heterosite, hydroxylapatite, hydroxylherderite, laueite, lepidolite, microcline, mitridatite, montebrasite, montmorillonite, muscovite, opal (hyalite), phosphosiderite, phosphuranylite, pollucite, pyrite, quartz, rhodochrosite, rockbridgeite, schoepite, schorl, spodumene, stewartite, strunzite, tantalite-(Mn), todorokite, triphylite, uraninite, uranophane, vivianite, xanthoxenite, zircon. **Dunton only:** anatase, arsenopyrite, beraunite, bermanite, beryllonite, beta-uranophane, biotite, bismuth, chalcopyrite, chrysoberyl, crandallite, cymatolite, dickinsonite, fairfieldite, ferrostrunzite, goyazite, greifensteinite, gummite, hureaulite, jahnsite, kaolinite, kastningite, löllingite, mangangordonite, metaswitzerite, microlite, moraesite, perhamite, phosphophyllite, rutherfordine, schoonerite, scorzalite, siderite, sphalerite, strengite, switzerite, torbernite, triploidite, uralolite, ushkovite, vandendriesscheite, vanmeerscheite, wardite, whitlockite, wodginite, wölsendorfite, zigrasite. **Crooker only:** pseudolaueite, pyrrhotite, tosudite, whitmoreite, zanazziite.

Special attraction: Steep Falls Preserve, Newry

Accommodations: Camping at Grafton Notch Campground, Newry. Lodging available in Bethel and Rumford.

Finding the site: From US 2 in Hanover, turn onto Howard Pond Road; proceed 2.2 miles. Turn right at Plumbago Mountain Farm sign; proceed 650 feet to parking area. High-clearance 4WD vehicles will be able to continue to mine, about 3.2 miles.

Rules and regulations: Safety goggles and sturdy footwear are required.

Rockhounding

A series of very rich gem-tourmaline (elbaite) pockets discovered in 1972 brought world fame to the Dunton mine. Tourmaline crystals were found in a rainbow of colors, including sapphire blue, pink, raspberry red, blue-green, green, colorless, and "watermelon." Pink tourmaline gems up to an astounding 60 carats were produced. The "Jolly Green Giant," a fabulous elbaite crystal, more than 10½ inches long and nearly 4 inches in diameter, is now at the Smithsonian. Unfortunately the glory days of the

Raspberry elbaite is a Dunton mine specialty; this faceted gemstone is 2.65 carats. (Cliff Trebilcock collection)

mine are long over and the dumps are not as productive as they once were. Still, sifting and screening in the dumps should produce some colorful small crystals and fragments of elbaite.

A rockhound's hound takes a refreshing dip in one of the Crooker quarries.

The Dunton mine was originally opened around 1898; pollucite was mined for cesium beginning in 1926, and montebrasite and spodumene were mined for lithium in 1935. But gems have been the most valuable product of the mine. Minerals new to science have been found at the site: Mangangordonite (1989) and zigrasite (2008) have Dunton as their type locality, and the mine is the co-type locality for perhamite (1977). Zigrasite occurs as tiny orange spheres on green elbaite; it was named for James Zigras, the mineral collector who discovered it, and so far this is its only known locality in the world.

Pink quartz crystals were discovered at the Dunton mine in 1927; they are also found at a site farther up Plumbago Mountain, where they are currently being mined. Fluorapatite crystals are very common, occurring in a variety of colors including purple, blue, gray, and white. The country rock surrounding the Dunton pegmatite is schist containing excellent brown crystals of dravite, some forming a starburst pattern.

The Crooker quarries, a stone's throw from the Dunton, are a series of hilltop excavations currently being worked. This area is especially noted for gem-quality blue elbaite (indicolite). Exceptional specimens of yellow-green zanazziite were found around 1992. Blue fluorapatite crystals are not uncommon. Large crystals of spodumene are abundant. Crystals of eosphorite and other rare phosphate minerals occur in small cavities in pegmatite in the dumps.

72. Newry II—Nevel Mine and Bell Pit

This cluster of purple fluorapatite crystals was found in the dumps adjacent to the Bell Pit. (Dana M. Jewell collection)

See map page 197.

Status: Restricted; no access, unless on an authorized field trip

Land manager: Private—Plumbago Timber and Quarries LLC

Land type: Pegmatite mines on a mountain

Type of deposit: Igneous (complex granitic pegmatite)

Location: Plumbago Mountain, Newry, Oxford County

GPS: Base parking, N44.5113 / W70.7276; Nevel, N44.5453 / W70.7219; Bell, N44.5447 / W70.7212

Elevation: Base parking, 1,200 feet; site, 1,355 to 1,435 feet

Vehicle: High-clearance 4WD

Best season: Mid-May through Oct

Tools: Crack hammer, chisels, digging tools, 10-power loupe, screen

Minerals: Nevel and Bell: albite, almandine, arsenopyrite, autunite, bertrandite, beryl, biotite, cassiterite, columbite-(Fe), cryptomelane, eosphorite, fairfieldite, fluorapatite, fluorite, goethite, hematite, heterosite, hydroxylherderite, laueite, microcline, mitridatite, montebrasite, montmorillonite, muscovite, pyrite, quartz, rockbridgeite, schoonerite, schorl, scorzalite, siderite, sphalerite, spodumene, strunzite, triphylite, uraninite, vivianite, wardite, whitlockite, zircon. **Nevel**

only: beta-uranophane, bismuthinite, cookeite, elbaite, gainesite, galena, greifensteinite, lepidolite, lithiophilite, microlite, schoepite, tapiolite. **Bell only:** augelite, beraunite, beryllonite, brazilianite, diadochite, ferrisicklerite, gorceixite, goyazite, greenockite, hydroxylapatite, jahnsite, ludlamite, magnetite, messelite, metaswitzerite, moraesite, perhamite, phosphophyllite, rhodochrosite, souzalite, switzerite, torbernite, whitmoreite, wurtzite, zanazziite.

Special attraction: Grafton Notch State Park, Grafton Township

Accommodations: Camping at Grafton Notch Campground, Newry. Lodging available in Bethel and Rumford

Finding the site: From US 2 in Hanover, turn onto Howard Pond Road; proceed 2.2 miles. Turn right at Plumbago Mountain Farm sign; proceed 650 feet to parking area. High-clearance 4WD vehicles will be able to continue to mine area, about 3.7 miles.

Rules and regulations: Eye protection and sturdy footwear are required.

Rockhounding

The Nevel mine (also called Twin Tunnels) and its neighbor the Bell Pit are not gem-mineral bonanzas, but from a mineralogical point of view are fascinating nonetheless. Spodumene is abundant at the Nevel mine in crystals as long as 12 inches. Triphylite is common as well; large, well-formed crystals have been found on the dumps. Columbite is another frequently collected mineral, often occurring in sharp black crystals. The Nevel mine is the type locality for the extremely rare phosphate mineral gainesite. When first found in 1941, it was mistaken for purple fluorapatite. Gainesite crystals are pyramidal, up to 2 millimeters long, and occur in albite (cleavelandite). It was eventually recognized as a new mineral and formally described in 1983. Gainesite is quite valuable; microcrystals of less than 1 millimeter in size can sell for $1,000 or more.

The Bell Pit is best known for its rare phosphate minerals, which are prized by micromineral collectors—beraunite, eosphorite, fairfieldite, goyazite, montebrasite, strunzite, and whitmoreite are among the better-known species that can be found. Siderite occurs in sharp, attractive crystals that can be tan, brown, or green. Pink rhodochrosite is also occasionally found. Sphalerite forms nice reddish-brown crystals. Fluorapatite occurs in colorless, white, blue, blue-green, and purple crystals. On a recent field trip, one observant collector found a plate of purple fluorapatite crystals lying on the ground near the Bell Pit. These were likely dug up by someone previously, but were probably covered with dirt or mud. No doubt rain later washed off the crystals, and the lucky rockhound who collected the specimen won an award from his mineral club for the find of the year!

73. Black Mountain

Black Mountain is known for world-class eosphorite. (Dana M. Jewell collection)

See map page 197.
Status: Restricted; no access, unless on an authorized field trip
Land manager: Private
Land type: Open-pit mines on a forested mountainside
Type of deposit: Igneous (complex granitic pegmatite)
Location: Rumford, Oxford County
GPS: N44.5860 / W70.6467
Elevation: Base of Tower Road, 1,057 feet; first quarry, 1,675 to 1,775 feet
Vehicle: High-clearance 4WD
Best season: Mid-May through Oct
Tools: Crack hammer, chisels, safety goggles, digging tools, screen, 10-power loupe
Minerals: Albite, almandine, amblygonite/montebrasite, autunite, beryl (golden, aquamarine), beryllonite, biotite, cassiterite, columbite-(Mn), cookeite, dickinsonite, dravite, eosphorite, fairfieldite, fluorapatite, goyazite, greifensteinite, gummite, heterosite, hurlbutite, hydroxylapatite, hydroxylherderite, kosnarite,

lepidolite, magnetite, microcline, microlite, mitridatite, montebrasite, montmorillonite, muscovite, opal (hyalite), phosphuranylite, pollucite, pyrite, quartz (rose), rhodochrosite, rockbridgeite, roscherite, rossmanite, schorl, siderite, sphalerite, spodumene, strunzite, tantalite-(Mn), titanite, todorokite, torbernite, triphylite, uraninite, uranophane, vivianite, wodginite, zircon

Special attraction: Maine Mineral and Gem Museum, Bethel

Accommodations: Camping at Honey Run Beach & Campground, Peru. Lodging available along US 2 in Rumford, Bethel, Wilton, and Farmington.

Finding the site: From the junction of US 2 and ME 120 in Rumford, follow ME 120 west for 8 miles. Turn left onto Horseshoe Valley Road; proceed 2.2 miles. Turn left onto Tower Road; drive uphill 0.7 mile to junction and continue straight for 0.4 mile.

Rules and regulations: Rules will be provided by field trip leaders.

Rockhounding

Black Mountain is a spectacular place for mineral collecting, with fabulous views of Maine's western mountains and New Hampshire's Presidential Range, often snowcapped in spring and fall. This site is called *Black* Mountain, but pink and purple are the colors that made it famous. Pink is the color of rubellite, a variety of the tourmaline species elbaite that occurs in large radiating sprays up to 2 feet across. Purple is the color of the mica species lepidolite, in which the rubellite is frequently embedded. Pink-and-purple specimens from Black Mountain can be seen in mineral museums around the world.

The mineralogical history of Black Mountain began in 1878 with the discovery of its abundant pegmatite minerals. Mining for tourmaline began in 1883, for muscovite mica in 1899, and for feldspar in 1904. In the 1930s and 1940s, beryl was mined for beryllium, and spodumene and lepidolite were mined for lithium.

Most of the pink tourmaline at the site is opaque and not gem quality, but the attractive fan-shaped sprays in lepidolite make exquisite specimens nonetheless. Tourmaline also occurs in blue, green, red, watermelon, reverse watermelon, and multicolored crystals. Masses of purple lepidolite are cut into slabs and polished for decorative purposes. Light gray or white spodumene crystals have been found up to 5 feet in length; some pink gemmy spodumene (kunzite) is known, associated with pink tourmaline and lepidolite.

Other Black Mountain mineral highlights include eosphorite (orange crystals to 1 inch), microlite (honey-yellow octahedrons), and tantalite-(Mn)

Elbaite is often found in fan-shaped crystal groups. (Dana M. Jewell collection)

in red to orange crystals. Pink fluorapatite has been found, and dark green, fluorescent manganese-bearing crystals are not uncommon. Good-quality uraninite crystals occur as cubes up to 5 millimeters across.

Black Mountain and Mount Mica (Site 82) are the co-type localities of the rare mineral kosnarite, which was first described in 1993. It occurs as pseudocubic microcrystals that are blue, blue-green, or colorless. To date, kosnarite is known from only two other localities in the world, one in Brazil and one in Australia. At Black Mountain it occurs with pink tourmaline and lepidolite.

74. Swift River—Gold Panning

The aptly named Swift River tumbles over quartzite and schist in Coos Canyon.

See map page 197.
Status: Open
Land manager: Various—private and public
Land type: Shallow, rocky river
Type of deposit: Alluvial placer deposit
Location: Byron, Oxford County
GPS: Coos Canyon Rest Area, N44.7205 / W70.6327; East Branch, N44.7361 / W70.6020
Elevation: Rest area, 870 feet; East Branch, 1,305 feet (at above coordinates)
Vehicle: Any
Best season: Mid-May to mid-Oct
Tools: Gold pan, plastic pail or bucket, screens, shovel, garden trowel, crow bar, tweezers, small plastic bottle or vial; sluice box and suction dredge (optional)
Minerals: Almandine, andalusite, gold, magnetite, scheelite, staurolite
Special attraction: Angel Falls, Township D
Accommodations: Coos Canyon Campground and Cabins, Byron
Finding the site: From the junction of US 2 and ME 17 in Mexico, follow ME 17 north for 13.4 miles to the Coos Canyon rest area. Take Byron Village Road over the bridge; proceed 2.2 miles to panning areas along the East Branch of the Swift River.

Rules and regulations: No permit is required for noncommercial gold-mining activities in sandy or gravelly streams (without vegetation), as long as stream banks are not disturbed and the equipment used is limited to a gold pan, a sluice of less than 10 square feet, or a suction dredge with a hose diameter of 4 inches or less.

Rockhounding

Ever since gold was discovered in Byron in the 1840s, prospectors have been panning for it in the Swift River and its East and West Branches. This is one of the best sites in New England to find your own gold. Commercial gold mining took place for a few years around the turn of the twentieth century, but it wasn't profitable; since that time only recreational prospectors have recovered gold from these streams. Swift River gold has long been used in jewelry. Admiral Robert Peary, the polar explorer, presented his wife with a necklace made from Swift River gold and Mount Apatite tourmaline in 1913.

Before you begin your hunt for gold, stop at Coos Canyon Rock and Gift, a veritable gold mine of information and a convenient place to obtain all the supplies you'll need. You can get directions in the shop to the best local panning areas. The display of nuggets found in the Swift River and its branches will whet your appetite, too. Gold-hunting equipment can be rented or purchased, and free demonstrations are offered to teach you how to successfully pan. Right across the street from the shop is Coos Canyon itself, a rocky gorge popular for fishing, swimming, and picnicking as well as gold panning.

The most productive panning area is along the East Branch of the Swift River. Gold is found in cracks and cavities in bedrock at the bottom of the stream. Check gravel bars and other areas of the river where gold might get trapped. The basic idea is to scoop up some gravel into your pan and swoosh the pan around just under the surface of the water so that the lighter minerals like quartz and feldspar get carried away by the current. After repeating this several times, only the heavy, darker magnetite-bearing sand will remain in the pan. Any gold that you have will show up in the remaining heavy sand.

Visitors to Coos Canyon (the canyon) can park for free at the town-operated rest stop on ME 17. The canyon bedrock consists of metamorphic rocks such as quartzite and schist—part of the Silurian-age Perry Mountain Formation. Farther upstream, crystals of andalusite up to 10 centimeters long occur in the schist. The crystals have been largely altered to muscovite, but some relict pink andalusite occurs as well.

75. Hedgehog Hill

Almandine crystals are abundant at this site. (Ingeborg Burggraf collection)

See map page 197.

Status: Open

Land manager: Private—Oxford County Mineral and Gem Association

Land type: Abandoned quarry on forested mountainside

Type of deposit: Igneous (granitic pegmatite)

Location: Peru, Oxford County

GPS: N44.4688 / W70.4565

Elevation: 850 to 1,000 feet

Vehicle: High-clearance 4WD

Best season: Mid-May to through Oct

Tools: Crack hammer, chisels, safety goggles, digging tools, screen

Minerals: Abite, almandine, beryl, biotite, chrysoberyl, fluorapatite, microcline, muscovite, quartz (smoky), schorl

Special attraction: Maine Mineral and Gem Museum, Bethel

Accommodations: Camping at Honey Run Beach & Campground, Peru, and Mountain View Campground, Dixfield. Lodging available in Rumford, Bethel, Wilton, and Farmington.

Finding the site: From the junction of US 2 and ME 108 in Rumford, follow ME 108 east for 4.9 miles. Turn right onto Main Street/Dickvale Road; continue for 3.1 miles. Turn left onto Mineral Spring Road; proceed 1 mile. Turn right onto Hammond Hill Road; continue for 1 mile. Walk along quarry road on right for 270 feet to fork; keep left. Continue for 675 to next fork; keep right. Proceed 900 feet to quarry.
Rules and regulations: Hand tools only.

Rockhounding

What was initially thought to be a valuable mica deposit was discovered on Hedgehog Hill (formerly called *Mount* Hedgehog) on the farm of Charles E. Knox in 1901; mining began the same year, conducted by the newly organized Big Gem Mica Company. Despite high hopes, the mine was never developed to any great extent. The site is famous today for abundant crystals of red almandine garnet that can be 3 inches or more across. Some crystals are gemmy enough to be cut;

Hedgehog Hill is one of the best localities in New England to collect large crystals of almandine. (Paul Young collection)

the Harvard Mineralogical & Geological Museum has a fine 1.81-carat red gemstone in its collection. The best-quality garnet crystals are embedded in massive quartz. Most of them occur as trapezohedrons, a crystal form that has twenty-four faces.

Good specimens can be found on Hedgehog Hill by digging through the dumps and tailings or by working the ledge. The hillside is very steep, so use abundant caution while collecting. Most of the minerals at the site are common pegmatite species and aside from almandine are not exceptional. However, greenish-yellow chrysoberyl is reported to have been found in the 1920s or earlier, and a small gem was faceted from the material. If there is any chrysoberyl remaining, it must be very rare. Keep an eye out for it just the same.

The name *hedgehog* was at one time frequently but incorrectly used in New England for the North American porcupine, an unrelated animal. True hedgehogs are found only in Europe, Asia, and Africa. There are no hedgehogs on Hedgehog Hill, but you may encounter a porcupine.

76. Emmons Quarry

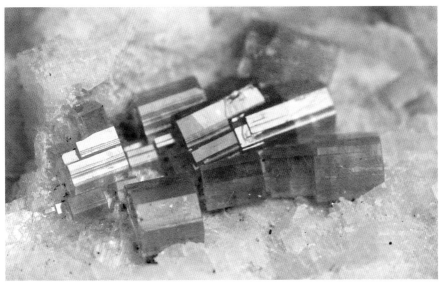

Fluorapatite crystals from the Emmons quarry are often light pinkish purple or lavender.

See map page 197.

Status: Restricted; no access, unless on an authorized field trip

Land manager: Private

Land type: Open-pit mine on a mountainside

Type of deposit: Igneous (complex granitic pegmatite)

Location: Greenwood, Oxford County

GPS: N44.3233 / W70.6956

Elevation: 1,175 to 1,305 feet

Vehicle: High-clearance 4WD

Best season: Mid-May through Oct

Tools: Crack hammer, chisels, safety goggles, digging tools, 10-power loupe

Minerals: Albite, almandine, arsenopyrite, autunite, beraunite, bermanite, bertrandite, beryl (aquamarine, goshenite, morganite), beryllonite, beta-uranophane, biotite, cassiterite, columbite, cookeite, crandallite, diadochite, dickinsonite, earlshannonite, elbaite, eosphorite, fairfieldite, fluorapatite, gahnite, goyazite, gummite, herderite, hureaulite, hydoxylapatite, hydoxylherderite, jahnsite, kastningite, landesite, laueite, lepidolite, leucophosphite, lithiophilite, löllingite, metaswitzerite, microcline, mitridatite, montebrasite, montmorillonite, moraesite, muscovite, nontronite, perhamite, petalite, phosphoferrite, phosphosiderite, phosphuranylite, pollucite, purpurite, quartz (rose, citrine, smoky), reddingite, rhodochrosite, robertsite, rockbridgeite, schorl, scorodite, siderite, spodumene, stewartite, strengite, strunzite, switzerite, tantalite-(Mn), todorokite, uraninite, vivianite, wodginite, zircon

Special attraction: Maine Mineral and Gem Museum, Bethel

Accommodations: Camping at Littlefield Beaches Lakeside Campground, Greenwood. Lodging available in Bethel and Rumford.

Finding the site: From the junction of ME 26 and ME 219 in West Paris, follow ME 219 west for 5.5 miles. Turn right onto Greenwood Road, then left onto Patch Mountain Road; proceed 0.6 mile. Turn right onto Willis Mills Road; proceed 1 mile. Turn right onto Horseshoe Trail; in 0.7 mile, turn left and proceed uphill 0.75 mile.

Rules and regulations: Hard hats must be worn in the pit.

Rockhounding

The Emmons quarry on Uncle Tom Mountain has been a source of interesting pegmatite minerals since about 1900. Though briefly mined for feldspar in the 1930s, the site has primarily been a producer of gemstones and mineral specimens, including beryl of exceptional quality. A large amount of gem pink beryl (morganite) was found during the feldspar mining period. Transparent colorless beryl (goshenite) was also found; an 11.8-carat faceted gemstone of this material is in the collection of the Harvard Mineralogical and Geological Museum in Cambridge, Massachusetts. Genuine citrine has been found at the Emmons quarry—a 27.5-carat faceted gem is in the collection of the Maine State Museum in Augusta.

Spodumene is a pyroxene mineral that commonly occurs in pegmatites enriched in lithium, which is the case at the Emmons quarry. Here the spodumene is found as large white or pale pink crystals. Very occasionally portions of the crystals are pink and transparent enough that they might be called kunzite. However, to date none of this material compares to worldwide examples of gem kunzite from places like Afghanistan.

Fluorapatite occurs at the site in clusters of small, lustrous hexagonal crystals. Some of the crystals are purple, but of a lighter shade than the famous ones from the Mount Apatite district. Blue, green, gray, white, and colorless

A tan, flowerlike crystal aggregate of perhamite rests on a bed of albite.

crystals are also found. Associated minerals include microcrystals of colorless bertrandite and metallic-brown aggregates of todorokite.

A long list of rare mineral species has been found here, making this a popular destination for collectors. Columbite-(Mn) occurs in red-brown to black rectangular crystals, sometimes with a core of wodginite, an uncommon manganese-tin-tantalum oxide. Phosphate minerals other than fluorapatite have been found as fine specimens, including eosphorite, goyazite, hydroxyl-herderite, purpurite, and strunzite. Perhamite, a mineral discovered in 1977 in Newry, occurs as small tan rosettes. It was named for the well-known, Maine-based miner and mineral collector Frank Perham.

77. Tiger Bill Quarries

A cluster of glassy hydroxylherderite crystals fills a small cavity in albite. (Dana M. Jewell collection)

See map page 197.
Status: Restricted; no access, unless on an authorized field trip
Land manager: Private
Land type: Open-pit mines
Type of deposit: Igneous (granitic pegmatite)
Location: Greenwood, Oxford County
GPS: N44.3302 / W70.7015
Elevation: 1,520 to 1,542 feet
Vehicle: High-clearance 4WD
Best season: Mid-May through Oct
Tools: Crack hammer, chisels, safety goggles, digging tools, 10-power loupe
Minerals: Albite, almandine, autunite, bertrandite, beryl (aquamarine, golden), biotite, fluorapatite, hydroxylherderite, microcline, muscovite, pyrite, quartz, schorl, uraninite
Special attraction: Greenwood Ice Caves, Greenwood

Accommodations: Camping at Littlefield Beaches Lakeside Campground, Greenwood. Lodging available in Bethel and Rumford.

Finding the site: From the junction of ME 26 and ME 219 in West Paris, follow ME 219 west for 5.5 miles. Turn right onto Greenwood Road; proceed 2.2 miles. Turn left onto Ames Lane; continue for 1.4 miles. Turn left onto Horseshoe Trail; proceed 0.25 mile. Follow mine road on right for 0.75 mile.

Rules and regulations: Rules to be provided by field trip leaders.

Rockhounding

Blue fluorapatite is well-known from this site. (Dana M. Jewell collection)

The name Tiger Bill might sound like the name of a rough-riding Wild West cowboy, but for Maine rockhounds it brings to mind a favorite collecting site on the northern shoulder of Uncle Tom Mountain. The Tiger Bill quarries are well-known for producing exceptional crystals of blue and purple fluorapatite and gem-quality aquamarine and golden beryl. While the purple fluorapatite is not equal to the famous royal purple crystals found at the Pulsifer quarry (Site 91), they are very attractive in their own right. But it's the blue fluorapatite crystals—often deep blue—that really say "Tiger Bill," and finding one would be a highlight of any visit to the site. Beryl is also a major attraction for rockhounds; it was actually mined at Tiger Bill during the 1950s. Today collectors can still find green, blue-green, and golden beryl by digging into the dumps—maybe even a gem piece or two.

Uncle Tom Mountain is also home to a group of talus caves known as the Greenwood Ice Caves. (Some references call them the Wentworth Caves after a former landowner.) Talus caves consist of openings between boulders that have fallen down and piled up at the base of a steep mountain slope or cliff. The Greenwood Ice Caves are fairly extensive, with several levels and a maze of passages. They were a popular destination for tourists in the nineteenth century, and daring souls with flashlight in hand (or on helmet) still visit them today. Ice often remains in the caves into July; in some of the deeper recesses, it might persist year-round.

78. Tamminen Quarry

Montmorillonite from the Tamminen quarry is often shocking pink.

See map page 197.
Status: Open
Land manager: Private
Land type: Open-pit mine and dumps
Type of deposit: Igneous (complex granitic pegmatite)
Location: Greenwood, Oxford County
GPS: Entrance, N44.2846 / W70.6401; site, N44.2830 / W70.6399
Elevation: Entrance, 794 feet; site, 730 to 805 feet
Vehicle: Any
Best season: May through Oct
Tools: Crack hammer, chisels, safety goggles, digging tools
Minerals: Albite, almandine, autunite, bertrandite, beryl (aquamarine, morganite), biotite, bismuth, cassiterite, chalcopyrite, chrysocolla, columbite-(Mn), cookeite, cryptomelane, dickinsonite, elbaite, eosphorite, fairfieldite, fluorapatite, fluorite, fourmarierite, gummite, hureaulite, hydroxylherderite, lepidolite, lithiophilite, microcline, montebrasite, montmorillonite, muscovite, petalite, phosphosiderite, pollucite, purpurite, quartz (smoky, rose), schorl, sphalerite, spodumene, tantalite-(Mn), tenorite, topaz, uraninite, uranophane, wölsendorfite, zircon
Special attraction: Maine Mineral and Gem Museum, Bethel

Accommodations: Camping at Bethel Outdoor Adventure, Bethel. Inns, motels, and bed-and-breakfasts also located in Bethel.

Finding the site: From the junction of ME 219 and ME 26 in West Paris, follow ME 219 west for 3 miles. Turn left onto Yates Road; proceed 300 feet. Bear left, then turn right onto Richardson Hollow Road; continue 4.2 miles. Walk along mine road on left 600 feet.

Rules and regulations: Hand tools only. Do not block the gate.

Rockhounding

The bubblegum-pink montmorillonite at this site is such a striking color that you might reasonably question whether or not it's a natural substance. It's weird-looking stuff, especially for something as "boring" as a clay mineral, which is what montmorillonite is. But it's just as real and natural as the lavender cookeite, bottle-green elbaite, and icy-blue albite that are also common here. These colorful minerals are a major reason the Tamminen quarry has long been a favorite destination for New England rockhounds.

But there's more—some of the quartz crystals at Tamminen are quite unusual, with prisms so short that the crystals look almost cubic. Pseudocubic quartz crystals like these are highly prized, and the Tamminen quarry is a well-known source. In addition, there are quartz crystals that have a moveable bubble trapped inside—you can see the bubble move when you flip the crystal over. This is sometimes called enhydro quartz and is another Tamminen specialty.

Opened in 1930 and first mined for feldspar, the Tamminen quarry has still other claims to fame. Tiny crystals of the rare mineral pollucite were found in the 1930s, the first such crystals discovered in the United States. Pollucite was abundant enough in massive form that it was mined for a time as an ore of cesium. Another rare pegmatite mineral, petalite, was mined for its lithium content. Petalite is found massive, never in crystals, and is off-white or cream-colored but usually stained a little pink by montmorillonite. It can be a tricky mineral to identify, as it somewhat resembles massive feldspar. Some exceptionally clear petalite from the Tamminen quarry has been faceted and made into exotic cut gemstones.

Elbaite tourmaline here is usually green, but on occasion the watermelon variety is found; only rarely is it gem quality. Fluorapatite is commonly green and fluorescent, but other colors have been found, including purple. Above the open pit where the pegmatite contacts the calc-silicate country rock, metamorphic minerals like diopside, titanite, and scheelite occur. Scheelite can be identified by its strong blue-white fluorescence under shortwave ultraviolet light.

79. Waisanen Quarry

This black crystal of tantalite-(Mn) was found on the dumps of the Waisanen quarry.

See map page 197.

Status: Open

Land manager: Private

Land type: Open-pit mine and associated dumps

Type of deposit: Igneous (complex granitic pegmatite)

Location: Greenwood, Oxford County

GPS: N44.2833 / W70.6389

Elevation: 725 to 767 feet

Vehicle: Any

Best season: May through Oct

Tools: Crack hammer, chisels, safety goggles, digging tools

Minerals: Albite, almandine, arsenopyrite, bertrandite, beryl (morganite), biotite, cassiterite, cookeite, elbaite, fluorapatite , goethite, graftonite, heterosite, hydroxylherderite, microcline, montmorillonite, muscovite, pyrite, quartz (smoky), schorl, sphalerite, tantalite-(Mn), topaz, triphylite, zircon

Special attraction: Maine Mineral and Gem Museum, Bethel
Accommodations: Camping at Bethel Outdoor Adventure, Bethel. Inns, motels, and bed-and-breakfasts also available in Bethel.
Finding the site: From the junction of ME 219 and ME 26 in West Paris, follow ME 219 west for 3 miles. Turn left onto Yates Road; proceed 300 feet. Bear left, then turn right onto Richardson Hollow Road; continue 4.2 miles. Walk along mine road on left 600 feet to Tamminen quarry; follow trail east for 200 feet to Waisanen.
Rules and regulations: Hand tools only.

Rockhounding

The Waisanen quarry is essentially the sister quarry to the larger Tamminen quarry (Site 78), literally a stone's throw away. The mine was operated for feldspar in the 1930s and for muscovite mica from 1943 to 1944. Originally there was a 200-foot open cut and a small shaft. Books of mica up to 3 feet in diameter and more than 1 foot thick were mined during the 1940s. The site is now worked only for mineral specimens.

The Waisanen quarry is perhaps best known in mineralogical circles for the extraordinarily large hydroxylherderite crystals—up to 3½ inches long—that were found in the 1960s. Hydroxylherderite is not uncommon in Oxford County pegmatites, but crystals are usually less than ½ inch in length. The white to tan hydroxylherderite crystals glow a pale yellow color under short-wave ultraviolet light.

Elbaite is found in green crystals but is usually not gem quality. Excellent bertrandite crystals are known in sizes up to 3 millimeters long. Recently new pockets in the pegmatite have been discovered, revealing large parallel-growth clusters of smoky quartz crystals. Most quartz at the site is colorless or stained yellow by iron oxides. Occasionally so-called phantom crystals are found; these are smaller ghostlike crystals inside of a larger one. Hexagonal crystals of fluorapatite occur in various colors including white, pale blue, and pale violet. Purple fluorapatite on yellowish-tan cookeite is especially attractive, as is pale blue fluorapatite sprinkled over clear quartz crystals. Mica (muscovite or lepidolite) occasionally exhibits an interesting "ball" habit. Beryl crystals up to 1½ feet long were seen during early mining operations. Recent blasting has unearthed some peach- to pink-colored morganite.

The Waisanen quarry is not a place where you're likely to find great stuff just lying on top of the ground. But if you are willing to do some digging and keep an open mind, this site can be very rewarding.

80. Harvard Quarry

Green tourmaline (elbaite) is common at this site. (Don Swenson collection)

See map page 197.

Status: Open

Land manager: Private

Land type: Open-pit mine and dumps on a forested mountainside

Type of deposit: Igneous (complex granitic pegmatite)

Location: Greenwood, Oxford County

GPS: Trailhead, N44.2850 / W70.6416; site, N44.2898 / W70.6422.

Elevation: Trailhead, 819 feet; site, 1,065 to 1,275 feet

Vehicle: Any

Best season: May through Oct

Tools: Crack hammer, chisels, safety goggles, digging tools

Minerals: Albite, almandine, amblygonite/montebrasite, arsenopyrite, autunite, bertrandite, beryl (morganite), beryllonite, biotite, cassiterite, columbite-(Mn), cookeite, elbaite, fairfieldite, fluorapatite, goethite, hydroxylherderite, lepidolite, microcline, montmorillonite, muscovite, pyrite, quartz (smoky, colorless), schorl, spodumene, todorokite, vivianite, zircon. In addition, axinite-(Fe), calcite, diopside, meionite, and vesuvianite occur in the calc-silicate country rock.

Special attraction: Maine Mineral and Gem Museum, Bethel

Accommodations: Camping at Bethel Outdoor Adventure, Bethel. Lodging also available in Bethel.

Finding the site: From the junction of ME 219 and ME 26 in West Paris, follow ME 219 west for 3 miles. Turn left onto Yates Road. In 300 feet bear left, then turn right onto Richardson Hollow Road. Continue 4.3 miles to trailhead on right. Hike uphill about 2,000 feet.

Rules and regulations: Hand tools only.

Purple mica (lepidolite) is abundant at the Harvard quarry. (John Chipman collection)

Rockhounding

Located high up on the steep western slope of Noyes Mountain, this scenic quarry is among the most popular mineral-collecting spots in Maine. The site was originally opened for quartz crystals by Isaac P. Noyes in the late 1800s. In 1917 mineral rights were leased by Harvard University; they mined it for specimens from 1923 to 1924, after which the name Harvard stuck. Except for a brief period in 1943 when the quarry was operated for mica, the site has been first and foremost a producer of mineral specimens, including many of outstanding quality.

After about a 20-minute hike up to the quarry, you'll be rewarded with a fabulous view of the countryside. The hike is moderately difficult, so you should be in good physical condition. Much of the quarry dump is on a steep slope, so be very careful while collecting. Tourmaline is common at the Harvard quarry, including excellent crystals of black schorl and rich green elbaite. One 5-foot-long tourmaline crystal collected in the 1960s was black on one end and green on the other. Tourmaline crystals with a green rind and a white core found at the quarry have been nicknamed "cucumber tourmaline," though the white core is often another mineral such as cookeite. Pseudomorphs of muscovite after tourmaline from the Harvard quarry can be quite large and are Maine classics.

The Harvard quarry is also well-known for beautiful fluorapatite crystals, often found associated with quartz crystals and cookeite. The best fluorapatite is found in shades of purple, but it can also be colorless, white, gray, pink, or green. Some of the crystals have been cut for gem use. Cassiterite occurs as shiny black crystals up to an inch long. There are so many interesting minerals here that this is one site you'll want to visit again and again.

81. Ryerson Hill Mine

A pitch-black crystal of uraninite is surrounded by lemon-yellow to yellow-orange "gummite."

See map page 197.

Status: Restricted; no access, unless on an authorized field trip
Land manager: Private
Land type: Open-pit mine on a hillside
Type of deposit: Igneous (complex granitic pegmatite)
Location: Paris, Oxford County
GPS: Entrance, N44.2977 / W70.4677; site, N44.2959 / W70.4670
Elevation: Entrance, 1,150 feet; site, 1,223 to 1,245 feet
Vehicle: High-clearance 4WD
Best season: May through Oct
Tools: Crack hammer, chisels, safety goggles, digging tools, pry bar, 10-power loupe
Minerals: Albite, almandine, arsenopyrite, beraunite, bertrandite, beryl (aquamarine, golden), columbite-(Fe), cookeite, diadochite, earlshannonite, eosphorite, fairfieldite, fluorapatite, gummite, gypsum, heterosite, hureaulite, hydroxylapatite, hydoxylherderite, jahnsite, laueite, ludlamite, messelite, microcline,

mitridatite, muscovite, opal (hyalite), phosphosiderite, pyrite, pyrrhotite, quartz, realgar, rockbridgeite, schorl, scorodite, siderite, sphalerite, stewartite, strunzite, switzerite, triphylite, uraninite, vivianite, whitmoreite, xanthoxenite, zircon

Special Attraction: Hamlin Memorial Library and Museum, Paris

Accommodations: Campgrounds located in Oxford, Poland, Hebron, and Greenwood. Lodging available in South Paris, Norway, and Woodstock.

Finding the site: From the junction of ME 26 and ME 219 in West Paris, follow ME 26 south for 4.2 miles. Turn left onto Paris Hill Road; proceed 1.1 miles. Turn left onto Ryerson Hill Road; proceed 2.9 miles. Walk or drive up mine road on the right 700 feet.

Rules and regulations: Rules to be provided by field trip leaders.

Rockhounding

The biggest attraction for most collectors at this scenic mountainside locality is beryl, which has been found as gem-quality aquamarine, golden beryl, and even bicolored crystals. The view from above the main pit is spectacular, especially in October when the autumn colors are at their peak. You have two choices here: Work the ledge with heavy hammers and chisels, or dig into the dump material to search for specimens. Much of the surface material has been picked over, so digging is a good idea.

Almandine is among the more common minerals at Ryerson Hill. It occurs as orange-red crystals, some displaying an interesting stepped-growth pattern. Uraninite associated with bright yellow and orange gummite has been collected from the ledge beside the main pit; these minerals are pretty distinctive, but if you have any doubts, check for radioactivity with a Geiger counter. Uraninite and gummite will cause it to click like crazy. Columbite-(Fe) is frequently associated with the uraninite. At least three arsenic minerals are found at the mine: One, arsenopyrite, is common in silvery-gray crystals; realgar, a very rare mineral in the eastern United States, occurs as red micro-crystals; and scorodite occurs as pale yellow micro-spheres on arsenopyrite.

Triphylite and a number of associated secondary phosphate minerals were collected during a period of active mining from 2002 to 2003. These rare species are highly sought after by micromineral collectors. Triphylite is green-gray or blue-gray with a greasy luster and can still be found on the dumps. Examine any you find closely for interesting secondary species including beraunite (tufted green balls), jahnsite (red-brown crystals), laueite (orange crystals), strunzite (silky white fibers), whitmoreite ("navel mine" habit), vivianite (sharp blue crystals), and rockbridgeite (black spherules).

82. Mount Mica

A road leads to the underground workings on Mount Mica.

See map page 197.
Status: Restricted; no access, unless on an authorized field trip
Land manager: Private—Coromoto Minerals, LLC
Land type: Gem tourmaline mine and associated dumps
Type of deposit: Igneous (complex granitic pegmatite)
Location: Paris, Oxford County
GPS: Entrance, N44.2671 / W70.4738; site, N44.2688 / W70.4733
Elevation: Entrance, 886 feet; site, 940 to 980 feet
Vehicle: 4WD
Best season: May through Oct
Tools: Crack hammer, chisels, safety goggles, digging tools, screen, 10-power loupe
Minerals: Albite, almandine, autunite, beraunite, bertrandite, beryl (aquamarine, golden, goshenite, morganite), biotite, cassiterite, columbite-(Mn), cookeite, crandallite, elbaite, eosphorite, fairfieldite, fluorapatite, foitite, glucine, goethite,

goyazite, graphite, greifensteinite, halloysite, hematite, heterosite, hureaulite, hydroxylapatite, hydroxylherderite, jahnsite, kaolinite, kosnarite, laueite, lepidolite, löllingite, mccrillisite, microcline, microlite, mitridatite, montebrasite, montmorillonite, moraesite, muscovite, opal (hyalite), petalite, phosphosiderite, phosphuranylite, pollucite, pyrite, quartz (smoky, pink crystals), rhodochrosite, rossmanite, schorl, scorodite, siderite, sphalerite, spodumene, stewartite, strunzite, tapiolite, torbernite, triphylite, uraninite, zircon

Special attraction: Hamlin Memorial Library and Museum, Paris

Accommodations: Campgrounds located in Oxford, Poland, Hebron, and Greenwood. Lodging available in South Paris, Norway, and Woodstock.

Finding the site: From the junction of ME 26 and ME 219 in West Paris, follow ME 26 south for 4.2 miles. Turn left onto Paris Hill Road; continue for 1.6 miles. Turn left onto Tremont Street; proceed 0.4 mile. Turn left onto Mt. Mica Road; continue for 1.1 miles to the mine access road.

Rules and regulations: Collect only in designated areas. Stay out of mine tunnels.

Rockhounding

On an autumn day in 1821, two young men—Elijah Hamlin and Ezekiel Holmes—found a beautiful green tourmaline crystal nestled in the roots of an upturned tree on Mount Mica. Unfortunately a snowstorm that night buried the mountain until spring, so they had a long wait before they could return to prospect the area. That tourmaline crystal was the first of countless gems found on Mount Mica over the next nearly 200 years. Today the site is without a doubt one of the most famous mineral localities in the world.

The most common tourmaline mineral on Mount Mica is elbaite, which occurs as blue, green, pink, red, colorless, or "watermelon" crystals, as long as 15½ inches. Underground mining in search of gem-bearing pockets is ongoing, and collectors have been fortunate in having the chance to search for fresh material in the dumps. The mine also produces excellent specimens of beryl, fluorapatite, cookeite, lepidolite, hydroxylherderite, and quartz. An unsuccessful attempt was made to mine cassiterite (tin ore) in 1881; this mineral is still encountered in the dumps as brownish-black masses. Many notable gems have been recovered from Mount Mica, including large crystals of pink morganite, a 12.25-carat light yellow heliodor (now at the American Museum of Natural History), and colorless goshenite crystals found in 1949 and 1979.

Blue tourmaline "eyes" are fairly common on the dumps; these consist of a tourmaline rind enclosing reddish garnet, grayish triphylite, silvery löllingite, or muscovite. Sometimes the eyes contain pyrite, quartz, siderite, rhodochrosite,

Minerals found at the Mount Mica mine include (clockwise from top left): phosphosiderite, elbaite (pink "rubellite"), fluorapatite, and elbaite (yellow-green).

or secondary phosphate minerals as well. One of these phosphates, mccrillisite, which was discovered on Mount Mica and formally described in 1994, is not known from anywhere else in the world. Mount Mica is also the co-type locality for kosnarite (1991), another extremely rare phosphate mineral.

Spodumene crystals up to 2 feet long have been mined at Mount Mica; they are usually gray, but sometimes contain pale pink or blue areas, and are often associated with pollucite and pink tourmaline. Fluorapatite is common and occurs as colorless, gray, green, blue, or purple crystals. A 17.6-carat oval gem of smoky quartz is in the collection of the Smithsonian.

The best collecting at Mount Mica is in the most recent dumps, where digging, sifting, and screening produces good results. Break up larger rocks that look promising, especially those containing pockets lined with quartz crystals, to see what you might find inside.

83. Mount Marie

Almandine and schorl are two of the many minerals that are found in good crystals at Mount Marie. (Paul Young collection)

See map page 197.

Status: Restricted; no access, unless on an authorized field trip

Land manager: Private—Durgin's of Maine

Land type: Gem tourmaline mine; open pits and prospects on hill

Type of deposit: Igneous (complex granitic pegmatite)

Location: Paris, Oxford County

GPS: N44.2218 / W70.4236

Elevation: 1,192 to 1,270 feet

Vehicle: 4WD

Best season: May through Oct

Tools: Crack hammer, sledgehammer, chisels, safety goggles, digging tools, screen

Minerals: Albite, almandine, arsenopyrite, bertrandite, beryl (aquamarine, morganite), cassiterite, columbite, cookeite, elbaite, eosphorite, fluorapatite, heterosite, hydroxylherderite, kaolinite, lepidolite, löllingite, malachite, metauranocircite, microcline, microlite, montebrasite, montmorillonite, muscovite, petalite, pharmacosiderite, pollucite, pyrite, quartz (citrine, smoky), rhodochrosite, schorl, siderite, sphalerite, spodumene, triphylite, uraninite, uranocircite, walentaite, zircon

Special attractions: Hamlin Memorial Library and Museum, Paris; Norway Historical Society Museum, Norway; Poland Spring Preservation Park, Poland
Accommodations: Campgrounds located in Oxford, Poland, Hebron, and Greenwood. Lodging available in South Paris, Norway, and Woodstock.
Finding the site: From the intersection of Fair Street/ME 26 and Main Street/ME 26/117 in South Paris, follow Main Street east for 1.2 miles. Bear right onto East Main Street/ME 117 north; proceed 0.4 mile. Turn left onto Buckfield Road/ME 117 north; continue for 2.8 miles. Turn right onto King Hill Road/Christian Ridge Road; proceed 2.2 miles to mine road on right.
Rules and regulations: Collecting allowed in designated areas only.

Rockhounding

In 1948 members of the newly formed Oxford County Gem and Mineral Association opened a pocket filled with smoky quartz crystals as well as blue, green, and pink elbaite tourmaline at the former feldspar mine on Mount Marie. Gem-quality blue-green aquamarine and pink morganite crystals were also found by the club members. In recent years the site has been operated commercially as a gem and specimen mine. Exceptional pockets of tourmaline crystals in a variety of colors including sapphire blue, yellow-green, mint green, pink, peach, orange, and red have been produced. One colorful specimen consisted of a green-and-pink "watermelon" tourmaline crystal encased in purple fluorapatite.

Other significant finds at Mount Marie are numerous. These include colorless crystals of quartz containing moveable bubbles, and eye-catching pink to purple aggregates of the lithium-bearing chlorite mineral cookeite. Fluorapatite has been found in shades of green, blue, and sometimes deep purple—the color most treasured by collectors and gemologists alike. Crystals of the cesium mineral pollucite are exceptionally rare worldwide but were found at Mount Marie in 1995 in sizes up to 2.5 centimeters across.

Naturally, the best new finds are made by the mine owner who has worked hard to reap the mine's rewards, but that doesn't mean that the scraps in the dumps are all that shabby. Collectors have done well sifting through tailings with a screen to find loose pieces of translucent green and pink tourmaline and blue-green beryl. You should have little trouble finding lepidolite at this site, often in large showy specimens. Search the dumps near the main pits, around the smaller prospects, and along the roads for interesting material. Interesting minerals also occur in the country rock—brown vesuvianite and orange grossular can be found along the mine access road. This is one of the most enjoyable collecting sites in Maine.

84. Bennett Quarry and Orchard Pit

Quartz crystals are abundant at the Bennett quarry.

See map page 197.

Status: Restricted; no access, unless on an authorized field trip

Land manager: Private; 2 adjacent but separately owned properties

Land type: Open-pit mines

Type of deposit: Igneous (complex granitic pegmatite)

Location: Buckfield, Oxford County

GPS: Entrance, N44.2860 / W70.4208; Bennett, N44.2932 / W70.4274; Orchard, N44.2941 / W70.4284

Elevation: Entrance, 650 feet; site, 645 to 764 feet

Vehicle: High-clearance 4WD

Best season: May through Oct

Tools: Crack hammer, chisels, safety goggles, digging tools, screen, 10-power loupe

Minerals: Bennett and Orchard: albite, autunite, bertrandite, beryl, cassiterite, columbite, fluorapatite, goethite, microcline, muscovite, quartz, schorl, uraninite.

Bennett only: almandine, arsenopyrite, beidellite, biotite, cookeite, elbaite, eosphorite, fairfieldite, fluorite, fluornatromicrolite, gorceixite, goyazite, hureaulite, hydroxylapatite, hydroxylherderite, kaolinite, landesite, laueite, lepidolite, lithiophilite, montebrasite, montmorillonite, opal (hyalite), pollucite, pyrite, pyrrhotite, reddingite, rhodochrosite, roscherite, siderite, spessartine, spodumene, tantalite-(Mn), tapiolite-(Fe), topaz, tosudite, triphylite, zircon. **Orchard only:** molybdenite, phenakite.

Special attraction: Maine Wildlife Park, Gray

Accommodations: Camping at Hebron Pines Campground, Hebron. Lodging available in South Paris, Norway, and Woodstock.

Finding the site: From the junction of ME 117 and ME 140 in Buckfield, follow ME 140 north across the bridge; immediately bear left onto High Street and proceed 1.3 miles. Turn left onto Paris Hill Road; continue for 2 miles. Turn right onto quarry road; proceed 0.6 mile to the Bennett and a few hundred feet more to the Orchard.

Rules and regulations: Rules will be provided by mine personnel and trip leaders.

Rockhounding

One of the most famous mineral specimens ever found in New England was a pink beryl (morganite) crystal collected at the Bennett quarry in 1989. The crystal was actually peach-colored when first unearthed but turned pink upon exposure to sunlight. The Rose of Maine, as it became known, was nearly 12 inches in diameter and 9 inches thick.

A 13-pound portion of the original crystal is now in the collection of the Harvard Mineralogical and Geological Museum; some of the remainder was cut into pink gemstones.

Opened in 1920, the Bennett quarry was mined for a time for feldspar and cesium ore (pollucite), but is best known for its history of producing fabulous gem and mineral specimens. Highlights include an enormous 800-pound milky quartz crystal extracted in 1924 and shipped to Acton, Massachusetts, for use as a cemetery stone. Gem-quality citrine

This specimen of orange-pink rhodochrosite with smoky quartz is from the Bennett quarry. (Cliff Trebilcock collection)

and high-quality lapidary-grade rose quartz have also been produced.

The list of minerals found here is a long one, and many are of exceptional quality, making this one of the very best sites to collect in New England. The Bennett quarry produces gem elbaite tourmaline, sometimes color-zoned in shades of pink and green: Watermelon crystals (pink core and green rind) and rare

Morganite from the Bennett quarry looks similar to rose quartz when not found in crystal form. (Don Swenson collection)

"reverse" watermelon crystals (green core and pink rind) both occur at the site. An enormous number of hydroxylherderite crystals have come out of the quarry, usually associated with colorless or milky quartz crystals and tan or orange cookeite. The crystals exhibit yellow fluorescence under shortwave ultraviolet light.

Several phosphate minerals are found at the Bennett quarry, including world-class examples of the rare mineral reddingite in crystals up to 1¾ inches long, and yellow-brown to orange-brown eosphorite associated with pink rhodochrosite. Fluorapatite is found in excellent crystals, often colorless, green, or blue. Massive pollucite is often tinted rose-red due to inclusions of montmorillonite. Sharply formed brown crystals of cassiterite are not uncommon. Pink rhodochrosite associated with truncated, quartzoid-habit smoky quartz crystals are outstanding.

The Orchard Pit is another fine mineral-collecting site, particularly known for its gem beryl. A 7.5-carat aquamarine gem from the quarry is now in the Maine State Museum. Fine crystals of aquamarine have been found up to 10 inches long. Gem-quality specimens of colorless and especially golden beryl have also been collected.

An enormous amount of hydroxylherderite has been found at the Bennett quarry. (Don Swenson collection)

85. G. E. Pollucite Mine

The rare mineral bavenite was found here by collectors in 1999. (Ingeborg Burggraf collection)

See map page 197.

Status: Restricted; no access, unless on an authorized field trip
Land manager: Private
Land type: Open pits and dumps in a forested area
Type of deposit: Igneous (complex granitic pegmatite)
Location: Buckfield, Oxford County
GPS: Entrance, N44.2600 / W70.3997; site, N44.2652 / W70.4032
Elevation: Entrance, 1,111 feet; site, 1,179 to 1,210 feet
Vehicle: High-clearance 4WD
Best season: May through Oct
Tools: Crack hammer, chisels, safety goggles, digging tools, 10-power loupe
Minerals: Albite, almandine, arsenopyrite, bavenite, beryl (aquamarine, goshenite), biotite, cassiterite, cookeite, elbaite, fluorapatite, hydroxylherderite, microcline, montebrasite, montmorillonite, muscovite, pollucite, pyrite, quartz, schorl

Special attraction: Maine Wildlife Park, Gray

Accommodations: Camping at Hebron Pines Campground, Hebron. Lodging available in South Paris, Norway, and Woodstock.

Finding the site: From the junction of ME 117 and ME 140 in Buckfield, follow ME 117 south for 2.2 miles. Turn left onto McAlister Road; continue for 0.5 mile. Follow mine road on the right 0.5 mile.

Rules and regulations: Rules to be provided by field trip leaders.

Rockhounding

In the 1920s General Electric mined pollucite at this site on the north side of Hodgdon Hill. Pollucite is the primary ore of cesium, a metal then used in the production of radio vacuum tubes. There are four open cuts and pits at the site, as well as several mine dumps now largely overgrown. Pollucite is found on the dumps in massive form, never in crystals, but is rare. It closely resembles quartz but is quite brittle and splintery, and has a resinous or greasy luster. Attractive specimens of beryl, montebrasite, and schorl have been collected from the dumps. Sizable masses of gray arsenopyrite have also been found. A yellow-green surface alteration on some of the arsenopyrite appears to be the secondary arsenic mineral scorodite, but has not been analyzed. More investigation into the mineralogy of the site will undoubtedly uncover additional species.

The surface of this massive arsenopyrite specimen is showing signs of alteration. (Don Swenson collection)

Amateur rockhounds made an important discovery in 1999, when colorless to pale yellow, transparent, bladed crystals of an unidentified mineral were found on a field trip to the mine. The crystals were minute, less than 1 millimeter long. Several collectors procured specimens at the time, but no one was able to say for sure what they were. Laboratory analysis later revealed the mineral to be bavenite, a rare beryllium species not previously reported from Maine. Bavenite is named for Baveno, Italy, in the Piedmont region, where the mineral was first discovered on Mount Camoscio.

86. B.B. #7 Quarry

Pollucite is the primary ore of cesium.

See map page 197.
Status: Restricted; no access, unless on an authorized field trip
Land manager: Private
Land type: Open pit and dumps
Type of deposit: Igneous (complex granitic pegmatite)
Location: Norway, Oxford County
GPS: N44.2701 / W70.6238
Elevation: 475 to 500 feet
Vehicle: 4WD
Best season: May through Oct
Tools: Crack hammer, chisels, safety goggles, digging tools
Minerals: Albite, almandine, autunite, bertrandite, beryl, cassiterite, columbite-(Mn), cookeite, elbaite, eosphorite, fairfieldite, fluorapatite, heterosite,

hydroxylapatite, hydroxylherderite, lepidolite, lithiophilite, microcline, montmorillonite, muscovite, pollucite, purpurite, quartz (rose, smoky), spodumene, strunzite, triphylite, uranophane, vivianite
Special attraction: Norway Historical Society Museum, Norway
Accommodations: Campgrounds located in Waterford, Oxford, and Greenwood. Lodging available in Norway, Woodstock, and Bethel.
Finding the site: From the junction of ME 117 and ME 118 in Norway, head west on ME 118 for 0.9 mile. Turn right onto Greenwood Road; proceed 3.7 miles. Follow unpaved road on the right to the site.
Rules and regulations: Rules will be provided by field trip leaders.

Rockhounding

The town of Norway was once known as the "Snowshoe Capital of the World" for its snowshoe-manufacturing industry, but for rockhounds it has long been known as a convenient base for seeking Oxford County's mineral and gem treasures. One of the county's best-known pegmatite localities, the B.B. #7, is located in Norway and is occasionally open to collectors on authorized field trips. B.B. #7 was named for the original landowners, Maurice Benson and Annie Brown, and because it was the seventh pit dug at the site. The pit was mined for muscovite mica and feldspar beginning in 1952; books of mica up to 6 feet across were found. Tons of pollucite (cesium ore) were also produced. A big discovery was made at the B.B. #7 on Friday, August 13, 1954, when a pocket of gem elbaite tourmaline was discovered by Stanley I. Perham. Crystals of green, blue-green, and blue tourmaline measuring up to 3 inches long were found in the Friday the 13th Pocket, as it became known. Pink crystals have also been found at the quarry, but are rare. Collectors today can still find tourmaline by searching the dumps.

Other minerals found at B.B. #7 include unusually large bertrandite crystals. Some of these measure more than an inch long and were found in pockets with tourmaline. Tabular, colorless or green fluorapatite crystals to about 3 millimeters across, are fairly common. Massive purpurite, formed through the alteration of lithiophilite, is popular because of its striking purple color, even though it never forms crystals. Associated with the purpurite are other phosphate minerals including eosphorite and fairfieldite. Spodumene is common and can be found in large white, tan, or pale pink opaque crystals. Columbite-(Mn) can be found in black crystals associated with lepidolite.

87. Chute Prospects

Vesuvianite is abundant at the Chute prospects.

See map page 197.
Status: Open
Land manager: Private
Land type: Rocky forested area
Type of deposit: Metamorphic (calc-silicate rock)
Location: Casco, Cumberland County
GPS: Prospects, N43.9357 / W70.5275, N43.9373 / W70.5272
Elevation: 365 to 500 feet
Vehicle: High-clearance 4WD
Best season: May through Oct
Tools: Crack hammer, sledgehammer, chisels, safety goggles, digging tools, rake
Minerals: Andesine, calcite, clinozoisite, diopside, fluorite, grossular, meionite, pyrite, pyrrhotite, quartz, titanite, vesuvianite
Special attraction: Maine Wildlife Park, Gray
Accommodations: Camping at Sebago Lake State Park, Naples. Lodging available along US 302 in Casco.

Finding the site: From the junction of US 302 and ME 85 in Raymond, follow US 302 west for 3.4 miles. Turn right onto Quaker Ridge Road; proceed 1 mile. Make a slight left onto New Road; proceed 0.4 mile. Turn right onto Deerfield Lane; continue straight, passing house on left, for 0.2 mile. Park and walk on trail on left for 1,200 feet to fork, stopping at small prospects along the road. Bear right at fork and continue 440 feet to sharp right curve. Walk up steep trail on left to prospect pit on ridge.
Rules and regulations: Do not leave any trash.

Rockhounding

For decades the Chute family has kindly permitted mineral collectors to visit their forested property in Casco to search for minerals in metamorphic rock. The scattered prospects on the land were originally dug by Edward Chute, a lifelong rockhound who built up a mineral collection that included fine specimens of vesuvianite and grossular. These and other minerals occur in calc-silicate rock formed when an impure limestone was subjected to contact metamorphism. The rock is very hard; heavy hammers are necessary to break it up. However, smaller loose stones can be found in the woods and along trails throughout the area. Examine the eroded material on steep trails, search the dumps around prospect pits, and look at boulders that have been worked by previous rockhounds. The weathered rock often has a "spongy" appearance, pitted where calcite has been dissolved away. Break open these rocks to see the fresh minerals inside.

Cinnamon-colored grossular crystals have been found at these prospects up to about an inch across; most of them are not gemmy, but those that are—a variety known as hessonite—are likely to be embedded in calcite. Vesuvianite commonly occurs in large brown masses. Parallel groups of brown or brownish-green crystals are often associated with green diopside. The best single vesuvianite crystals occur in pockets and are an inch or more in length.

Titanite from the Chute prospects is very pale tan or brown and exhibits yellow fluorescence under shortwave ultraviolet light. Very few other localities in the world produce fluorescent titanite, making this a favorite site for fluorescent mineral collectors. Gray-green clinozoisite is very common in bladed crystals and masses associated with light green diopside and dark green actinolite. Again, the best crystals are found embedded in calcite. Groups of parallel-growth milky-white meionite crystals are fairly common as well.

This is not an easy site. However, advanced rockhounds with enough time and patience to really explore the area and anyone who would enjoy a "treasure hunt" in the woods should find it rewarding.

88. Heath Quarry

Interesting minerals are found in several different types of rock at the Heath quarry.

See map page 197.

Status: Restricted; no access, unless on an authorized field trip

Land manager: Private—P & K Sand & Gravel, Inc.

Land type: Active crushed stone quarry

Type of deposit: Metamorphic (calc-silicate rock) and igneous (granite, granitic pegmatite, mafic dikes)

Location: Casco, Cumberland County

GPS: N44.0022 / W70.4711

Elevation: 330 to 462 feet

Vehicle: Any

Best season: May through Oct

Tools: Crack hammer, chisels, pry bar, shovel, 10-power loupe

Minerals: Albite, almandine, anatase, ankerite, beryl, biotite, calcite, chalcopyrite, chamosite, clinozoisite, diopside, epidote, grossular, microcline, muscovite, opal (hyalite), pyrite, quartz, rutile, schorl, titanite, vesuvianite

Special attraction: Maine Wildlife Park, Gray

Accommodations: Camping at Sebago Lake State Park, Naples. Lodging available along US 302 in Casco.

Finding the site: From the junction of ME 85 and ME 11 in Ca[...]
north for 1.3 miles. Turn left onto Indian Acres Road and proceed[...]
Rules and regulations: Safety gear is required: hard hat, reflective [...]
steel-toed boots, safety goggles, and gloves.

Rockhounding

Few collecting sites in Maine have as large a variety of rock types as the Hea[...]
quarry. The quarry first came to the attention of collectors for its calc-silicate
minerals, which are like those found at the Chute prospects (Site 87) in the same
town. Cinnamon-orange grossular and brown vesuvianite have been found in
crystals over an inch in size, though the smaller ones are better quality. Grass-
green crystals of diopside, brown titanite, and pale green or brown clinozoisite
are associated.

Pegmatites in the quarry are mineralogically simple, but nonetheless have
produced sizable crystals of black schorl, golden beryl, and pink, red, and orange-
red almandine. Small cavities in granite are often filled with crystals of calcite,
ankerite, or albite along with microcrystals of quartz, brassy pyrite, golden chalcopyrite, red to black rutile, and dark blue to black anatase. White to tan microcline crystals coated with dark green chamosite are reminiscent of alpine veins
typical of some of the crushed stone quarries in eastern Massachusetts. Quartz
veins have produced quartz crystals to several inches long. Black basalt in dikes
is sometimes sprinkled with perfect little pyrite cubes.

The Heath quarry is worked commercially for crushed stone. Depending
on what area of the quarry is being worked, visiting collectors might find a
bonanza of interesting material or come away practically empty-handed. Be
sure to check out piles of recently quarried material, looking for telltale signs
of mineralization, especially crystal-filled cavities. You'll definitely need to use
your crack hammer and chisels here.
Most of the rock is pretty manageable and can be readily broken, but
the calc-silicate rock is hard and may
require the use of heavy hammers.
There is no shade in this quarry, and
it can feel brutally hot in the summer, so be sure to use sunscreen and
drink plenty of water.

Vesuvianite crystals can be found in calc-silicate rock.

co, follow ME 11
0.4 mile.
afety vest,

Green tourmaline (elbaite) is abundant on Mount Apatite.

See map page 197.

Status: Open

Land manager: City of Auburn, Parks and Recreation Department

Land type: A 344-acre wooded park with abandoned quarries

Type of deposit: Igneous (complex granitic pegmatite)

Location: Mount Apatite Park, Auburn, Androscoggin County

GPS: Parking, N44.0855 / W70.2790; quarry area, N44.0880 / W70.2907

Elevation: Parking, 252 feet; collecting area, 350 to 430 feet

Vehicle: Any

Best season: May through Oct

Tools: Crack hammer, hand sledge, chisels, safety goggles, digging tools, rake, screen

Minerals: Albite, almandine, arsenopyrite, autunite, bertrandite, beryl (aquamarine, morganite), biotite, cassiterite, columbite-(Mn), cookeite, damourite, diadochite, dickinsonite, elbaite, eosphorite, fluorapatite, gahnite, goethite, hydroxylherderite, landesite, lepidolite, lithiophilite, löllingite, ludlamite, microcline, microlite, mitridatite, molybdenite, montebrasite, montmorillonite, muscovite, opal (hyalite), pyrite, quartz (smoky), rhodochrosite, schorl, siderite, sphalerite, spodumene, strunzite, tantalite-(Mn), topaz, torbernite, triplite, uraninite, zircon

Special attraction: Maine State Museum, Augusta

Accommodations: Camping at Bradbury Mountain State Park, Pownal. Lodging available in Auburn.

Finding the site: From the junction of US 202 and ME 11/121 in Auburn, follow ME 11/121 west for 2 miles. Turn right onto Garfield Road; proceed 0.5 mile. Turn left onto Stevens Mill Road. Park near the ball field; walk past the armory, straight onto the woods trail, and continue 0.25 mile to the quarries.

Rules and regulations: Hand tools only. Digging for minerals is permitted to a depth of 2 feet. No camping, fires, or swimming.

Rockhounding

Mount Apatite Park is a large forested city park that is a major attraction for rockhounds as wells as hikers, mountain bikers, dog walkers, and snowmobilers. The City of Auburn acquired the land in the early 1970s and allows recreational mineral collecting. The two principal quarries in the park are the Maine Feldspar and Greenlaw. Mining for feldspar began in 1902 at the now long-abandoned quarries, but the extensive rock dumps still contain plenty of mineral and gem treasures.

As you might expect, there's apatite on Mount Apatite—specifically fluorapatite—and it can be found in a variety of colors including purple, especially at the Greenlaw quarry. Colored tourmaline (elbaite) is fairly common—crystals are usually green but some are blue-green, blue, pink, or "watermelon." Many collectors like to dig and screen for loose tourmaline crystals in the mine tailings. At the Greenlaw quarry, an unusual pseudomorph can be found consisting of pink damourite after elbaite.

Columbite-(Mn), an important ore of niobium, occurs in many pegmatite deposits in Maine. (Dana M. Jewell collection)

The trail to the quarries is wide and well-marked.

(Damourite is a fine-grained, compact variety of muscovite.) While the pseudomorphs have the same shape as the original elbaite crystals, they are easily distinguished by their softness.

Beryl on Mount Apatite is usually not gem quality, but there are exceptions. A large pink morganite crystal was found at the Maine Feldspar quarry in 1914, and small pieces of morganite are still occasionally found. Gem aquamarine has also been reported. Transparent smoky quartz occurs at both quarries—one crystal, nearly 20 inches long, was found a century ago; smaller quartz crystals are not uncommon in the dumps. Garnet crystals are abundant on Mount Apatite; at the Maine Feldspar quarry, red almandine crystals have been collected measuring more than 2 inches across. Good garnet crystals can also be found at the Greenlaw quarry. Other commonly found minerals in the park include brown cassiterite, black columbite, tan cookeite, and purple lepidolite.

90. Hatch Ledge Prospect

Mount Apatite Farm is the starting point for exploring Hatch Ledge.

See map page 197.

Status: Open on a fee basis (children free)

Land manager: Private—Carol Segal (Cookin' Carol), Mount Apatite Farm; www.cookincarol.com

Land type: Pegmatite prospect on a wooded hillside

Type of deposit: Igneous (complex granitic pegmatite)

Location: Auburn, Androscoggin County

GPS: N44.0849 / W70.2946

Elevation: 405 to 435 feet

Vehicle: Any

Best season: May through Oct

Tools: Crack hammer, chisels, safety goggles, digging tools, pry bar

Minerals: Albite, beryl (morganite), elbaite, fluorapatite, lepidolite, microcline, montebrasite, muscovite, quartz (smoky, citrine), schorl, spessartine

Special attraction: Old Fort Western, Augusta

Accommodations: Camping at Poland Spring Campground, Poland. Lodging available along ME 4 in Auburn.

Finding the site: From the junction of ME 11 and ME 119 in Minot, head east on ME 11 for 2.3 miles. Turn left onto Hatch Road; proceed 0.4 mile to Mount Apatite Farm.

Rules and regulations: No parking allowed on Hatch Road.

Rockhounding

Gem tourmaline was discovered in 1868 on the farm of Gilbert C. Hatch, and mining began in 1883. Nearly 1,500 crystals were found, measuring up to 4 inches long. The crystals were pink, green, blue, colorless, white, or multi-colored. A 39.8-carat emerald-cut gem is in the collection at Harvard. Today the Hatch Ledge prospect is located in the woods at the edge of Mount Apatite Farm, a 29-acre farm bordering the City of Auburn's Mount Apatite Park. White-tailed deer, wild turkeys, and other wildlife are commonly seen in the woods and in the fields of the farm.

Groups visiting Mount Apatite Farm can enjoy a catered meal prepared by the farm's owner, Cookin' Carol, a professional chef. Fresh vegetables grown on the farm are used in her recipes when in season. Rockhounds work up an appetite digging and screening for minerals, break for an excellent lunch, and then head back out for more collecting. In October 2008 a new pocket was discovered at the site that contained superb smoky quartz crystals, pink beryl, and gemmy tourmaline. Named the Halloween Pocket, this lucky gem strike proved that the old locality still has potential.

Lepidolite crystals to over 10 centimeters have been found at Hatch Ledge, but of course, most specimens are much smaller. Fluorapatite is common in crystals that are colorless or a light shade of blue, green, pink, or purple. Digging and screening in the dumps will produce these minerals as well as green elbaite, books of muscovite, quartz crystals, and orange to red garnet.

There are three small pits and dumps located about 150 feet north of the Hatch Ledge prospect, which are called the Turner quarries. Opened in the 1890s for feldspar, the quarries are now within Mount Apatite Park. While the dumps are not known for rare or gem minerals, nice crystals of almandine and schorl can be found, so it's worth exploring the area to see what might turn up.

This colorless fluorapatite crystal was found at the Hatch Ledge prospect.

91. Mount Apatite West— Pulsifer, Groves, Keith, and Wade Quarries

The Groves quarry is well-known for large crystals of gahnite. (Don Swenson collection)

See map page 197.

Status: Restricted; no access, unless on an authorized field trip

Land manager: Private

Land type: Open-pit gem mines

Type of deposit: Igneous (complex granitic pegmatite)

Location: Auburn, Androscoggin County

GPS: Pulsifer, N44.0894 / W70.3030; Groves, N44.0898 / W70.3048; Keith, N44.0892 / W70.3015

Elevation: 365 to 455 feet

Vehicle: Any

Best season: Late May through Sept

Tools: Crack hammer, chisels, safety goggles, digging tools, screen

Minerals: Albite, almandine, arsenopyrite, autunite, bertrandite, beryl (aquamarine, golden, morganite, goshenite), biotite, cassiterite, columbite, cookeite, diadochite, dickinsonite, elbaite, eosphorite, fairfieldite, fluorapatite, gahnite, goethite, landesite, lepidolite, lithiophilite, hydroxylapatite, hydroxylherderite, lepidolite, löllingite, ludlamite, microcline, microlite, mitridatite, molybdenite, montebrasite, montmorillonite, muscovite, nontronite, pollucite, purpurite, pyrite, quartz (smoky, citrine), rhodochrosite, schorl, siderite, sphalerite, spessartine, spodumene, strunzite, tantalite-(Mn), todorokite, topaz, torbernite, triplite, uraninite, uranophane, zircon

Special attraction: Maine Geological Survey, Augusta

Accommodations: Camping at Poland Mining Camps, Poland. Lodging available in Auburn.

Finding the site: From the junction of ME 11 and ME 119 in Minot, head east on ME 11 for 2.3 miles. Turn left onto Hatch Road; proceed 0.9 mile to a mine road on the left.

Rules and regulations: Rules will be provided by field trip coordinator.

Rockhounding

The four privately owned gem mines on the western side of Mount Apatite are in close proximity to one another, and in fact are in the same pegmatite body. A visit to any one of them could be a rockhound's dream come true.

The famous Pulsifer quarry is named for Pitt P. Pulsifer, who first mined tourmaline at the site in 1901. Pulsifer tourmaline (elbaite) is frequently gem quality and comes in a variety of colors including green, pink, blue, gray, lavender, pinkish brown, and cinnamon. The quarry's main claim to fame, however, is not gem tourmaline, but rather royal-purple fluorapatite. There are Pulsifer fluorapatite specimens at Harvard and the Smithsonian that are simply amazing. Fluorapatite also occurs as pink, blue, blue-green, green, and gray crystals. And if gem tourmaline and fluorapatite aren't reason enough to get excited, there's a third exquisite gem species here: morganite, the pink gem variety of beryl. One astounding 18.48-carat round-cut morganite gem is in the collection at Harvard.

The Pulsifer quarry abounds in the platy type of albite called cleave-landite, often an attractive light blue color. Cookeite occurs in tan, gray, or purple clusters. Gahnite, in dark green octahedral crystals up to 2 centimeters long, has been found and makes very nice thumbnail specimens. The Groves quarry (originally called the Hole in the Ground) is also well-known for

The Pulsifer quarry is famous for royal-purple fluorapatite. (Paul Young collection)

gahnite; dark green, almost black crystals up to nearly 6 inches long have been produced. Groves quarry gahnite has been faceted into gems of more than 5 carats. Many of the same minerals are found at the Wade quarry, a small pit adjacent to the Pulsifer.

The Keith quarry (formerly the Towne quarry) opened in 1907 for tourmaline and produced green, blue, blue-green, pink, lilac, and watermelon varieties. Gemmy blue topaz was found at the Keith quarry; a faceted gem of 43.75 carats is at the Smithsonian. If you visit the Keith quarry, look for gem aquamarine, crystals of hydroxylherderite up to ¼ inch long, and pink, blue, and purple fluorapatite.

92. Pitts-Tenney Prospects

Grossular from Pitts-Tenney is a New England classic; these crystals are ½ to ⅝ inch across.

See map page 197.

Status: Restricted; no access, unless on an authorized field trip

Land manager: Private

Land type: Small prospects on a forested hill

Type of deposit: Metamorphic (calc-silicate rock)

Location: Minot, Androscoggin County

GPS: N44.1022 / W70.3311

Elevation: 390 to 400 feet

Vehicle: Any

Best season: May through Oct

Tools: Heavy hammers, chisels, safety goggles, digging tools

Minerals: Actinolite, calcite, clinochlore, clinozoisite, diopside, grossular, meionite, molybdenite, quartz, titanite, vesuvianite

Special attraction: Poland Spring Museum, Poland

Accommodations: Camping at Poland Spring Campground, Poland. Lodging available in Auburn and Lewiston.

Finding the site: From the junction of ME 11/121 and ME 119 in Minot, follow ME 119 north for 1.1 miles. Park and walk uphill on woods road on left for about 1,000 feet.

Rules and regulations: Hand tools only.

Rockhounding

The Pitts-Tenney garnet (grossular) prospects were likely opened as long ago as the 1880s, but the name is for Frank Pitts and Harold Tenney, two men who began working the site in the 1930s. Although the grossular crystals are usually not especially gemmy, the clusters of the crystals make fine display specimens and are New England classics. The calc-silicate rock (or skarn) at the site belongs to the Patch Mountain Limestone Member of the Silurian-age Sangerville Formation. This rock formed through contact metamorphism of the original limestone, caused by a nearby intrusion of granitic magma during Devonian time.

Cinnamon and orange-brown grossular crystals up to an inch across are common at Pitts-Tenney. During the early decades of mining, individual crystals up to 5 inches across could be obtained in large clusters. The crystals occur either in massive quartz or garnet and are dodecahedral (twelve-sided) in form. Complete, isolated crystals are rare, however, because they are usually intergrown. Other calc-silicate minerals at the site include clusters of small grass-green diopside crystals, dark green bladed actinolite, blocky white crystals of meionite up to 2½ inches, and sharp tan to brown wedge-shaped crystals of titanite.

The calc-silicate rock at Pitts-Tenney is very hard, and heavy hammers and chisels are necessary to break it. Trimming specimens to best expose the crystals is usually necessary and takes practice and patience. Bring home specimens containing calcite; when you get home you can dissolve the calcite in a very mild acid like vinegar to expose hidden crystals. Soak the specimens in water afterwards to remove all traces of the acid.

Meionite, a mineral in the scapolite group, occurs as white crystals at this site. (Don Swenson collection)

93. Havey Mine and Berry Mine

Beautiful crystals of watermelon tourmaline have been collected at the Havey mine.

See map page 197.
Status: Restricted; no access, unless on an authorized field trip
Land manager: Private; mine properties are adjacent but are separately owned
Land type: Open-pit gem tourmaline mines
Type of deposit: Igneous (complex granitic pegmatite)
Location: Poland, Androscoggin County
GPS: Havey, N44.0712 / W70.2984; Berry, N44.0721 / W70.2984
Elevation: 240 to 290 feet
Vehicle: 4WD recommended
Best season: May through Oct
Tools: Crack hammer, chisels, safety goggles, 10-power loupe, whisk broom, trowel or small shovel, screen
Minerals: Albite, almandine, arsenopyrite, autunite, bertrandite, beryl (aquamarine, morganite), biotite, cassiterite, columbite-(Mn), cookeite, correianevesite, cryptomelane, dickinsonite, elbaite, eosphorite, fairfieldite, fluorapatite, foitite,

goethite, gummite, hureaulite, hydoxylherderite, kaolinite, landesite, lepidolite, lithiophilite, microcline, microlite, mitridatite, montebrasite, montmorillonite, muscovite, phosphosiderite, purpurite, pyrite, quartz (rose, smoky), reddingite, rhodochrosite, rockbridgeite, rossmanite, schoepite, schorl, siderite, spodumene, stewartite, strunzite, todorokite, triplite, uraninite, uranophane, wardite, zircon

Special attraction: Poland Spring Museum, Poland

Accommodations: Camping at Poland Spring Campground, Poland. Lodging available in Auburn and Lewiston.

Finding the site: From the Maine Turnpike, take exit 75 to US 202/ME 4/ME 100; turn right and continue for 0.4 mile. Turn right onto Kittyhawk Avenue and proceed 0.8 mile. Turn right onto Hotel Road and continue for 1.3 miles. Turn left onto Lewiston Junction Road and proceed 0.2 mile. Turn right onto West Hardscrabble Road. To get to the Havey, continue for 1.4 miles and turn right onto Levine Road; the entrance to the mine road will be 500 feet on the left. For the Berry mine, continue along West Hardscrabble Road another 0.1 mile past Levine Road; the mine road will be on the right.

Rules and regulations: Do not climb on walls, large rocks, or rock piles. Keep away from mining equipment. Do not leave any trash.

Rockhounding

The Havey and Berry mines are separate excavations in the same pegmatite and are famous for producing outstanding gem-quality tourmaline (elbaite) crystals. The colors include emerald green, bright pink, red, rich blue, blue-green, yellow-green, yellow, orange, cinnamon, and watermelon (pink on the inside with a green rind). The Havey mine produces a mint-green to teal shade of elbaite that is cut and sold under the trade name SparHawk tourmaline, as well as large slabs of purple lepidolite containing radiating sprays of pink tourmaline. Collectors can find crystals in freshly blasted material in

The Berry gem mine has produced some outstanding crystals of elbaite. (Cliff Trebilcock collection)

Colorful minerals found at the Havey mine include (clockwise from top left): elbaite (blue, green, pink, orange); almandine (red); stewartite (yellow) with strunzite (white) and rhodochrosite (pink); and zircon (red-brown).

the pit or by digging and sifting through the dumps. Both approaches have been very productive.

Interesting minerals are abundant in the pegmatite; among them are fluorapatite crystals in shades of blue and purple, hydroxylherderite crystals up to ½ inch, red almandine, yellow-green platy autunite, metallic-brown todorokite, and flat-black columbite with a bluish surficial alteration. Sharply formed brown zircon crystals are not uncommon, sometimes associated with gray-black uraninite. Quartz crystals can be colorless or smoky and are sometimes associated with unusual muscovite crystal aggregates that look like cones. Rare phosphate minerals at the site include green dickinsonite, honey-yellow stewartite, and white fibrous strunzite; these are associated with pink masses of rhodochrosite. The metamorphic country rock hosts good crystals of calc-silicate minerals such as greenish-brown titanite, dark green hornblende or actinolite, white plagioclase, and green diopside.

The Berry was mined for feldspar beginning in 1911 and is the type locality for the rare phosphate mineral landesite (1930). The dumps still contain minerals of interest to collectors, but the mine is not now actively worked.

94. Sandy Point Beach

Garnet sand has a distinctive reddish-purple color.

Status: Open
Land manager: Town of Yarmouth
Land type: Ocean beach
Type of deposit: Beach sand
Location: Yarmouth, Cumberland County
GPS: Parking, N43.7731 / W70.1452
Elevation: Sea level
Vehicle: Any
Best season: May through Oct
Tools: Small plastic container, magnifying glass or 10-power loupe, magnet
Minerals: Almandine, magnetite
Special attraction: Littlejohn Island Preserve, Yarmouth
Accommodations: Camping at Bradbury Mountain State Park, Pownal. Lodging available in Yarmouth, Freeport, and Brunswick.

Sites 94-98

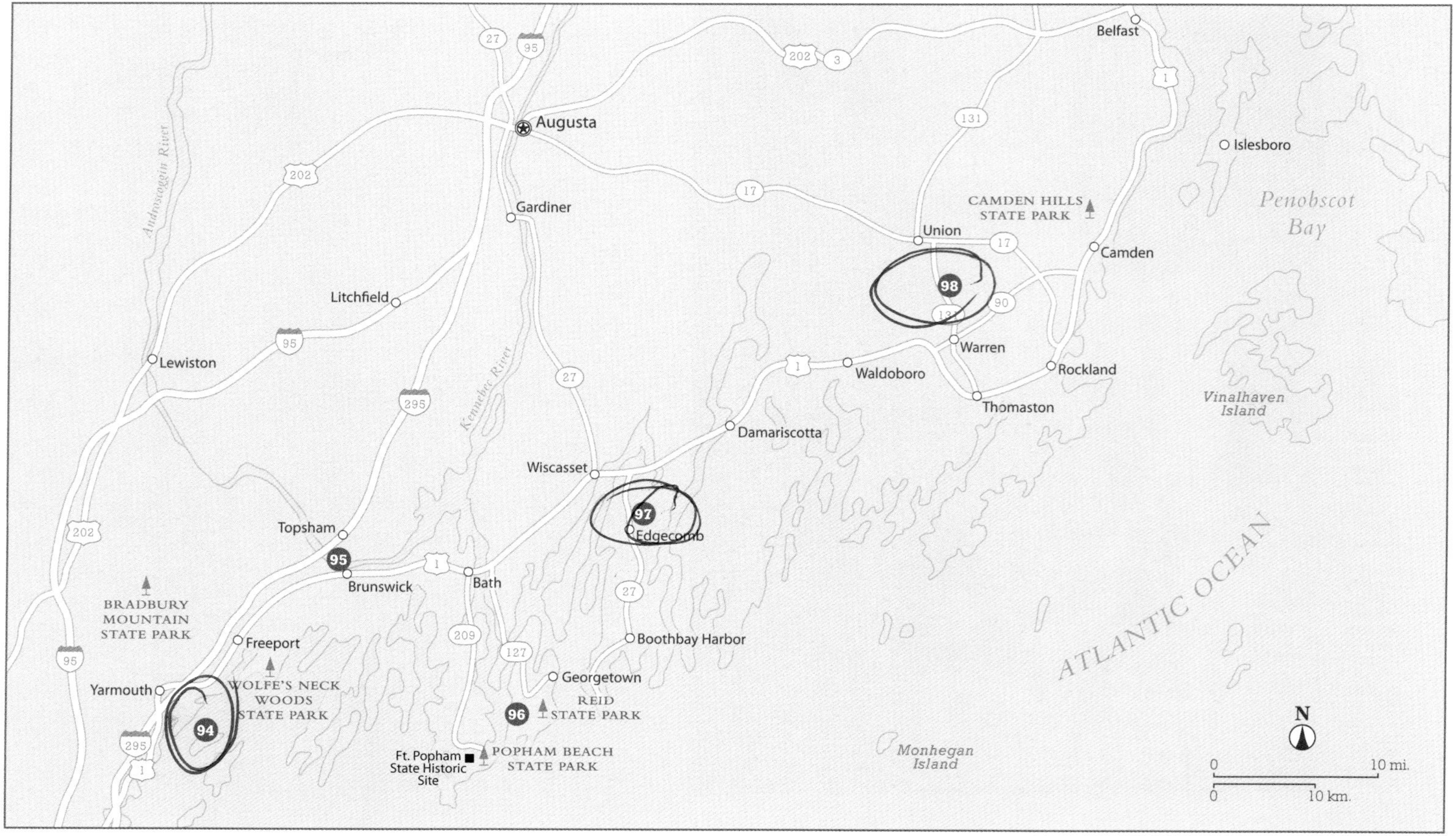

Penobscot Bay

o Islesboro

Vinalhaven Island

Monhegan Island

ATLANTIC OCEAN

N

0 _____ 10 mi.
0 _____ 10 km.

o Belfast

Camden

CAMDEN HILLS STATE PARK

o Rockland

Union

Warren

Thomaston

Waldoboro

98

Augusta

Gardiner

Damariscotta

Kennebec River

Wiscasset

Edgecomb

97

Boothbay Harbor

Georgetown

REID STATE PARK

27

96

POPHAM BEACH STATE PARK

Bath

Ft. Popham State Historic Site

Litchfield o

Brunswick

Topsham

95

Freeport

WOLFE'S NECK WOODS STATE PARK

Lewiston o

Androscoggin River

BRADBURY MOUNTAIN STATE PARK

Yarmouth o

94

Finding the site: From the junction of US 1 and ME 88 in Yarmouth, follow ME 88 south for 1.8 miles. Turn left onto Gilman Road and proceed 2.1 miles, crossing the bridge to Cousins Island.

Rules and regulations: No dogs in summer. Do not leave any trash.

Rockhounding

Reddish-purple areas of sand can be seen on Sandy Point Beach, colored largely by grains of almandine garnet. If you examine a handful of this sand closely with a magnifying glass or 10-power loupe, you'll see abundant red grains (garnets) along with pink, yellow, green, and black ones. The black grains are mostly magnetite; these can be readily identified by their attraction to a magnet.

Almandine and magnetite are heavier than the lighter-colored minerals such as quartz that make up the largest portion of most sand. These and other heavy minerals are often segregated into small areas of a beach by the action of wind and water. In some parts of the world, heavy sands such as these contain mineral deposits of significant economic importance. Reddish garnet sands like the ones on Sandy Point Beach are not uncommon; this beach, which was featured on the Maine Geological Survey's website, is easily accessible. Scoop up a thimbleful of sand to examine later with a microscope. If you want to start a sand collection, just be sure to label the container.

Sand collecting is not a new hobby, even among rockhounds. In fact, *Rocks & Minerals* magazine formerly had a monthly column dedicated to the specialty. Sand collectors, or psammophiles, are hobbyists who are fascinated by all the various minerals, shells, and other components of sand, and their colors, textures, and shapes. Sand can easily be collected at ocean and lake beaches, along rivers, and in deserts. There is little expense involved—you'll just need small plastic containers and labels. A high-quality magnifying loupe or microscope will help you get the most out of the hobby.

Heavy mineral sands can be found on many beaches in New England. Most commonly they are red or black, colored by such minerals as garnet, magnetite, and ilmenite. But exotic minerals are occasionally found, too— scientists examining heavy beach sands on the island of Martha's Vineyard in Massachusetts found grains of gold, native copper, staurolite, and blue and red corundum that were carried there by glaciers thousands of years ago.

95. Russell Brothers Quarry

This 0.55-carat stone was faceted from Russell Brothers aquamarine. (Cliff Trebilcock collection)

See map page 262.
Status: Restricted; no access, unless on an authorized field trip
Land manager: Private
Land type: Former open-pit feldspar and mica mine
Type of deposit: Igneous (complex granitic pegmatite)
Location: Topsham, Sagadahoc County
GPS: N43.9215 / W69.9814
Elevation: 75 to 112 feet
Vehicle: Any
Best season: May through Oct
Tools: Crack hammer, chisels, safety goggles, digging tools
Minerals: Albite, almandine, arsenopyrite, beryl (aquamarine), biotite, bismuthinite, columbite-(Fe), ishikawaite, microcline, monazite-(Ce), muscovite, quartz, schorl, uraninite
Special attractions: Desert of Maine and Wolfe's Neck Woods State Park, Freeport

Accommodations: Campgrounds located in Brunswick, Bath, and Freeport. Lodging available along US 1 in Brunswick.

Finding the site: From I-295, exit 31, follow ME 196 east for 0.2 mile; turn right onto Mallet Drive and proceed 0.8 mile. Turn right onto Winter Street, then left onto Granite Hill Drive; continue for 0.3 mile and park. Walk south along woods road for 540 feet, then follow trail heading west for 1,200 feet.

Rules and regulations: Rules will be provided by field trip leaders.

Rockhounding

The Russell Brothers quarry is one of many pegmatite localities in the Topsham area that produce fine mineral specimens. This site, consisting of three open cuts, was originally mined for feldspar beginning about 1930 and later for mica as well. Books of muscovite mica were recovered as large as 30 inches across and 18 inches thick. Much of what the miners didn't want ended up on the dumps, including crystals of beryl and garnet!

During the years of active mining, crystals of beryl were observed up to 2 feet long. The beryl is usually opaque, ranging in color from pale green to yellow-green or blue-green, but gem-quality aquamarine has been found and faceted into dazzling blue gems. Some of the crystals have a peculiar cone-shaped termination and are highly prized by collectors. Dark red almandine crystals are another well-known Russell Brothers specialty, often occurring in sharp crystals of up to an inch or more across. One remarkable gem crystal uncovered on the quarry floor in the 1990s was said to be the size of a basketball!

Fine specimens of radioactive minerals have been found in many Topsham-area pegmatites, and this site is no exception. These include fairly large black crystals of uraninite, brown crystals of the rare-earth mineral monazite-(Ce), and black ishikawaite. It is quite possible that there are other radioactive species in the quarry that are yet to be reported. Other minerals found at the site include well-formed brown zircon crystals, gray masses of the sulfides arsenopyrite and bismuthinite, and excellent crystals of columbite and schorl.

A large number of other pegmatites have been worked in the Topsham area; some of these may be open from time to time. As always, the best way to obtain up-to-date information about potential collecting sites is to join one of the local mineral clubs. Clubs are continually looking for new sites at which to conduct authorized field trips; most carry insurance, and all seek to maintain good relationships with property owners in order to maintain access.

96. Consolidated Feldspar Quarries

This rare specimen of natural citrine was found at the Consolidated quarries. (Cliff Trebilcock collection)

See map page 262.
Status: Restricted; no access, unless on an authorized field trip
Land manager: Private
Land type: Open-pit and underground workings and associated dumps
Type of deposit: Igneous (complex granitic pegmatite)
Location: Georgetown, Sagadahoc County
GPS: Entrance, N43.7764 / W69.7657
Elevation: Entrance, 90 feet; site, 40 to 122 feet
Vehicle: Any
Best season: May through Oct
Tools: Crack hammer, chisels, safety goggles, digging tools, 10-power loupe
Minerals: Albite, almandine, autunite, bertrandite, beryl (aquamarine, golden, goshenite), beryllonite, biotite, cassiterite, columbite, cookeite, elbaite, eosphorite, fluorapatite, greifensteinite, gummite, hydroxylherderite, lepidolite, microcline, montebrasite, montmorillonite, moraesite, muscovite, phosphuranylite, pyrite,

quartz (citrine, rose, smoky), schorl, spodumene, tantalite-(Mn), torbernite, uraninite, zircon (cyrtolite)

Special attractions: Reid State Park, Georgetown; Fort Popham State Historic Site, Phippsburg; Peary-MacMillan Arctic Museum, Brunswick

Accommodations: Oceanfront camping available at Sagadahoc Bay Campground, Georgetown. Lodging available in Bath and Brunswick.

Finding the site: From the junction of US 1 and ME 127 in Woolwich, follow ME 127 south for 8.4 miles. Turn right onto Bay Point Road and proceed 1.8 miles.

Rules and regulations: Collect in authorized areas only.

Rockhounding

Feldspar was mined at this site near the eastern shore of Todd Bay beginning in 1868 or 1869. The quarries grew into one of the largest open-pit pegmatite operations in the United States. In 1908 Golding Sons Company of Trenton, New Jersey, operated three open pits covering about 3 acres. Besides the larger openings, smaller prospect pits were dug as well. Consolidated Feldspar Company was the operator in 1942, at the end of the site's feldspar-mining era. In recent years one of the prospects, the Howard-Collins quarry (formerly the Harvard cut), has been operated for crushed stone and mineral specimens.

Mineralogically, most of the pegmatites are relatively simple, but there are occasional zones containing lithium minerals including spodumene, montebrasite, and elbaite. Tourmaline was discovered at the site just after the turn of the twentieth century, when gemmy pink, green, and watermelon elbaite crystals were found. Since then yellow-green, blue (indicolite), and colorless crystals have been found as well. Black tourmaline (schorl) has been found in huge crystals, some more than a foot in length.

Common beryl occurs as pale yellow or pale green crystals as long as 15 inches. Transparent, gem-quality golden beryl and aquamarine crystals have been collected as well, but are scarce. Interesting two-toned beryl crystals consisting of a greenish core and pale yellow rind are known. Colorless to white beryl crystals up to 4 inches long were discovered in 2012.

Spodumene in pale shades of blue or green has been found, some of it gemmy. Quartz, almandine, autunite, and zircon (cyrtolite) crystals are all common. Several secondary phosphate minerals are found at the site, with eosphorite being by far the most common. The eosphorite occurs in attractive tan or orange-brown radiating crystal groups sometimes associated with hexagonal white crystals of carbonate-rich fluorapatite and tiny crystals of hydroxylherderite.

97. Edgecomb Feldspar Mine

The Edgecomb mine was abandoned over a century ago.

See map page 262.
Status: Open
Land manager: Town of Edgecomb
Land type: Abandoned open-pit feldspar mine in forest
Type of deposit: Igneous (granitic pegmatite)
Location: Schmid Land Preserve, Edgecomb, Lincoln County
GPS: Parking, N43.9669 / W69.6136; site, N43.9645 / W69.6141
Elevation: Parking, 207 feet; site, 200 to 215 feet
Vehicle: Any
Best season: May through Oct
Tools: Crack hammer, chisels, safety goggles, digging tools, screen, rake
Minerals: Almandine, beryl (aquamarine), biotite, fluorapatite, microcline, muscovite, quartz (smoky), schorl

Special attraction: Fort Edgecomb State Historic Site, Edgecomb
Accommodations: Campgrounds located in Boothbay. Lodging available in Edgecomb and Boothbay Harbor.
Finding the site: From the junction of US 1 and ME 27 in Edgecomb, follow ME 27 south for 3.1 miles. Turn left onto Old County Road; continue for 1 mile to the kiosk and parking area for the Schmid Preserve. Walk south on the woods road for 850 feet.
Rules and regulations: Hobby mineral collecting only.

Rockhounding

Two open pits in pegmatite were worked at this site as early as 1883 for feldspar (microcline) and possibly mica (muscovite). The main pit is 150 by 50 feet; the smaller is 50 by 25 feet. The operation must have been relatively short-lived because when USGS geologist Edson S. Bastin visited in August 1906, he found that it had already been "abandoned for many years." Today the pits are flooded, and the walls above water are mostly covered with moss. The dumps are largely obscured by forest debris, but portions have been exposed by mineral collectors.

The feldspar that was mined is a buff- to cream-colored microcline; origi-nally it occurred in masses of up to 3 feet across. Lathe-shaped black biotite crystals as long as 3 feet were frequently embedded in the feldspar, lowering the feldspar's value substantially, as the min-ers had no cost-effective way to remove the biotite. The most common miner-als on the dumps today are microcline, biotite, muscovite, and quartz, and schorl is occasionally seen. But you'll have to look harder to find the two most desir-able minerals, almandine and beryl.

A lucky break with a hammer revealed this small, gemmy almandine crystal in quartz.

Almandine most commonly occurs as tiny pink to red crystals associated with biotite, microcline, or quartz; larger and better crystals are embedded in masses of compact smoky quartz. These can be ½ inch or so across, and some are rather gemmy. Beryl, too, is found as crystals solidly frozen in smoky quartz; it is typi-cally pale green, but gem aquamarine has been reported as well. Break open any large pieces of smoky quartz on the dumps showing even a trace of almandine. There could be good crystals of almandine or beryl inside.

It's a good idea to use bug spray here in the late spring and summer, as blackflies and mosquitoes abound due to the water-filled pits.

98. Warren Nickel Prospect

Pentlandite, the principal ore of nickel, is intermixed with pyrrhotite and chalcopyrite at this site.

See map page 262.

Status: Believed to be open for recreational mineral collecting unless otherwise posted

Land manager: Private (timberland)

Land type: Abandoned open-pit prospect in a wooded area

Type of deposit: Igneous (sulfide deposit in gabbro)

Location: Warren, Knox County

GPS: Entrance, N44.1772 / W69.2577; site, N44.1771 / W69.2554

Elevation: Entrance, 193 feet; site, 216 to 226 feet

Vehicle: High-clearance 4WD

Best season: May through Oct

Tools: Crack hammer, chisels, safety goggles

Minerals: Augite, biotite, bornite, bravoite, calcite, chalcocite, chalcopyrite, clinochlore, cummingtonite, diopside, enstatite, fluorapatite, forsterite, galena, graphite, hematite, hercynite, hornblende, ilmenite, mackinawite, magnetite, molybdenite, niggliite, pentlandite, plagioclase, pyrite, pyrrhotite, quartz, rutile, sperrylite, sphalerite, spinel, valleriite

Special attraction: Camden Hills State Park, Camden

Accommodations: Camping available at Camden Hills State Park, Camden. Lodging available in Rockland, Rockport, and Camden.

Finding the site: From the junction of ME 90 and ME 131 in Warren, proceed north on ME 131 for 4.1 miles. Turn right onto woods road and continue for 500 feet.

Rules and regulations: Do not park on or block woods road.

Rockhounding

Discovered in 1965, the Warren nickel deposit was periodically the subject of significant interest from mining companies. However, actual mining never took place; the last company to consider developing the site dropped its plans after the town of Warren adopted a restrictive metallic-mining ordinance in 1992. According to the Maine Geological Survey, the deposit contains an estimated 2.6 million tons of massive sulfide ore that contains valuable amounts of nickel, copper, and cobalt. The ore is made up almost entirely of three minerals: pyrrhotite (about 90–95%), pentlandite, and chalcopyrite. Pentlandite (nickel ore) is intermixed with pyrrhotite and chalcopyrite at the site, so the hand specimens of ore you find are likely to be a mixture of all three minerals.

Pieces of ore are scattered about the dumps near the flooded prospect pit. These have a rusty, weathered exterior and are noticeably heavier than stones not containing ore minerals. Crack one of the heavier stones open and you'll see that it has a fresh metallic-brown to brassy interior. While somewhat resembling pyrite, this is mostly pyrrhotite. Pyrrhotite is magnetic, so the ore specimens will easily attract a strong magnet. You'll notice an unpleasant sulfurous smell in the dump area due to the decomposing sulfide minerals. If you are sensitive to odors, you might want to skip this site.

While several rare minerals have been reported from the prospect, including species containing platinum and palladium, these are all microscopic. Just the same, it's surprising to learn that minerals containing platinum-group metals have been found in New England.

99. Jasper Beach

Ocean-tumbled rhyolite stones from Jasper Beach exhibit many colors and patterns.

Status: Open
Land manager: Town of Machiasport
Land type: Ocean beach
Type of deposit: Beach gravel
Location: Howard Cove, Machiasport, Washington County
GPS: N44.6279 / W67.3888
Elevation: Sea level to 14 feet
Vehicle: Any
Best season: May through Oct
Tools: Pail
Rocks: Granite, quartzite, rhyolite
Special attractions: Machias Bay petroglyphs, Machiasport; Reversing Falls Park, Pembroke
Accommodations: Camping at Cobscook Bay State Park, Edmunds Township. Lodging available in Machias.

Jasper Beach is located in a remote part of "Downeast" Maine. Photo by Paul Young

Finding the site: From US 1 in Machias, follow Route 92 east for 9.5 miles, passing through the villages of Machiasport and Bucks Harbor. Turn left onto Jasper Beach Road and continue to the end.

Rules and regulations: Do not leave any trash.

Rockhounding

The warm rays of the sun, fresh salty air, and the hypnotic sound of pebbles being jostled by waves make Jasper Beach an appealing spot for all beach lovers, rockhounds or not. On foggy days you might hear the lonely, haunting sound of a lobster boat's foghorn. Harbor seals are known to frequent the cove, so keep an eye out—maybe you'll see one pop its head above water. On the backside of the spit that makes up the beach, you'll find both fresh- and saltwater lagoons and a salt marsh as well. Countless colorful stones, seashells, driftwood, and other beachcombing treasures all await you on the beach.

Jasper Beach is a half-mile-long pocket beach made up of attractive, naturally polished pebbles and cobbles. Most of the stones are made of rhyolite, a fine-grained volcanic rock that can resemble jasper. The rhyolite on Jasper Beach originated in local outcrops of the Eastport and Leighton Formations, both probably Silurian in age. The stones are often red with black stripes, but an enormous variety of patterns can be found. Granite also occurs on the beach as white, gray, pink, or yellow-orange stones with a speckled appearance. Find a spot that feels right and sit down to take a closer look. Each stone has a unique combination of colors, lines, swirls, and splotches. The colors are richer when the stones are wet, so if it looks good dry, you've got a great one.

Elsewhere in Machiasport, fossiliferous purple-red shale of the Silurian-age Hersey Formation is exposed in outcrops. You can see it on the gravel

Sites 99-100

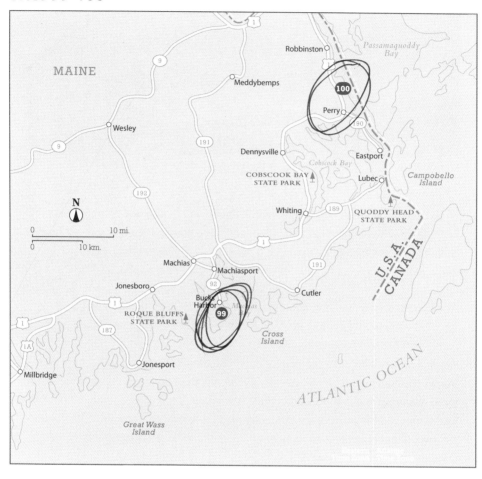

beaches near the village of Starboard at the southern end of Route 92. This formation contains marine fossils such as ostracods. Inquire locally for permission to access and collect on the beaches.

Shamans of the Passamaquoddy tribe left rock carvings called petroglyphs in Machiasport and elsewhere around Machias Bay between 380 and 3,000 years ago. Various figures are depicted on the rocks, including moose, snakes, canoes, and stylized humans—all of which are believed to have had spiritual significance. This is the largest concentration of such rock art on the East Coast. You can view some of the petroglyphs by taking a guided kayak tour of the bay. Inquire locally or check online for more information about these tours.

100. Perry Agate Localities

These beach stones from Perry were polished in a rock tumbler. (Dana M. Jewell collection)

See map page 274.

Status: Open

Land manager: Public and private

Land type: Gravel beaches and shoreline rock outcrops

Type of deposit: Igneous (amygdaloidal basalt) and beach gravel

Location: Perry, Washington County

GPS: Loring Cove, N45.0170 / W67.0774; Gleason Cove, N44.9748 / W67.0511; Lewis Cove, N45.0335 / W67.1008

Elevation: Sea level

Vehicle: Any

Best season: May through Oct

Tools: Collecting bucket

Minerals: Analcime, calcite, datolite, hematite, natrolite, prehnite, pumpellyite-(Mg), quartz (agate, amethyst, bloodstone, carnelian, chalcedony), saponite, stilbite

Special attraction: Quoddy Head State Park, Lubec

Accommodations: Seaview Campground in Eastport has campsites, cottages, and a motel. Camping also available at Cobscook Bay State Park, Dennysville, and Quoddy Head State Park, Lubec.

Finding the site: Loring Cove: From the junction of US 1 and ME 190 in Perry, follow US 1 north for 0.3 mile. Turn right onto Shore Road; proceed 3.3 miles. Turn right onto Gin Cove Road; proceed 0.4 mile. Get permission at Loring's Auto Body to park and access the beach. **Gleason Cove:** From the junction of US 1 and ME 190, follow US 1 north for 0.3 mile. Turn right onto Shore Road; proceed 0.3 mile. Turn right onto Gleason Cove Road; continue for 0.9 mile to beach. **Lewis Cove:** From the junction of US 1 and ME 190, follow US 1 north for 4.5 miles. Turn right onto Gin Cove Road; proceed 0.4 mile. Park and walk down Horse Landing Road; at curve, continue straight onto public-access trail to beach.

Rules and regulations: Permission is required when crossing private property.

Rockhounding

The rocky beaches in Perry have been known as a source of gemstones as far back as the early nineteenth century. These are gorgeous places to collect beach treasures—however, you must beware of the tides! (Plan to visit at low tide, and watch carefully for the rapidly incoming tide.) Agates are found among the waterworn beach pebbles; typically they are banded gray-and-white or pale shades of red, orange, or yellow. While most of the agates don't compare in quality with those from worldwide sources, there are exceptions. For instance, an outstanding 42-carat cabochon of gray-and-white agate from Loring Cove is in the collection of the Smithsonian Institution.

Agate is not as common as it once was on the beaches, but it still keeps popping up, especially after winter storms. Local lapidaries have turned peach-colored Perry agates into beautiful cabochons. Other quartz gems on the seashore include carnelian, red or yellow jasper (often brecciated), and botryoidal chalcedony. Bloodstone (also known as heliotrope) consists of dark green chalcedony with red spots resembling blood, and is a prized find.

Minerals also occur in the amygdaloidal basalt of the Devonian Perry Formation, exposed in sea cliffs. Erosion of the rock outcrops sometimes reveals cavities containing interesting species. Dark green pumpellyite lines vugs that can also contain zeolite minerals such as analcime, natrolite, and stilbite.

There's an interesting historical marker in Perry on US 1, about 1.5 miles south of Shore Road, that says "This stone marks latitude 45 degrees north, halfway from the equator to the pole." (Actually, because the earth is not a perfect sphere, the true halfway line is 10.1 miles to the north, but we won't quibble.) The pink granite marker, dated 1896, is said to be the oldest existing "halfway north marker." It was made by the Maine Red Granite Company in Red Beach, and was set in place in a ceremony on July 4, 1899.

APPENDIX A: CLUBS

Connecticut

Bristol Gem & Mineral Society
Founded: 1972 Meetings: Monthly, 2nd Tues
Place: Douglas Beals Senior/Community Center, Bristol
Website: http://bristolgem.org

Danbury Mineralogical Society
Founded: 1948 Meetings: Monthly, 1st Thurs; Feb–June, Oct–Dec
Place: Broadview Middle School, Danbury
Website: www.danburymineralogicalsociety.org

Lapidary and Mineral Society of Central Connecticut
Founded: 1970 Meetings: Monthly, 4th Mon; Sept–June
Place: Maloney High School, Meriden
Website: www.lmscc.org

Manchester Gem & Mineral Club
Founded: 1996 Meetings: Monthly, 3rd Tues
Place: Lutz Children's Museum, Manchester
Website: N/A

New Haven Mineral Club
Founded: 1933 Meetings: Monthly, 2nd Mon; Oct–May
Place: Veterans Memorial Building, Brooksvale Park, Hamden
Website: www.newhavenmineralclub.org

Nutmeg Prospectors
Founded: 2007 Meetings: Monthly, 1st Sat
Place: Killingly Library, Danielson
Website: www.nutmegprospectors.org

Stamford Mineralogical Society
Founded: 1954 Meetings: Monthly, 2nd Tues; July, Sept–May
Place: Eastern Greenwich Civic Center, Greenwich
Website: www.stamfordmineralsociety.org

Thames Valley Rockhounds
Founded: 1966 Meetings: Monthly, 1st Mon; Apr–June, Sept–Nov
Place: Bill Library, Ledyard
Website: N/A

Maine

Kennebec Rocks and Minerals Club
Founded: 1960 Meetings: Monthly, 3rd Fri; Mar–Dec
Place: Kennebec Savings Bank, Winthrop
Website: www.kennebec-rocksandminerals.com

Maine Gold Prospectors
Founded: 1996 Meetings: Monthly, 3rd Sat; Jan–Apr, Oct
Place: Town Office, Windsor
Website: www.mainegoldprospectors.com

Maine Mineralogical and Geological Society
Founded: 1927 Meetings: Monthly, 3rd Sat; Sept–May
Place: University of Southern Maine, Portland
Website: www.mainemineralclub.org

Oxford County Mineral and Gem Association
Founded: 1948 Meetings: Monthly, 1st Fri; Aug–June
Place: Oxford Hills Comprehensive High School, South Paris
Website: www.oxfordcountymineralandgemassociation.blogspot.com

Penobscot Mineral and Lapidary Club
Founded: 2004 Meetings: Monthly, 2nd Sat
Place: PMLC Club House, Milford
Website: http://penobscotminerallapidaryclub.com

Water-Oak Gem and Mineral Society
Founded: 1970 Meetings: Monthly, 1st Sat
Place: Mount Merici School, Waterville
Website: N/A

Massachusetts

Boston Mineral Club
Founded: 1936 Meetings: Monthly, 1st Tues; Sept–June
Place: Harvard University (Haller Hall), Cambridge
Website: www.bostonmineralclub.org

Connecticut Valley Mineral Club
Founded: 1940 Meetings: Monthly, 1st Wed; Mar–June, Sept–Jan
Place: Springfield Science Museum, Springfield
Website: www.cvmineralclub.org

Gold Prospectors Association of America—Western Mass. Chapter
Founded: 2012 Meetings: Monthly, 3rd Sun
Place: Republican Masonic Lodge, Greenfield
Website: www.goldprospectorsofwmass.org

Micromounters of New England
Founded: 1966 Meetings: Monthly, 3rd Sat; Jan–June, Sept–Nov
Place: Trinity Lutheran Church, Chelmsford
Website: www.micromountersofnewengland.org

Nashoba Valley Mineralogical Society
Founded: 1963 Meetings: Monthly, 2nd Tues; Sept–June
Place: J.V. Fletcher Library, Westford
Website: N/A

New England Rockhounds
Founded: 2012 Meetings: N/A (field trips only)
Website: www.meetup.com/new-england-rockhounds

North Shore Rock and Mineral Club
Founded: 1958 Meetings: Monthly, 3rd Fri; Sept–June
Place: Hamilton Wenham Community House, Hamilton
Website: www.northshorerock.org

Northern Berkshire Mineral Club
Founded: 1959 Meetings: Monthly, 3rd Thurs; Oct–Apr
Place: North Adams Public Library, North Adams
Website: http://nbmclub.webs.com

Southeastern Massachusetts Mineral Club
Founded: 1969 Meetings: Monthly, 2nd Thurs; Sept–June
Place: Bridgewater State University (Conant Science Building), Bridgewater
Website: www.semmc.com

Worcester Mineral Club
Founded: 1938 Meetings: Monthly, 3rd Tues; Sept–June
Place: Trinity Episcopal Church, Shrewsbury
Website: www.worcestermineralclub.org

New Hampshire
Capital Mineral Club
Founded: 1961 Meetings: Monthly, 1st Sat; Sept–May
Place: Salvation Army Building, Concord
Website: http://capital.questblue.com

Keene Mineral Club
Founded: 1948 Meetings: Monthly, 1st Sat; Sept–May
Place: Keene State College Science Building, Keene
Website: www.keenemineralclub.50webs.com

Presidential Gem and Mineral Society
Founded: 1991 Meetings: Monthly, 2nd Fri
Place: Jefferson Town Hall, Jefferson
Website: N/A

Saco Valley Gem and Mineral Club
Founded: 1965 Meetings: Monthly, 3rd Tues
Place: Tin Mountain Conservation Center, Albany
Website: www.sacovalleygemandmineralclub.org

Southeastern New Hampshire Mineral Club
Founded: 1956 Meetings: Monthly, 2nd Wed; Sept–June
Place: St. John's Methodist Church, Dover
Website: http://senhmineralclub.org

Rhode Island
Museum Mineral Society
Founded: 2010 Meetings: Six per year
Place: Museum of Natural History, Roger Williams Park, Providence
Website: www.providenceri.com/museum/mineral-society

Rhode Island Mineral Hunters
Founded: 1962 Meetings: Monthly, 2nd Tues; Mar–July, Sept–Dec
Place: Community College of Rhode Island, Knight Campus, Warwick
Website: www.rimh.us

Vermont
Burlington Gem and Mineral Club
Founded: 1966 Meetings: Monthly, last Thurs; Jan–June, Aug–Oct
Place: Community Lutheran Church, South Burlington
Website: www.burlingtongemandmineralclub.org

Green Mountain Prospectors of Vermont
Founded: 2002 Meetings: Schedule varies; spring and summer only
Place: Locations vary
Website: www.gmpv.org

Mineralogical Society of Brattleboro
Founded: 1981 Meetings: Monthly, 1st Tues; Sept–June
Place: Brooks Memorial Library, Brattleboro
Website: N/A

APPENDIX B: ROCK, MINERAL, AND FOSSIL DISPLAYS

Connecticut

Bruce Museum
1 Museum Dr., Greenwich, CT 06830
http://brucemuseum.org; (203) 869-0376

Connecticut Museum of Mining & Mineral Science
31 Kent Cornwall Rd., Kent, CT 06757
www.ctamachinery.com; (860) 927-0050

Connecticut State Museum of Natural History
2019 Hillside Rd., Storrs, CT 06269
www.cac.uconn.edu/mnhhome.html; (860) 486-4460

Dinosaur State Park Museum
400 West St., Rocky Hill, CT 06067
www.dinosaurstatepark.org; (860) 529-8423

Joe Webb Peoples Museum
Wesleyan University, 265 Church St., Middletown, CT 06459
www.wesleyan.edu/ees/museum1.html; (860) 685-2000

Old Quarry Nature Center
5 Maple Ln., Danbury, CT 06810
www.danbury.org/oldquarry; (860) 354-7592

Peabody Museum of Natural History
Yale University, 170–210 Whitney Ave., New Haven, CT 06511
http://peabody.yale.edu; (203) 432-5050

Stamford Museum and Nature Center
39 Scofieldtown Rd., Stamford, CT 06903
www.stamfordmuseum.org; (203) 322-1646

Maine

Deer Isle Granite Museum
51 Main St., Stonington, ME 04681
http://deerislegranitemuseum.wordpress.com; (207) 367-6331

George B. Dorr Museum of Natural History
105 Eden St., Bar Harbor, ME 04609
www.coamuseum.org; (207) 288-5395

Hamlin Memorial Library and Museum
16 Hannibal Hamlin Dr., Paris, ME 04281
www.hamlin.lib.me.us; (207) 743-2980

L. C. Bates Museum
Good Will-Hinckley, 14 Easler Rd., Hinckley, ME 04944
www.gwh.org/lcbates; (207) 238-4250

MacDonald's Mineral Museum
34 Moody St., Saco, ME 04072
(207) 284-4633; open by appointment

Maine Geological Survey
Ray Building, Hospital St., Augusta, ME 04333
www.maine.gov/doc/nrimc/mgs/mgs.htm; (207) 287-2801

Maine Granite Industry Museum
62 Beech Hill Crossroad, Mount Desert, ME 04660
www.mainegraniteindustry.org; (207) 244-7299

Maine Mineral and Gem Museum
103 Main St., Bethel, ME 04217
www.mainemineralmuseum.org; (207) 824-0218

Maine State Museum
230 State St., Augusta, ME 04330
http://mainestatemuseum.org; (207) 287-2301

Northern Maine Museum of Science
181 Main St., Presque Isle, ME 04769
www.umpi.edu/nmms; (207) 768-9482

Norway Historical Society Museum
471 Main St., Norway, ME 04268
www.norwayhistoricalsociety.org; (207) 743-7377

Nylander Museum of Natural History
657 Main St., Caribou, ME 04736
www.nylandermuseum.org; (207) 498-6156

Poland Spring Museum and Environmental Education Center
115 Preservation Way, Poland, ME 04274
www.polandspringps.org; (207) 998-7143

Spratt-Mead Museum
Bridgton Academy, 11 Academy Ln., North Bridgton, ME 04057
(207) 647-3322, ext. 214; open by appointment

Wilson Museum
120 Perkins St., Castine, ME 04421
www.wilsonmuseum.org; (207) 326-9247

Massachusetts

Bartlett Museum
270 Main St., Amesbury, MA 01913
http://bartlettmuseum.org; (978) 388-4528

Beneski Museum of Natural History
Amherst College, 11 Barrett Hill Rd., Amherst, MA 01002
www.amherst.edu/museums/naturalhistory; (413) 542-2165

Berkshire Museum
39 South St., Pittsfield, MA 01201
http://berkshiremuseum.org; (413) 443-7171

Blue Hills Trailside Museum
1904 Canton Ave., Milton, MA 02186
www.massaudubon.org/get-outdoors/wildlife-sanctuaries/blue-hills; (617) 333-0690

Cape Cod Museum of Natural History
869 Main St., Brewster, MA 02631
www.ccmnh.org; (508) 896-3867

Capen Hill Nature Sanctuary
56 Capen Rd., Charlton, MA 01508
www.capenhill.org; (508) 248-5516

EcoTarium
222 Harrington Way, Worcester, MA 01604
www.ecotarium.org; (508) 929-2700

Great Falls Discovery Center
2 Avenue A, Turners Falls, MA 01376
http://greatfallsdiscoverycenter.org; (413) 863-3221

Greenfield Community College Rock Park
1 College Dr., Greenfield, MA 01301
http://web.gcc.mass.edu/science/rock-park; (413) 775-1000

Hamilton Memorial Library
195 Route 20, Chester, MA 01011
www.hamiltonmemoriallibrary.org; (413) 354-7808

Keep Homestead Museum
35 Ely Rd., Monson, MA 01057
www.keephomesteadmuseum.org; (413) 267-4137

Maria Mitchell Association Aquarium and Science Center
33 Washington St., Nantucket, MA 02554 (opening 2015)
www.mariamitchell.org; (508) 228-9198

Marion Natural History Museum
8 Spring St., Marion, MA 02738
www.marionmuseum.org; (508) 748-2098

Millers River Environmental Center
100 Main St., Athol, MA 01331
www.millersriver.net; (978) 248-9491

Mineralogical & Geological Museum at Harvard University
Harvard Museum of Natural History, 26 Oxford St., Cambridge, MA 02138
www.geomus.fas.harvard.edu/icb/icb.do; (617) 495-3045

Museum of Science, Boston
1 Science Park, Boston, MA 02114
www.mos.org; (617) 723-2500

Nash Dinosaur Track Site and Rock Shop
594 Amherst Rd., South Hadley, MA 01075
www.nashdinosaurtracks.com; (413) 467-9566

Neponset Valley Natural History Museum
Samuel J. Pavadore, 217 Walpole St., Canton, MA 02021
(781) 389-1298; open by appointment

Skinner Museum
Mount Holyoke College, Lower Lake Rd., South Hadley, MA 01075
www.mtholyoke.edu/artmuseum/skinner; (413) 538-2085

Springfield Science Museum
Springfield Museums, 21 Edwards St., Springfield, MA 01103
www.springfieldmuseums.org/the_museums/science; (800) 625-7738

New Hampshire
The Libby Museum
755 North Main St., Wolfeboro, NH 03894
http://wolfeboronh.us/Pages/WolfeboroNH_Museum/index; (603) 569-1035

The Little Nature Museum
18 Highlawn Rd., Warner, NH 03278
www.littlenaturemuseum.org; (603) 746-6121

Ruggles Mine & Museum
Ruggles Mine Rd., Grafton, NH 03240
www.rugglesmine.com; (603) 523-4275

Squam Lakes Natural Science Center
23 Science Center Rd., Holderness, NH 03245
www.nhnature.org; (603) 968-7194

Tin Mountain Conservation Center
1245 Bald Hill Rd., Albany, NH 03818
www.tinmountain.org; (603) 447-6991

Woodman Institute Museum
182 Central Ave., Dover, NH 03820
http://woodmaninstitutemuseum.org; (603) 742-1038

Rhode Island
Babcock-Smith House Museum
124 Granite St., Westerly, RI 02891
www.babcock-smithhouse.com; (401) 596-5704

Edna Lawrence Nature Lab
Rhode Island School of Design, 13 Waterman St., Providence, RI 02903
http://naturelab.risd.edu; (401) 454-6451

Museum of Natural History and Planetarium
Roger Williams Park, 1000 Elmwood Ave., Providence, RI 02907
www.providenceri.com/museum; (401) 785-9457

Portsmouth Historical Society Museum
870 East Main Rd., Portsmouth, RI 02871
http://portsmouthhistorical.com; (401) 683-9178

University of Rhode Island Department of Geosciences
45 Upper College Rd., Kingston, RI 02881
http://cels.uri.edu/geo; (401) 874-1000

Vermont

Fairbanks Museum and Planetarium
1302 Main St., St. Johnsbury, VT 05819
www.fairbanksmuseum.org; (802) 748-2372

Goodsell Ridge Preserve Visitor Center & Museum
Quarry Rd., Isle La Motte, VT 05463
www.ilmpt.org/ilmpt/Visitor_Center.html; (802) 928-3364

Hitchcock Memorial Library and Museum
1252 Route 100, Westfield, VT 05874
http://hitchcocklibrary.blogspot.com; (802) 744-6621

Montshire Museum of Science
1 Montshire Rd., Norwich, VT 05055
www.montshire.org; (802) 649-2200

Nature Museum at Grafton
186 Townshend Rd., Grafton, VT 05146
http://nature-museum.org; (802) 843-2111

New England Via Vermont—Geology and Vermont History Room
4 Milk St., Alburgh, VT 05440
http://newenglandviavermont.net; (802) 796-3665

Perkins Geology Museum
University of Vermont, 180 Colchester Ave., Burlington, VT 05405
www.uvm.edu/perkins/geology.htm; (802) 656-8694

Southern Vermont Natural History Museum
7599 Route 9, West Marlboro, VT 05363
www.vermontmuseum.org; (802) 464-0048

Vermont Granite Museum and Stone Arts School
7 Jones Bros. Way, Barre, VT 05641
www.stoneartsschool.org; (802) 476-4605

Vermont Marble Museum
52 Main St., Proctor, VT 05765
www.vermont-marble.com; (800) 427-1396

Vermont Museum of Mining and Minerals
55 Pleasant St., Grafton, VT 05146
www.vtmmm.org; (802) 843-2300

APPENDIX C: SHOPS

Connecticut
A to Z Mineral Shop and Ancient Fossils Shop
The Shops at Nature's Art Village
1650 Hartford New London Turnpike, Oakdale, CT 06370
www.naturesartvillage.com; (860) 443-4367

Connecticut Museum of Mining & Mineral Science—Gift Shop
31 Kent Cornwall Rd., Kent, CT 06757
www.ctamachinery.com; (860) 927-0050

Earth Lore Gems & Minerals
27 North Main St., Kent, CT 06757
www.earthlorekent.com; (860) 927-2059

Essence of the Earth
1783 Meriden Waterbury Turnpike, Milldale, CT 06467
(860) 628-7906

Lucky 33 Gemstone Flume Mine
1353 Boston Post Rd., Old Saybrook, CT 06475
www.lucky33mine.com; (860) 575-6750

Middle Earth Lapidary Shop
186 Hartford Ave., East Granby, CT 06026
www.middleearthlapidary.com; (860) 653-0664

Mother Earth Gallery & Mining Co.
806 Federal Rd., Brookfield, CT 06804
www.motherearthcrystals.com; (203) 775-6272

Rock Garden
17 South Main St., Branford, CT 06405
www.rockgarden.com; (203) 488-6699

Stone Age Rock Shop
17 Kibbe Dr., Somers, CT 06071
(860) 749-3807 (call first)

Yale Peabody Museum Store
170 Whitney Ave., New Haven, CT 06511
http://peabody.yale.edu; (203) 432-3740

Maine

Bennett's Gems & Jewelry
45 Searsport Ave., Belfast, ME 04915
www.bennettsgems.com; (207) 338-5530

Coos Canyon Rock & Gift
472 Swift River Rd., Byron, ME 04275
www.cooscanyonrockandgift.com; (207) 364-4900

Creaser Jewelers
145 Main St., South Paris, ME 04281
www.creaserjewelers.com; (207) 744-0290

Jack's Jewelry
23 and 27 Main St., Bar Harbor, ME 04609
www.jacksjewelry.com; (800) 303-8297

Kennebec Jewelry and Repair
501 Maine Ave., Farmingdale, ME 04344
http://kennebecjewelry.com; (207) 582-5200

L. C. Bates Museum—Gift Shop
Route 201, Hinckley, ME 04944
www.gwh.org/lcbates; (207) 238-4250

Maine Mineral and Gem Museum—Gift Shop
103 Main St., Bethel, ME 04217
www.mainemineralmuseum.org; (207) 824-0218

Maine State Museum Store
230 State St., Augusta, ME 04330
www.mainestatemuseum.org/visit/museum_store; (207) 287-2938

Mainestone Jewelry
179 Broadway, Farmington, ME 04938
www.mainestonejewelry.com; (207) 778-6560

Mineral Collector
178 North Main St., Bryant Pond, ME 04219
(207) 665-2759

Mount Mica Rarities
162 Main St., Bethel, ME 04217
(207) 875-3060

Mt. Mann Jewelers
57 Main St., Bethel, ME 04217
www.mtmann.com; (207) 824-3030

Rochester's Eclectic Emporium
403 Main St., Oxford, ME 04270
(207) 539-4631

The Rock & Art Shop
36 Central St., Bangor, ME 04401
1584 Bangor Rd., Ellsworth, ME 04605
http://therockandartshop.com; (207) 947-2205

Scallops Mineral & Shell Emporium
12 Perkins Cove Rd., Ogunquit, ME 03907
(207) 646-5644

Sonny's Museum and Mineral Shop
226 Water St., Augusta, ME 04330
(207) 623-9685

Stones & Stuff
556 Congress St., Portland, ME 04101
www.stonesandstuff.com; (207) 874-0789

Sunday River Gems
251 Sunday River Rd., Newry, ME 04261
(207) 824-3414

The Unique Rock Shop
131 US 1, Verona Island, ME 04416
www.uniquerockshop.com; (207) 469-7040

Village Jewelers
1 Main St., Cornish, ME 04020
(207) 625-8958

Willis' Rock Shop
69 Main St., Bar Harbor, ME 04609
(207) 288-4935

Massachusetts

Down to Earth Crystals & Minerals
9 Treasure Ln., Mashpee, MA 02649
www.downtoearthcrystals.com; (508) 477-3500

Geoclassics Gems & Minerals
Faneuil Hall Marketplace, Boston, MA 02109
www.geoclassics.com; (617) 523-6112

Harvard Museum of Natural History—Gift Shop
26 Oxford St., Cambridge, MA 02138
www.hmnh.harvard.edu; (617) 495-4473

Heart of Stone
130 Route 6A, Sandwich, MA 02563
www.heartofstoneonline.com; (508) 833-8500

Nash Dinosaur Track Site and Rock Shop
594 Amherst Rd., South Hadley, MA 01075
www.nashdinosaurtracks.com; (413) 467-9566

The Rock, Fossil and Dinosaur Shop
213 Greenfield Rd., South Deerfield, MA 01373
www.georgesrocks.com; (413) 665-7625

Springfield Museums—Gift Shop
21 Edwards St., Springfield, MA 01103
www.springfieldmuseums.org; (800) 625-7738

The Stone Store
682 West Falmouth Hwy., Falmouth, MA 02540
(508) 548-8411

Treasure Mountain Mining—Showroom
40 Church St., Greenfield, MA 01301
www.treasuremountainmining.com; (413) 774-5707 (call first)

Treasures Over Time
139 Washington St., Salem, MA 01970
www.treasuresovertime.com; (978) 745-2330

Village Silversmith (3 locations)
138 Main St., Gloucester, MA 01930
Northshore Mall, 210 Andover St., Peabody, MA 01960
20 Bearskin Neck, Rockport, MA 01966
www.villagesilversmith.net; (978) 283-8811

New Hampshire

A Broader Concept: Crystal, Mineral & Fossil Shop
143 Londonderry Turnpike, Hooksett, NH 03106
www.abroaderconcept.com; (603) 641-1323

Alpine Valley Gems & Minerals
221 Main St., Gorham, NH 03581
(603) 466-5198

America's Stonehenge—Gift Shop
105 Haverhill Rd., Salem, NH 03079
www.stonehengeusa.com; (603) 893-8300

Dondero's Rock Shop
2730 Main St., North Conway, NH 03860
(603) 356-5359

Gemstar Gemstone Company
427 Shaker Blvd., Enfield, NH 03748
(603) 632-7115

Lost River Gorge & Boulder Caves—Gift Shop
1712 Lost River Rd., North Woodstock, NH 03262
www.lostrivergorge.com; (603) 745-8031

North Star Gems
252 Mayhew Turnpike, Bridgewater, NH 03222
www.nstargems.com; (603) 744-6338

Polar Caves Park—Gift Shops
705 Route 25, Rumney, NH 03266
www.polarcaves.com/gift-shops; (603) 536-1888

The Quartz Source Rock & Mineral Shop
503 Nashua St., Milford, NH 03055
http://thequartzsource.com; (603) 673-0481

Ruggles Mine—Gift Shop
Ruggles Mine Rd., Grafton, NH 03240
www.rugglesmine.com; (603) 523-4275

Santerre's Stones 'n Stuff Bead and Mineral Store
42 Water St., Exeter, NH 03833
www.santerresstones.com; (603) 773-9393

Scallops Mineral & Shell Emporium
65 Daniels St., Portsmouth, NH 03901
(603) 431-7658

Toad Hollow Minerals
2517 Wakefield Rd., Wakefield, NH 03872
http://anitanh.com/minerals; (603) 522-6529

Toveco Gemstones & Fine Jewelry
7 Wilton Rd., Milford, NH 03055
www.toveco.com

Rhode Island

Geoclassics Gems & Minerals
Bowen's Wharf, Newport, RI 02840
www.geoclassics.com; (401) 849-5587

Natures! The Rock Shop
1782 Main Rd., Tiverton, RI 02878
www.naturestherockshop.com; (401) 624-4367

Vermont

Earth Rock & Oils
29 West Main St., Wilmington, VT 05363
(802) 464-7319

Evans' News
434 Main St., Bennington, VT 05201
(802) 442-6326

Global Pathways Jewelry
126 Church St., Burlington, VT 05401
http://globalpathwaysjewelry.com; (802) 651-1006

Manchester Gem & Mineral Gallery
4732 Main St., Manchester Center, VT 05255
(802) 362-4008

Middle Earth Crystals
28 Church St., Burlington, VT 05401
(802) 489-5191

New England Via Vermont
4 Milk St., Alburgh, VT 05440
http://newenglandviavermont.net; (802) 796-3665

Riverknoll Rock Shop
Route 100, Stockbridge, VT 05772
(802) 746-8198

Rock of Ages—Gift Shop
558 Graniteville Rd., Barre, VT 05641
www.rockofages.com; (802) 476-3119

Stowe Gems
70 Pond St., Stowe, VT 05672
www.stowegems.com; (802) 253-7000

APPENDIX D: ADDITIONAL RESOURCES

COMMERCIAL GUIDES
Businesses That Conduct Fee-Based Field Trips
Maine Mineral Adventures
1148 South Main St., Woodstock, ME 04219
www.digmainegems.com; (207) 674-3440

Maine Mineralogy Expeditions
c/o Bethel Outdoor Adventure
121 Mayville Rd., Bethel, ME 04217
www.rocksme.biz; (207) 824-4224

Poland Mining Camps
34 Groves Ln., PO Box 26
Poland, ME 04274
(207) 998-2350

EDUCATIONAL EVENTS WITH FIELD TRIPS
Maine Pegmatite Workshop
www.pegworkshop.com.
Annual weeklong workshop conducted by leading pegmatite experts. Field trips to sites in Maine and New Hampshire.

New England Mineral Conference
www.nemineralconference.org
Annual three-day conference held in Maine, with lectures, exhibits, dealers, and a field trip.

WEBSITES
Handbook of Mineralogy
www.handbookofmineralogy.org
Free online version of the five-volume *Handbook of Mineralogy,* courtesy of the Mineralogical Society of America.

Maine Geological Survey
www.maine.gov/doc/nrimc/mgs
Extensive geological information about the state, including sections on mining, mineral collecting, and fossils.

Massachusetts Geological Survey
www.geo.umass.edu/stategeologist
Comprehensive earth science information for Massachusetts; downloadable maps.

Mindat
www.mindat.org
International mineral and locality database with over 500,000 photos.

New Hampshire Geological Survey
http://des.nh.gov/organization/commissioner/gsu
Information about the geology of the state; downloadable publications and maps.

New Hampshire Mineral Species
http://mindatnh.org
A site dedicated to documenting mineral species in New Hampshire; many excellent photos and articles.

Rhode Island Geological Survey
http://cels.uri.edu/geo/GEO_risurvey.aspx
Source for geological publications and maps covering Rhode Island.

United States Geological Survey
www.usgs.gov
The number one source for geological publications and maps, many downloadable.

Vermont Geological Survey
www.anr.state.vt.us/dec/geo/vgs.htm
All about Vermont's geology and natural resources; downloadable maps and publications.

Webmineral
http://webmineral.com
Comprehensive mineralogy database with descriptions of more than 4,700 mineral species.

White Mountain National Forest
www.fs.usda.gov/whitemountain
Official national forest information, including rules for rockhounding and gold panning.

APPENDIX E: BIBLIOGRAPHY

Connecticut

Betts, John. 1999. "The Quarries and Minerals of the Dayton Road District, South Glastonbury, Connecticut." *Rocks & Minerals* 74 (2): 110–21.

Foye, W. 1922. "Mineral Localities in the Vicinity of Middletown, Connecticut." *American Mineralogist* 7 (1): 4–12.

Hiller, J. 1971. *Connecticut Mines and Minerals.* Shelton, CT: Hiller's Crystal Shop Press.

Januzzi, R. 1976. *Mineral Localities of Connecticut and Southeastern New York State.* Danbury, CT: Mineralogical Press.

Jarnot, Bruce. 1995. "Connecticut Gems & Gem Minerals." *Rocks & Minerals* 70 (6): 378–82.

Ryerson, K. 1968. *Rock Hound's Guide to Connecticut.* Stonington, CT: Pequot Press.

Shannon, E. 1921. "The Old Tungsten Mine in Trumbull, Connecticut." *American Mineralogist* 6 (8): 126–28.

Skehan, J. 2008. *Roadside Geology of Connecticut and Rhode Island.* Missoula, MT: Mountain Press.

Sohon, J. A. 1951. *Connecticut Minerals—Their Properties and Occurrence.* Connecticut Geological and Natural History Survey, Bulletin 77.

Sullivan, Earle C. 1985. *History and Minerals of Old Mine Park.* 2nd ed. Trumbull, CT: Trumbull Historical Society.

Weber, M., and E. Sullivan. 1995. "Connecticut Mineral Locality Index." *Rocks & Minerals* 70 (6): 396–409.

Maine

Bastin, E. S. 1911. *Geology of the Pegmatites and Associated Rocks of Maine.* USGS Bulletin 445.

Caldwell, D. W. 1998. *Roadside Geology of Maine.* Missoula, MT: Mountain Press.

Churchill-Dickson, Lisa. 2007. *Maine's Fossil Record: The Paleozoic.* Augusta, ME: Maine Geological Survey.

Falster, A. U., J. W. Nizamoff, G. T. Bearss, and W. B. Simmons. 2011. "A Second US Location for Väyrynenite." 38th Rochester Mineralogical Symposium program and abstracts.

Francis, Carl A. 1985. "Maine Tourmaline." *Mineralogical Record* 16 (5): 365–88.

King, Vandall T., and Eugene E. Foord. 1994. *Mineralogy of Maine, Volume 1: Descriptive Mineralogy.* Augusta, ME: Maine Geological Survey.

King, Vandall T., ed. 2000. *Mineralogy of Maine, Volume 2: Mining History, Gems, and Geology.* Augusta, ME: Maine Geological Survey.

Morrill, Philip. 1958. *Maine Mines and Minerals, Vol. 1: Western Maine.* Naples, ME: Dillingham Natural History Museum.

Morrill, Philip, and W. P. Hinckley. 1959. *Maine Mines and Minerals, Vol. 2: Eastern Maine.* Naples, ME: Dillingham Natural History Museum.

Perham, Frank. 1964. "Waisanen Mine Operation." *Rocks & Minerals* 39 (7–8): 341–47.

Perham, Jane C. 1987. *Maine's Treasure Chest: Gems and Minerals of Oxford County.* 2nd ed. West Paris, ME: Quicksilver Publications.

Shaub, B. M. 1957. "Garnet Locality of Minot, Maine." *Rocks & Minerals* 32 (5–6): 227–31.

———. 1958. "The Quartz Crystal Pocket Discovered on Deer Hill, Maine, in 1956." *Rocks & Minerals* 33 (8–9): 407–10.

Stevens, C. J. 1989. *The Next Bend in the River.* Phillips, ME: John Wade.

Stevens, Jane Perham. 1972. *Maine's Treasure Chest: Gems and Minerals of Oxford County.* 1st ed. West Paris, ME: Perham's Maine Mineral Store.

Thompson, W. B, D. L. Joyner, R. G. Woodman, and V. T. King. 1988. *A Collector's Guide to Maine Mineral Localities.* 1st ed. Augusta, ME: Maine Geological Survey.

———. 1991. *A Collector's Guide to Maine Mineral Localities.* 2nd ed. Augusta, ME: Maine Geological Survey.

———. 1998. *A Collector's Guide to Maine Mineral Localities.* 3rd ed. Augusta, ME: Maine Geological Survey.

———. 2005. *A Collector's Guide to Maine Mineral Localities.* Online ed. Maine Geological Survey Bulletin 41, June 2005.

Thompson, Woodrow B. 1994. "Amethyst Discovery on Deer Hill." *Rocks & Minerals* 69 (1): 44–51.

Thompson, Woodrow B., et al. 2000. "The Estes Quarry, Cumberland County, Maine: A New Pegmatite Mineral Locality." *Rocks & Minerals* 75 (6): 408–18.

Watts, Douglass. 1996. "A New Find of Phosphates at the Maine Feldspar Quarry, Mt. Apatite, Auburn, Maine." *Mineral News* 12 (5): 1–5.

Wilson, W. E. 1977. "Famous Mineral Localities: The Pulsifer Quarry." *Mineralogical Record* 8 (2): 72–77.

Massachusetts

Biggart, Norman. 1974. "Ashland B & M Quarry." In *Souvenir Guide to New England Mineral Collecting,* 41–43. Privately published.

Cahoon, James C. 1985. "Massachusetts: A Classic Swiss Alpine Cleft Mineral Region." Boston Mineralogical Symposium program book, May 1985.

Chamberlain, Barbara Blau. 1964. *These Fragile Outposts.* New York: Natural History Press.

Clapp, C. H., and W. G. Ball. 1909. "The Lead-Silver Deposits at Newburyport, Massachusetts, and Their Accompanying Contact-Zones." *Economic Geology* 4 (3): 239–50.

Dunn, P. J., and J. H. Marshall. 1975. "The Loudville Lead Mines." *Mineralogical Record* 6 (6): 293–98.

Emerson, B. K. 1917. *Geology of Massachusetts and Rhode Island.* USGS Bulletin 597.

Gleba, Peter. 1978. *Massachusetts Mineral and Fossil Localities.* Cambridge, MA: Krueger Enterprises.

Greene, E., and J. Marshall. 2001. "Loudville Pyromorphite." *Rocks & Minerals* 76 (2): 92–101.

Hitchen, C. S. 1935. "The Pegmatites of Fitchburg, Massachusetts." *American Mineralogist* 20 (1): 1–24.

Hovey, H. 1901. "The Lead and Silver Mines of Newbury." *Scientific American,* supp. 1328:21, 284.

Jackson, Charles. 1865. "Discovery of Emery in Chester, Massachusetts." *American Journal of Science 2nd series,* 39 (116): 87–90.

Lincks, G. Fred. 1978. "The Chester Emery Mines." *Mineralogical Record* 9 (4): 235–42.

Marshall, John H., Jr. 1970. "The Chipman Lead-Silver Mine." *Rocks & Minerals* 45 (5): 306.

Médard, Etienne, Peter Cristofono, and William A. Henderson. 2007. "Kamphaugite-(Y) from Ashland, MA." *Micromounters of New England Newsletter* 284: 2–5.

Mosier, M. 1949. *Investigation of Anson Betts Manganese Mine, Hampshire County, Massachusetts.* Washington, DC: Bureau of Mines.

Palache, Charles. 1950. "Chipman Lead-Silver Mine in Newbury, Massachusetts." *Rocks & Minerals* 25 (5–6): 247.

Plante, A. 1992. *Western Massachusetts Mineral Localities.* Greenfield, MA: Valley Geology Press.

Quinn, Alonzo W. 1945. "Geology of the Plainfield-Hawley area: with special reference to deposits of manganese and iron minerals." USGS Open-File Report 45-28.

Sawyer, Alfred. 1913. "Early Mining Operations near Lowell." In *Contributions of the Lowell Historical Society,* vol. 1. Lowell, MA: Lowell Historical Society.

Sears, John Henry. 1905. *The Physical Geography, Geology, Mineralogy and Paleontology of Essex County, Massachusetts.* Salem, MA: Essex Institute.

Shaub, B. M. 1953. "Chiastolite of Lancaster, Massachusetts." *Rocks & Minerals* 28 (1–2): 3–8.

Shaub, B. M, and B. J. Schenck. 1954. "Pollucite from Lithia, Massachusetts." *American Mineralogist* 39 (7–8): 661–64.

Skehan, J. 2001. *Roadside Geology of Massachusetts.* Missoula, MT: Mountain Press.

New Hampshire

Bearss, Gene T. 1984. "The Weeks (Ham) Mine, Wakefield, NH." Micromounters of New England Northeast Meeting, May 19, 1984, program guide.

Bothner, W., and H. Tischler. 1990. "Fossils of New Hampshire." *Rocks & Minerals* 65 (4): 314–20.

Bradshaw, John J. 1990. "Gemstones of New Hampshire." *Rocks and Minerals* 65 (4): 300–5.

Cox, Dennis P. 1970. *Lead-zinc-silver deposits related to the White Mountain Plutonic Series in New Hampshire and Maine.* USGS Bulletin 1312-D.

Cristofono, P., T. Mortimer, J. W. Nizamoff, A. Wilken, and R. Wilken. 2011. "The Chickering Mine in Walpole, NH." 38th Rochester Mineralogical Symposium program and abstracts.

Dallaire, Donald, and Robert Whitmore. 1990. "Mines & Minerals of North Groton, New Hampshire." *Rocks & Minerals* 65 (4): 350–60.

Eusden, J. Dykstra, et al. 2013. *The Geology of New Hampshire's White Mountains.* Lyme, NH: Durand Press.

Freedman, Jacob. 1950. *The Geology of the Mt. Pawtuckaway Quadrangle, New Hampshire.* Concord, NH: New Hampshire State Planning and Development Commission.

Hitchcock, Charles H. 1877. *Geology of New Hampshire, Vol. II.* Concord, NH: Edward A. Jenks, State Printer.

Jackson, Charles. 1844. *Final Report on the Geology and Mineralogy of the State of New Hampshire.* Concord, NH: Carroll and Baker.

Janules, Bob. 1991. "Beryllium Minerals of New Hampshire." Micromounters of New England, Northeast Meeting, May 11, 1991, program guide.

———. 2005. "The Oliver Trench on Middle Moat Mountain, Hales Location, NH." *Micromounters of New England Newsletter,* no. 263 (April 2005).

Kampf, A. R., S. J. Mills, W. B. Simmons, J. W. Nizamoff, and R. W. Whitmore. 2012. "Falsterite, a new secondary phosphate mineral from the Palermo No. 1 pegmatite, North Groton, New Hampshire." *American Mineralogist* 97 (4): 496–502.

Meyers, T. R., and Glenn W. Stewart. 1956. *The Geology of New Hampshire, Part III: Minerals and Mines.* Concord, NH: State Planning and Development Commission.

Morong, Dana. 1986. "Update on the Parker Mountain Mine." *Micromounters of New England Newsletter*, no. 108.

Morrill, Philip. 1960. *New Hampshire Mines and Mineral Localities.* 2nd ed. Hanover, NH: Dartmouth College Museum.

Nizamoff, James. 2006. "The Mineralogy, Geochemistry and Phosphate Paragenesis of the Palermo #2 Pegmatite, North Groton, New Hampshire." University of New Orleans Theses and Dissertations, Paper 398.

Page, J. J., and D. M. Larabee. 1962. *Beryl Resources of New Hampshire.* US Geological Survey Professional Paper 353.

Smith, A. 2001. "Climbing and Collecting on Iron Mountain, Jackson, Carroll County, New Hampshire." *Mineral News* 17 (3): 1, 6–7.

———. 2005. "Madison Mine, Madison, Carroll County, NH." *Mineral News* 21 (3): 1.

———. 2005. "New Hampshire Mineral Locality Index." *Rocks & Minerals* 80 (4): 242–61.

Smith, Arthur E., and Gene T. Bearss. 1991. "The Weeks Pegmatite Mine, Wakefield, Carroll County, New Hampshire." *Rocks & Minerals* 66 (2): 129–35.

Switzer, George. 1938. "The paragenesis of the Center Strafford, New Hampshire, pegmatite." *American Mineralogist* 23 (11): 811–20.

Van Diver, B. 1987. *Roadside Geology of Vermont and New Hampshire.* Missoula, MT: Mountain Press.

Whitmore, R. W., and R. C. Lawrence Jr. 2004. *The Pegmatite Mines Known As Palermo.* North Groton, NH: Friends of Palermo Mines.

Whittemore, Scott, and Bob Janules. 1990. "Pegmatite and Miarolitic Cavity Minerals of North Sugarloaf Mountain, Bethlehem, NH." *Rocks & Minerals* 65 (4): 338–47.

Young, James. 1990. "Fluorite Deposits of Westmoreland, NH." *Rocks & Minerals* 65 (4): 328–35.

Rhode Island

Carr, R., and J. Edwards. 1986. "A Field Trip in Northeastern Rhode Island." *Rocks & Minerals* 61 (5): 286–89.

Emerson, B. K. 1917. *Geology of Massachusetts and Rhode Island.* USGS Bulletin 597.

Miller, Clarence E. 1972. *Minerals of Rhode Island.* Kingston, RI: University of Rhode Island.

Miller, F. W., and J. Cares. 1986. "Rhode Island Minerals & Collectors." *Rocks & Minerals* 61 (5): 264–75.

Morrill, Phillip, and Willard S. Winslow Jr. 1969. *Rhode Island Mines and Minerals.* Winthrop, ME: Winthrop Mineral Shop.

Quinn, Alonzo W. 1976. *Rhode Island Geology for the Non-Geologist.* Providence, RI: Rhode Island Department of Natural Resources.

Skehan, J. 2008. *Roadside Geology of Connecticut and Rhode Island.* Missoula, MT: Mountain Press.

Teixeira, Angie. 1990. "Bowenite—The Rhode Island State Mineral." Micromounters of New England Northeast Meeting, May 12, 1990, program guide.

Vermont

Carlsen, K., and A. Bentley. 1996. "Early Vermont Mining." *Rocks & Minerals* 71 (4): 267–74.

Grant, Raymond W. 1968. *Mineral Collecting in Vermont*. Montpelier, VT: Vermont Geological Survey.

Hadden, Sue H. 1996. "Minerals of the Quarries of Lowell-Eden, Vermont." *Rocks & Minerals* 71 (4): 236–44.

King, Vandall T., and Janet W. Cares. 1996. "Vermont Mineral Locality Index." *Rocks & Minerals* 71 (5): 324–38.

Meeks, H. 1986. *Vermont's Land and Resources*. Shelburne, VT: New England Press.

Morrill, Philip, and Robert G. Chaffee. 1957. *Vermont Mines and Mineral Localities, Part 1: Southern Vermont*. Hanover, NH: Dartmouth College Museum.

———. 1960. *Vermont Mines and Mineral Localities, Part 2: Northern Vermont*. Hanover, NH: Dartmouth College Museum.

Van Diver, B. 1987. *Roadside Geology of Vermont and New Hampshire*. Missoula, MT: Mountain Press.

General

Barton, William R., and Carl E. Goldsmith. 1968. *New England Beryllium Investigations*. Washington, DC: Bureau of Mines.

Cameron, E., et al. 1954. *Pegmatite Investigations, 1942–45, in New England*. US Geological Survey Professional Paper 255.

Kuchera, Roger W. 1986. "Gold in New England." In *This Is New England 1986*. Warwick, RI: Rhode Island Mineral Hunters.

Schlichter, Ernie. 1986. "On Collecting Tools." In *This Is New England 1986*. Warwick, RI: Rhode Island Mineral Hunters.

Shelton, Bill, and Bud Webster. 1979. *Mineral Collector's Field Guide: The Northeast*. Wallingford, CT: Mineralogy.

Sinkankas, J. 1988. *Field Collecting Gemstones and Minerals*. Prescott, AZ: Geoscience Press.

———. 1959. *Gemstones of North America, Vol. 1*. New York: Van Nostrand Reinhold.

———. 1976. *Gemstones of North America, Vol. 2*. New York: Van Nostrand Reinhold.

———. 1997. *Gemstones of North America, Vol. 3*. Tucson, AZ: Geoscience Press.

Zabriskie, Daniel, and Carolyn Zabriskie. 2006. *Rockhounding in Eastern New York and Nearby New England*. 7th ed., rev. Albany, NY: Many Facets.

SITE INDEX

INDEX

chrysoberyl
  Maine, 208, 217
  New Hampshire, 163, 166, 187
chrysocolla
  Maine, 224
  Massachusetts, 79, 92, 104
  Rhode Island, 61
Chute Prospects (ME), 197,
  244–45
clinochlore
  Maine, 256, 271
  Massachusetts, 107, 109, 112
  New Hampshire, 151
  Rhode Island, 64
  Vermont, 127
clinozoisite
  Connecticut, 24, 28
  Maine, 244, 246, 256
  Massachusetts, 79, 88, 90, 108
  Rhode Island, 58
cobaltite (MA), 112
collinsite (NH), 173, 175
columbite
  Connecticut, 33, 46
  Maine, 203, 207, 219, 235,
    237, 254, 266
  Massachusetts, 110
  New Hampshire, 139, 145,
    160, 166, 173
columbite-(Fe)
  Connecticut, 38, 41, 44
  Maine, 196, 199, 201, 205,
    210, 230, 264
  New Hampshire, 163, 175
columbite-(Mn) (ME), 212, 224,
  228, 232, 242, 248, 258
columbite/tantalite (NH), 182
concretions (VT), 131–32
Conklin Quarry (RI), 56, 61–63
Connecticut facts, 5–7
Consolidated Feldspar Quarries
  (ME), 262, 266–67
cookeite
  Maine, 207, 211, 212, 219,
    224, 226, 228, 230, 232,
    235, 238, 240, 242, 248,
    254, 258, 266
  New Hampshire, 160
coral (VT), 116
Cordaites (MA), 71, 73
cordierite
  Connecticut, 44
  Massachusetts, 108
  New Hampshire, 151
corkite (NH), 160
correianevesite (ME), 258
corundum (MA), 108
Cory's Lane Fossil Locality (RI),
  54–57

covellite
  Massachusetts, 85, 104
  New Hampshire, 173
crandallite
  Maine, 208, 219, 232
  New Hampshire, 173, 175
Cranston Quarry (RI), 56, 58–60
crinoid stems
  Massachusetts, 112
  Vermont, 116
cryptomelane (ME), 201, 203,
  207, 210, 224, 258
cumberlandite, (RI), 64
cummingtonite
  Maine, 271
  Massachusetts, 108, 112
cuprite
  Massachusetts, 104
  New Hampshire, 173, 184
cuprobismutite (CT), 44
curite (NH), 139
cymatolite
  Maine, 208
  Massachusetts, 110
  New Hampshire, 160

damourite (ME), 248
danalite (NH), 182, 187, 189, 193
datolite
  Maine, 275
  Rhode Island, 61
Deer Hill, ME, 197, 199–200
diadochite
  Maine, 196, 207, 211, 219,
    230, 249, 254
  New Hampshire, 160, 173, 175
diaspore
  Connecticut, 24
  Massachusetts, 108
dickinsonite
  Maine, 208, 212, 219, 224,
    249, 254, 258
  New Hampshire, 139, 173
dinosaur footprints (CT), 49–50
diopside
  Connecticut, 24, 28, 30
  Maine, 228, 244, 246, 256, 271
  Massachusetts, 88, 90, 97
  New Hampshire, 187
  Rhode Island, 61
diorite (NH), 153, 154
djurleite (NH), 173
dolomite
  Connecticut, 30
  Maine, 196
  Massachusetts, 90
  New Hampshire, 148
  Rhode Island, 61
  Vermont, 119, 127

Dracut Quarry, (MA), 84, 88–89
dravite
  Maine, 212
  Massachusetts, 108
  New Hampshire, 151, 155
  Rhode Island, 61
dufrénite (NH), 173

earlshannonite (ME), 207,
  219, 230
Edgecomb Feldspar Mine, (ME),
  262, 268–69
elbaite
  Connecticut, 46
  Maine, 196, 201, 207, 211,
    219, 224, 226, 228, 232,
    235, 238, 240, 242, 249,
    251, 254, 258, 266
  Massachusetts, 110
  New Hampshire, 139, 145
Emmons Quarry (ME), 197,
  219–21
enstatite
  Maine, 271
  Massachusetts, 88
eosphorite
  Maine, 196, 201, 207, 210,
    212, 219, 224, 230, 232,
    235, 238, 242, 249, 254,
    258, 266
  New Hampshire, 173, 175
epidote
  Connecticut, 25, 51
  Maine, 246
  Massachusetts, 75, 77, 79, 82,
    88, 92, 108, 112
  New Hampshire, 153, 155, 189
  Rhode Island, 58, 61, 64
Estes Quarry (ME), 196–98
Eubrontes (CT), 49
eucryptite (NH), 160
extrusive rocks, 4

fairfieldite
  Maine, 196, 208, 210, 212,
    219, 224, 228, 230, 232,
    238, 242, 254, 258
  New Hampshire, 139, 173, 175
fairfieldite-messelite (NH), 145
Falls Village Marble Quarries
  (CT), 30–32
falsterite
  Maine, 196
  New Hampshire, 173
ferberite (CT), 25
fergusonite (NH), 182, 189
ferrimolybdite
  New Hampshire, 148
  Rhode Island, 61

hinsdalite (NH), 173
hisingerite (NH), 173, 193
hollandite (NH), 173
Hooksett Crushed Stone
  Quarry (NH), 155–57
hopeite (NH), 173
hornblende
  Connecticut, 25, 51
  Maine, 271
  Massachusetts, 77, 82, 88,
    92, 97
  Hoyt Hill Mica Mine (NH),
    168, 170–71
humite group (MA), 90
hureaulite
  Maine, 201, 208, 219, 224,
    230, 233, 238, 259
  New Hampshire, 145, 173
hurlbutite (ME), 212
hydromagnesite (RI), 61
hydrothermal vein deposits, 4
hydroxylapatite
  Maine, 196, 201, 204, 207,
    211, 212, 219, 230, 233,
    238, 243, 254
  New Hampshire, 173, 176
hydroxylherderite
  Maine, 196, 201, 204, 207, 210,
    212, 219, 222, 224, 226, 228,
    230, 233, 235, 238, 240, 243,
    249, 254, 259, 266
  New Hampshire, 161, 173
hydrozincite
  Massachusetts, 104
  New Hampshire, 184, 193

igneous rocks, 4
ilmenite
  Connecticut, 51
  Maine, 271
  Massachusetts, 77, 79, 88, 99,
    108, 112
  New Hampshire, 182
  Rhode Island, 58, 61, 64
ilvaite (RI), 64
Iron Mine Hill (RI), 56, 64–66
Iron Mountain Mines (NH),
  178, 187–88
ishikawaite (ME), 264

jacobsite (MA), 112
jahnsite
  Maine, 196, 201, 208, 211,
    220, 230, 233
  New Hampshire, 161, 173, 176
jarosite (RI), 61
Jasper Beach, ME, 272–74

kamphaugite-(Y) (MA), 79

kaolinite
  Maine, 199, 201, 204, 208,
    233, 235, 238, 259
  Rhode Island, 61
kasolite (NH), 167
kastningite (ME), 208, 220
keckite (NH), 173
kosnarite (ME), 212, 233
kryzhanovskite (NH), 173, 176
kulanite (NH), 173
kutnahorite (MA), 112
kyanite
  Connecticut, 51
  Massachusetts, 97, 108
  New Hampshire, 151

labradorite
  Massachusetts, 82, 88
  Rhode Island, 64
Lancaster Chiastolite Locality
  (MA), 93, 95–96
landesite (ME), 220, 238, 249,
  254, 259
langite (MA), 104
laueite
  Maine, 207, 210, 220, 230,
    233, 238
  New Hampshire, 145, 161,
    173, 176
laumontite (MA), 79, 82, 88
lazulite (NH), 173
lazulite-scorzalite (NH), 176
leadhillite (MA), 104
lepidocrocite (RI), 61
Lepidodendron
  Massachusetts, 71, 73
  Rhode Island, 55
lepidolite
  Connecticut, 46
  Maine, 207, 211, 213, 220,
    224, 228, 233, 235, 238,
    243, 249, 251, 254, 259, 266
  New Hampshire, 139, 145
leucophosphite
  Maine, 220
  New Hampshire, 173, 176
liandratite (CT), 44
linarite
  Massachusetts, 104
  New Hampshire, 184
lithiophilite
  Maine, 196, 211, 220, 224,
    238, 243, 249, 254, 259
  New Hampshire, 139
Littleton Quarry (MA), 92–94
löllingite
  Maine, 196, 208, 220, 233,
    235, 249, 254
  Massachusetts, 112

New Hampshire, 145, 161,
  167, 173, 176
Lord Hill (ME), 197, 201–2
ludlamite
  Maine, 211, 230, 249, 254
  New Hampshire, 145, 161,
    173, 176
Lunenburg Quarry (MA), 93,
  97–98
Lyme disease, 17

Machias Bay petroglyphs, 272, 274
Maclurites (VT), 118
Madison Mine (NH), 178,
  193–94
magnesiohornblende
  New Hampshire, 151
  Rhode Island, 62
magnesite
  Massachusetts, 108
  Rhode Island, 62
  Vermont, 127
magnetite
  Connecticut, 51
  Maine, 211, 213, 215, 261, 271
  Massachusetts, 79, 82, 88,
    108, 112
  New Hampshire, 161, 163,
    173, 176, 177, 180, 187, 189
  Rhode Island, 58, 62, 64
  Vermont, 123, 127, 129
Maine facts, 9–10
malachite
  Connecticut, 25
  Maine, 235
  Massachusetts, 77, 79, 85, 92,
    97, 104, 108
  New Hampshire, 148, 155,
    163, 173, 184
  Rhode Island, 62
mangangordonite (ME), 208
manganite (RI), 62
Manhan Lead-Silver Mine
  (MA), 104
marble
  Massachusetts, 91
  Rhode Island, 62
  Vermont, 119, 120
marcasite
  Connecticut, 25
  Massachusetts, 68, 112
  New Hampshire, 173
margarite
  Connecticut, 25
  Massachusetts, 108
Mariopteris (MA), 71
Mascot Mine (NH), 178,
  184–86
Massachusetts facts, 7–8

triphylite
  Maine, 196, 208, 210, 213, 226, 231, 233, 235, 238, 243
  New Hampshire, 146, 161, 167, 173, 176
triplite (ME), 202, 249, 254, 259
triploidite
  Maine, 208
  New Hampshire, 173
Tripp Mine (NH), 135, 141–42
trögerite (NH), 189
tungstite (CT), 25
Tunnel Brook-Gold Panning (NH), 178, 180–81
turgite (NH), 137
Turner Mine (NH), 135, 139–40

unconsolidated deposits, 4
uralolite (ME), 208
uraninite
  Connecticut, 25, 33, 38, 41, 44, 46
  Maine, 196, 202, 204, 208, 210, 213, 220, 222, 224, 231, 233, 235, 237, 249, 254, 259, 264, 267
  Massachusetts, 99
  New Hampshire, 134, 139, 146, 161, 163, 167, 173, 176, 189
uranocircite (ME), 235
uranophane
  Connecticut, 38, 44
  Maine, 202, 205, 208, 213, 224, 243, 254, 259
  New Hampshire, 134, 139, 161, 167, 173
uranpyrochlore (CT), 44
ushkovite
  Maine, 208
  New Hampshire, 173, 176

uvite (NH), 182, 193
valleriite (ME), 271
vandendriesscheite
  Maine, 208
  New Hampshire, 167, 173
vanmeerscheite (ME), 208
väyrynenite (ME), 196, 198
Vermont facts, 8
vesuvianite
  Maine, 228, 244, 246, 256
  New Hampshire, 187
vivianite
  Maine, 196, 202, 204, 208, 210, 213, 220, 228, 243
  New Hampshire, 146, 161, 167, 173, 176

Waisanen Quarry (ME), 197, 226–27
walentaite (ME), 235
wardite
  Maine, 208, 210, 259
  New Hampshire, 146–47, 173
Warren Nickel Prospect (ME), 262, 270–71
West Nile Virus (WNV), 16–17
West Redding Grossular Locality (CT), 26, 28–29
whiteite (NH), 173, 176
whitlockite
  Maine, 208, 210
  New Hampshire, 161, 173
whitmoreite
  Maine, 208, 211, 231
  New Hampshire, 146, 173, 176
Wild Ammonoosuc River-Gold Panning (NH), 177–79
William Wise Fluorite Mine (NH), 135, 148–49
Wilton Crushed Stone Quarry (NH), 135, 153–54

wodginite (ME), 208, 213, 220, 221
wolfeite (NH), 173, 176
wollastonite (CT), 30
wölsendorfite (ME), 208, 224
worm burrows (VT), 116
Wrentham Quarry (MA), 68–70
wroewolfeite (MA), 104
wulffenite
  Massachusetts, 104
  New Hampshire, 148, 189, 193
wurtzite (ME), 211

xanthoxenite
  Maine, 208, 231
  New Hampshire, 173
xenotime-(Y) (NH), 176, 182, 187

zanazziite
  Maine, 208, 211
  New Hampshire, 173
zigrasite (ME), 208
zinnwaldite (NH), 182
zircon
  Connecticut, 38, 44, 46
  Maine, 196, 202, 204, 205, 208, 210, 213, 220, 224, 226, 228, 231, 233, 235, 238, 249, 254, 259, 267
  Massachusetts, 82, 99, 110
  New Hampshire, 134, 139, 146, 153, 158, 161, 163, 167, 170, 173, 176, 182, 187
  Rhode Island, 62
zoisite (RI), 62